Indigeneity
and Politics

Edited by
Franke Wilmer
Montana State University

A ROUTLEDGE SERIES

Indigenous Peoples and Politics
Franke Wilmer, *General Editor*

Inventing Indigenous Knowledge
Archaeology, Rural Development, and the Raised Field Rehabilitation Project in Bolivia
Lynn Swartley

The Globalization of Contentious Politics
The Amazonian Indigenous Rights Movement
Pamela L. Martin

Cultural Intermarriage in Southern Appalachia
Cherokee Elements in Four Selected Novels by Lee Smith
Katerina Prajnerova

Storied Voices in Native American Texts
Harry Robinson, Thomas King, James Welch, and Leslie Marmon Silko
Blanca Schorcht

On the Streets and in the State House
American Indian and Hispanic Women and Environmental Policymaking in New Mexico
Diane-Michele Prindeville

Chief Joseph, Yellow Wolf, and the Creation of Nez Perce History in the Pacific Northwest

Robert R. McCoy

Routledge
Taylor & Francis Group
NEW YORK AND LONDON

Published in 2004 by
Routledge
711 Third Avenue, New York, NY 10017
2 Park Square, Milton Park, Abingdon, Oxfordshire OX14 4RN

Routledge is an imprint of the Taylor and Francis Group.

First issued in paperback 2012

Copyright © 2004 Routledge

All rights reserved. No part of this book may be printed or utilized in any form or by any electronic, mechanical or other means, now known or hereafter invented, including photocopying and recording, or any other information storage or retrieval system, without permission in writing from the publisher.

Library of Congress Cataloging-In-Publication data
McCoy, Robert R. (Robert Ross), 1962-
Chief Joseph, Yellow Wolf, and the creation of Nez Perce history in the Pacific northwest / Robert R. McCoy
p. cm.—(Indigenous peoples and politics)
Includes bibliographical references and index.
ISBN: 0-415-94889-4 (hardback : alk. paper)
 1. Nez Percé Indians—Historiography. 2. Nez Percé Indians—Cultural assimilation. 3. Nez Percé Indians—Public opinion. 4. Ethnohistory—Pacific, Northwest. 5. Assimilation (Sociology)—Northwest, Pacific. 6. Joseph, Nez Percé Chief, 1840-1904. 7. Yellow Wolf, 1855-1935. 8. National characteristics, American. 9. Public opinion—Northwest, Pacific. I. Title. II. Series.

E99.N5M22 2004
979.5004'974124'0072073—dc22

2003021146

ISBN 978-0-415-94889-0 (hbk)
ISBN 978-0-415-64650-5 (pbk)

Contents

List of Figures — vii

Foreword — ix

Preface — xiii

Chapter One
Ghosts of the Whitmans — 1

Chapter Two
Coyote and the Nez Perce — 13

Chapter Three
Coyote Meets Monster — 43

Chapter Four
Words and Boundaries: Missionaries, Settlers, and Treaties — 69

Chapter Five
Monster Inhaled the People — 99

Chapter Six
The Consuming Silence: The Nez Perce in the Stomach of Monster — 145

Epilogue	185
Notes	191
Bibliography	233
Index	239

List of Figures

Figure 1	The Stick Game played by Columbia Plateau Indian People	33
Figure 2	A Sweathouse used for ritual cleansing	37
Figure 3	Heart of the Monster near Kamiah, Idaho	40
Figure 4	Chief Lawyer, circa 1861	89
Figure 5	Ollokot, Brother of Chief Joseph	113
Figure 6	Yellow Wolf, 1909	116
Figure 7	Chief Joseph	119
Figure 8	Peo Peo Thalekt wearing historical headdress	121
Figure 9	Map of the Nez Perce War, Scene of the Outbreak	122
Figure 10	Bear Paw Battlefield	126
Figure 11	Engravings of Eagle of the Light, Chief Joseph, and the Dreamer	131
Figure 12	Illustrations of various scenes from the Nez Perce War of 1877	141
Figure 13	Nez Perces Chief Joseph and Red Thunder pose with Edmond S. Meany	155
Figure 14	Chief Joseph posed on horseback	156
Figure 15	Chief Yellow Bull delivering speech at Chief Joseph Monument ceremony	157
Figure 16	Map of Pacific Northwest Indian Reservations, 1879	161
Figure 17	Map of Nez Perce Reservation, 1911	164
Figure 18	Parade Day, Toppenish Round-up	180
Figure 19	Drunken Indian Ride, Toppenish Round-up	181
Figure 20	Chief Joseph	188

Foreword

By Clifford E. Trafzer

Yellow Wolf, the famed warrior and war chief of the Nimipu, ended his account of the Nez Perce War by saying, "the whites told only one side." He believed that scholars told their story: "Told it to please themselves." Yellow Wolf stated that historians had "Told much that is not true," including the "best deeds" of whites and "only the worst deeds of the Indians." The Nez Perce elder understood the power of the written word, and although illiterate, Yellow Wolf knew what white historians had said about the war and his people. He was not pleased with the past presentations of the Nez Perce, and he never forgot the injustices forced on his people by white Americans. Yellow Wolf represented the views of many Nez Perce when he told rancher L.V. McWhorter that non-Indian scholars understood little about the Nimipu and their culture. In their writings, historians had justified the invasion of Nez Perce lands, and they had downplayed the role of the United States and its citizens in bringing a devastating war to his people who had befriended white explorers, soldiers, and government agents only to have them turn against the Nimipu out of greed and racial hatred.

Rob McCoy examines these topics and far more, weaving an original analysis about the ways in which academics appropriated the Nez Perce story to enhance their own regional and national identities. He demonstrates the way in which historians in the Northwest created a regional history that glorified Westward expansion, the settlement of the "wilderness," and exploitation of the rich natural resources. He maintains that Indians play a role in the "winning" of the West by being noble barriers to white expansion, barriers that had to be overcome by gallant pioneers, like the rivers and mountains. McCoy argues that no individual symbolized the so-called "Indian barrier" better than Chief Joseph, the famous Nez Perce chief who heroically fought the United States, but lost to a "superior" people who promised to open the west and plant true culture, civilization, and progress. McCoy provides details about the development of the Anglo-American myth about the positive development of the west that helped frame the manifest destiny of the country into the Pacific and beyond. He informs us about the way the creation of a regional identity mirrored the national identity, fostered by the lectures and writings of leading scholars who produced history in the early twentieth century, a history that influenced the way in which people around the world viewed and interpreted American history.

McCoy links the Northwest with Frederick Jackson Turner, the mentor professor of Edmond Meany, the leading historian of Washington State, whose work still influences history education in the region. McCoy offers us windows from which we can view historical productions and images that continue to affect our lives today. He also takes us into the world of Nez Perce history as created by whites, not Indians, offering new ways of thinking about the way "others" have constructed Native American history, representing Nez Perces without significant knowledge or in-depth interest in the Nimipu. McCoy uses part of the Nez Perce creation story recorded by Archie Phinney as a metaphor to deconstruct white presentations of Nez Perce history. He invites readers into the Native story to illustrate the symbolic way in which Monster (the United States and scholars) consumed Coyote (Nez Perce people), swallowing the trickster but not killing him. Monster believed that by eating Coyote, the wily hero would disappear. For a brief time, Monster eliminated Coyote. The hero did not die or surrender. From the outset, Coyote conceded that Monster would swallow him, so the hero prepared for the inevitable by hiding five knives in his fur. After Coyote found himself in the stomach of Monster, he began to destroy Monster from within. So Coyote used his five knives to cut at Monster's body, an action that Monster realized immediately but could not prevent. Coyote cut Monster until he reached the ogre's heart, and the hero killed Monster, reemerging into the daylight. Coyote used Monster's body to create all the Indian peoples, tossing parts of the body in every direction and using Monster's blood to create the strongest people on earth, the Nimipu.

Like Coyote, Monster swallowed Nez Perces but could not kill them. The people survived disease, death, war, removal, reservations, and government policies bent on destroying Nez Perce language, culture, religion, and history. They used their experiences and Monster's body of knowledge through the written and spoken work to revitalize themselves. The people turned the power against Northwestern scholars to construct their own history with a deep understanding of Native American culture, religion, and oral narratives. The Nez Perce and their friends used community-based research and oral history to re-envision, reclaim, and reconstruct a new history of the Nimipu, one that included the knowledge of the Nez Perce people themselves without the goal of regional or national building. Rob McCoy allows us to emerge from the belly of Monster so that we can see the academic world differently. He encourages us to reinterpret Nez Perce history with a new lens centered on the first historians who ignored the rich panorama of American Indian culture and the historical stories kept by families of Nez Perce people themselves.

Clifford E. Trafzer is professor of History and American Indian Studies at the University of California, Riverside. His books include *Death Stalks the Yakama*, *Chief Joseph's Allies*, *The Native Universe*, and *As Long As the Grass Shall Grow and the Rivers Flow*.

Preface

While writing this book in California, I often returned to my hometown in Oregon during the summer for brief vacations to clear my head and visit my family. During one of those brief holidays, my family and I traveled to Joseph, Oregon, to watch the start of Chief Joseph Days, a yearly celebration held in the small town of Joseph, located in Oregon's northeastern corner. As with many other small town celebrations, Chief Joseph Days included a parade, rodeo, street fair and other activities that all hoped would attract tourists and locals to spend time and money in the town. Fortunately for the organizers of Chief Joseph Days, the trip to Joseph was remarkably beautiful and while the day was cool, the sights and sounds of Wallowa Lake and the Eagle Cap Mountain Range made the trip worthwhile. During the day we watched a parade, ate barbecue, shopped at small stores and admired the growing number of sculptures created by the recent influx of artists to this region. As we participated in the day's festivities, a growing unease emerged in my mind. I was puzzled by the absence of Nez Perce people or any other native people at the celebration. My family and I were ostensibly celebrating the "Great" Indian Chief Joseph of the Nez Perce, but none or very few of his people seemed to be present at the event. During the weeks to come, I began to wonder what we, the people present during Chief Joseph Days, were actually celebrating. Were we celebrating Joseph and his life? Were we celebrating the "conquering" of a people and the theft of their land by the United States? Or were we simply celebrating for celebrating's sake, out to have a good time while attaching some significance to the event by pasting Joseph's name to the festivities? The purpose of the celebration escaped me, especially in the light of those attending, who were probably descendants of the very people who pushed the Nez Perce out of their beloved homeland in the Wallowa Valley and Northeast Oregon.

These questions lay dormant in my mind until the day that I began reading *Yellow Wolf: His Own Story*. This semi-autobiographical sketch of Yellow Wolf's life contained within it the answers to my questions concerning Chief Joseph Days and the relative scarcity of Native American voices in the recitation of Pacific Northwestern history. Yellow Wolf, a remarkable warrior and chief, believed that Anglo Americans told the story of his people and their struggle to maintain their homeland in a distorted and self-serving manner. Yellow Wolf asserted that Anglo Americans narrated the story "to please themselves." In all my studies, this brief biographical assessment caught my attention like no other. Yellow Wolf understood the power of controlling and telling of stories and succinctly described what Anglo Americans had been doing to the story of his people for a very long time. During those summer days in Joseph, Oregon, we celebrated ourselves and our ability to control and manipulate history. In reality, the public celebration of Chief Joseph was a sanitized version of history, created and presented to celebrate the completion of a dream, the dream of manifest destiny, a dream rooted in violence and in the expulsion of a people from their homeland.

My work in memory and public history led me down a path that eventually brought me back to the above questions. The "public" memory in the Pacific Northwest, while giving "voice" to Chief Joseph, silenced Nez Perce voices. While celebrating the "mythic," white-generated and sanitized image of "the greatest Indian who ever lived," people in the Northwest relegated the Nez Perce and other Plateau peoples to a realm of silence, a realm not understood or allowed to speak for itself. When my friend and fellow historian, Clifford Trafzer, recommended that I explore a topic in Native American history, concentrating on the Columbia Plateau region of the Pacific Northwest, I was skeptical. While interested in the Nez Perce and other native peoples of the Columbia Plateau, I initially believed that the "story" of the Nez Perce and Chief Joseph had been "overnarrated." The prospect of developing a "new" topic and approach did not seem favorable, but this was not the case. The very overnarration of the Nez Perce story by non-Indians signaled its importance in the historical consciousness of non-native people in the Pacific Northwest and the United States. The systematic exclusion of Nez Perce voices from metanarratives developed over generations by Anglo-American historians became the topic of my work. Native American history is rich in topics requiring the study of the way in which Anglo-Americans produced history about Native Americans. In particular, the story of the Nez Perce and Chief Joseph offered a unique opportunity to deconstruct and understand the creation of narratives and themes that persist in the historical consciousness of all American people. These concerns about memory and the creation of public history led to the research premise of this work: why did Anglo Americans narrate the story of the Nez

Perce and other Plateau peoples the way they did? What purposes did this story serve for Anglo American culture and society? Did narration from various parts of Anglo American society share common themes and do these themes persist into the present?

This work focuses on the following questions: In what ways did the various discursive practices, histories, and images about the Nez Perce created by missionaries, settlers, academics, and government officials, become necessary for white regional and national identity? To what ends were the history and images of the Nez Perce put to use by certain groups within the Anglo-American community? Finally, how does the production of history and historical knowledge about the Nez Perce change or remain the same over time? The production of history concerning the Nez Perce serves as an example of the processes that occurred generally in the Pacific Northwest. This work focuses on how whites used Nez Perce history, images, activities, and personalities in the production of history, to develop a regional identity and integrate this identity into a national framework.

These questions are investigated through a re-narration of the history of the Nez Perce with an eye to illuminating and critiquing how Anglo Americans used their narratives to provide identity, meaning and significance for their new communities in the Pacific Northwest. One of the main tools used in this investigation of the Anglo-American historical production has Nez Perce origins. The story of Coyote and Monster is one of the most familiar oral narratives of the Nez Perce. I have used the story of Coyote and Monster as a metaphor for the experience of the Nez Perce in dealing with the historical production of Anglo Americans. Each chapter begins with an excerpt from the Coyote and Monster story that parallels the analysis of Anglo-American historical production. This Nez Perce story is very important because it not only describes the battle between Monster and Coyote, but also tells of Monster's swallowing of Coyote and Coyote's subsequent escape with all the animal people. It is a story of conflict and regeneration. Only through the swallowing of Coyote and his defeat of Monster can the creative process continue with the eventual creation of mankind. In the same way, "Monster" swallowed the Nez Perce, but the people, through their efforts to retain their culture and history, defeated "Monster" and now are engaged in the creative process of regenerating their history.

Many people made my journey to complete this work possible. While it is difficult to truly repay their sacrifices, I hope that these words will express my deep gratitude and indebtedness to my family, friends, mentors and colleagues. My family played an essential role in the creation and completion of this project. My deep appreciation and love goes to my family in the Pacific Northwest for their support and patience as I slowly worked on this volume. In particular, I am indebted to my grandmother, Lillian McCoy, who taught me to love stories and gardening. Her patience and devotion throughout my life supplied me with strength and perseverance.

During my days at the University of California, Riverside, I relied on the gifts and skills of many friends and companions. Working as an intern at the City of Riverside Planning Department, I met Anthea Hartig, a true friend and good colleague. Her confidence in my skills and abilities, as well as her friendship, helped me to see the possibilities and joys of a profession as an historian while maintaining my sanity and compassion. Gail Bouslough, a friend from my high school teaching days and a graduate student at The Claremont Colleges, also helped keep me sane. Not only did she discuss the writing process and offer encouragement, but she also copy-edited drafts of this manuscript, and made insightful suggestions.

A number of institutions and their staffs assisted my work on this project. Trevor James Bonds and Laila Miletic-Vejzovic of Manuscripts, Archives, and Special Collections, Holland Library, Washington State University helped me greatly as I worked through the Lucullus Virgil McWhorter Collection. The staff of the University Archives Division, University of Washington Libraries provided valuable assistance during my research in the Edmond Meany Collection. Judith McWhorter Goodwin, granddaughter of Lucullus Virgil McWhorter shared her memories and insights of her grandfather. The staff of the National Archives and Records Administration, Washington, D.C. assisted my efforts to wade through the enormous materials contained in Record Group 75. John Ferrell, Archivist at the National Archives and Records Administration – Pacific Alaska Region also supplied invaluable insight into the records of the Northern Idaho Indian Agency and other pertinent records relating to the Nez Perce.

I wish to thank Rebecca Kugel and Brian Lloyd of the University of California, Riverside for their insightful suggestions, all of which improved my manuscript. I appreciate their investment of time and energy in this project. I also thank Clifford Trafzer for his guidance and friendship. In all ways, Cliff gave of his wisdom and insight, providing his time and effort to help me craft the best possible book. He shared his experience, knowledge and love of the Pacific Northwest with me, helping me give voice to the Nez Perce and their story.

In the end, it is always those closest to us who share the greatest burden during the process of writing. Without the support of my wife, Julie Regnier McCoy, this book would have remained only thoughts and aspirations bouncing around my mind. Her faith and confidence in my work helped me research and write. She provided an atmosphere conducive to creativity. I owe much to her as she patiently endured my ups and downs and faithfully believed that we would reach the end of the writing tunnel.

Finally, I acknowledge and thank the Nez Perce people for their strength and endurance over the past century and a half. Without their perseverance, this work would have been impossible, since it was their desire to retain and pass on their history and culture that inspired me to write about their struggle. I am not Nez Perce, but I have tried my best to represent the views and voices of the people through their own writings and beliefs. I hope I have provided some measure of success and that my work will encourage others to use native voices in framing their own work. A few years back, some Nez Perce returned to the Wallowa Valley to live. Perhaps the next time I visit Joseph, Oregon, I will meet some of the original inhabitants of Northeastern Oregon and learn their assessment of Chief Joseph Days and the myths that surround the patient leader and his people.

Chapter One
Ghosts of the Whitmans

Words have power. Both Native Americans and Anglo Americans recognize this power and set boundaries on the use of words. "The word became flesh and dwelt among us." These words from the Gospel of John graphically emphasize the power of the word in western European culture. The word, the power, the creative force, the ability to change and create a new history "dwelt among us." History is essentially about words, both oral and written, that express forms of memory or embody the creative forces of a particular culture. Analyzing the means that a culture uses to create its story or telling how the "word" is made alive to dwell among the people is the subject of this work. The "word" in this instance is the history of the Nez Perce people and Anglo Americans created a very specific "word" to dwell among them and animate their past.

Words carry not only creative force but also a destructive capacity, killing or at least severely restricting the creativity of words used by other cultures. Nez Perce War Chief Yellow Wolf's admonition to Anglo Americans that they told the story of his people to please themselves is a poignant reminder of the destructive power of words. Words provided by others circumscribed the experience of the Nez Perce or restricted Nez Perce voices to the periphery of society, sometimes completely silencing Nez Perce words or relegating them to exile. Anglo Americans failed to understand native viewpoints and worldviews and therefore archived, wrote, researched, and recorded history from a non-native perspective, while consigning Nez Perce words to the void. I am using biblical or Judeo-Christian imagery since most Anglo Americans presented in this work were familiar with these images. They worked within a written and oral framework that actively pursued the word, using words to create a society that conformed to the creative power of their own voices.

The failure to understand Native American worldviews produced a distorted and less creative version of history. A lesson from my own life constantly reminds me of the dilemma facing those attempting to use words to create a new vision of our collective history and to include Native American voices in the history of the United States. Baker City is a small town located in the northeastern corner of Oregon, near the borders of Idaho and Washington. In many respects, Baker City shares many of the same characteristics of rural towns across the American West. The town's economy relies on farming, ranching, extractive industries, and tourism to survive. Mainly Anglo Americans of European ancestry populate Baker City. In Baker City elementary school, students are exposed to the story of the United States, and, in particular, introduced to the story of the Pacific Northwest. As an elementary school student, I remember that our class had the opportunity to take a field trip to an important historical site of Pacific Northwest history. While numerous historical sites existed within a short distance from Baker City itself, our teachers decided that a field trip to the Whitman Mission near Walla Walla, Washington, some ninety miles west of Baker City, would be the most interesting and profitable use of field trip funds and provide a tactile and visual historical experience.

The trip to the mission site was the standard yellow school bus type, filled with overanxious and loud students, exultant to be outside of the classroom for the day. During the trip, my mind went back to the only reference point that I had for the Whitman Mission. As with most field trips, our teachers attempted to prepare us for the experience and present material to familiarize the class with the field trip activity. While I forgot most of the "factual" information presented by our teacher, I distinctly remember a particular drawing, which depicted the Whitman Massacre and painted a scene of fear. Bursting through the door on the right side of the picture was a Cayuse warrior with his war tomahawk raised and a facial expression that, in my mind, the mind of an elementary school student, conjured up images of crazy people or even demons. The left side of the drawing contained images of white women and children, cowering before the warrior, frightened and facing their deaths. Since I was an impressionable child, this image popped into my mind as we traveled to the mission site. I identified with the children and their fear.

When we arrived at the site, the customary tour began led by a guide from the National Park Services Whitman Mission historical site. The guide probably was quite familiar with taking children from surrounding communities through the site and pointed out the various points of interest. Most of the students, though, were more interested in finding some place to escape the clutches of our chaperones. At least superficially we understood the importance of this site. At the Whitman Mission, white Christian missionaries gave their lives to open the Pacific Northwest for other Anglo Americans and to secure the area for the United States. The story of the Whitmans and their demise is consistent with many other iconic stories of the "West." As missionaries, the Whitmans followed the Word, the creative force of Christian religion that in the nineteenth century rapidly flowed out into the world to bring "civilization" and "Christianity" to "heathen savages." The interesting part of the story is that the Whitmans did not respond to words from their fellow Anglo Americans, but supposedly they heard their missionary call in the voices of a Nez Perce delegation that had traveled in 1833 to St. Louis in search of the white man's book of power. The exhibits in the interpretive center and around the site emphasized the Whitmans' call, their journey to the Northwest, and their mission to the Plateau Indians, motivated by the voices and actions of Nez Perce people.

While presenting a great deal of information about the Whitmans and their activities at Waiilatpu, the interpretive center gave far less information about the Cayuse, Nez Perce, Walla Walla, Umatilla and other Native American communities that frequented the mission site before, during, and after the establishment of the mission. At most, the depiction of the massacre informed the visitor that the Cayuse participating in the attack believed that the Whitmans were responsible for the measles epidemic that killed many people in their community, but these exhibits also subtly communicated that the killings were more akin to superstitious persecution of witches in New England rather than a rational response to the epidemic. In fact, this part of the story was negated by a reminder to the visitor that the "irrational" Cayuse killed the very people who were trying to help cure them, namely Dr. Marcus Whitman and the staff of the mission.

The creative power of words spoken about the Whitmans and their fate failed to communicate the source of conflict and the ultimate reason for the "massacre." Instead the park's staff created a story, a myth that was told to please themselves on behalf of many non-natives, words that informed everyone in the Anglo-American community that no matter the consequences, those who pursue the "word," those who work for civilization, progress, the advancement of American culture will ultimately see their work completed by those who follow. The death of Whitman, at least in this story, was a necessary sacrifice, one imbued with a significance that far outstripped the original event. White people in western Oregon ultimately punished the Cayuse for their actions against those who brought the word to the Pacific Northwest. The only problem is that the punishment continued and expanded to other Indian communities. The Anglo-American word was always accompanied by hordes of white people who were attempting to bring the vision of Manifest Destiny and Christian civilization into being in a new land populated by people with a different vision of history and knowledge. Words were not used to make connections to the past and to draw it into the present, but Anglo Americans destroyed the connections of Native American communities with their past and disrupted their connection with the land. The power of this story rested in its ability to justify the eventual assault on Plateau Indian communities and their confinement to the peripheries of Pacific Northwest history, like being exiled to the Indian Territory or to reservations. As early as elementary school, the power of words created boundaries, divided cultures and fashioned a world that had little or no room for the power of Nez Perce words.

HISTORY: SKIRMISHES AROUND THE POWER OF THE WORD

The research premise guiding this present work is that Europeans, and in particular Anglo Americans, used discursive practices, historical knowledge, and memory about Native Americans from initial contact to the present as a self-perpetuating means to advance and justify the subjugation of Indians and to secure group identity. In essence, this work is about the power of words and in particular the power of words when transformed in our culture into "history." History, at least until recently, was not the integrative use of words and memory, but expressed itself in dualities of oral versus written, myth versus fact, sacred versus scientific. Native Americans labored under a number of historical representations and narrative models that flattened and froze their experience and memory into simplistic narratives that denied agency or the presence of historical knowledge as defined by Anglo-American culture. Too often Anglo Americans, especially in the late nineteenth and early twentieth centuries, portrayed Native Americans as doomed impediments to progressive, liberal and democratic history, reducing the Nez Perce and other native people to the status of "victims" without recourse or resistance, while their culture slowly faded into oblivion. The dualities of history in our culture favored the Anglo-American version, while placing the words and knowledge of the Nez Perce in isolation and outside the course of historical action by labeling Nez Perce knowledge as myth, primitive or imbued with mystical meanings.

At the heart of "silencing" Nez Perce memory and historical knowledge was the process of Anglo-American historical production in the late nineteenth and early twentieth century. The production of history occurs within specific historical contexts that shape and re-shape narratives to meet current societal needs.[1] Is the context for Anglo-American historical production about the Nez Perce the mythological confrontation of the "democratic," "civilized" Anglo-American man and the "Indian" or some other context? The specific historical context for the creation of Anglo-American historical narratives was, as William Robbins noted, the emergence and dominance of industrial and corporate capitalism in the United States during the late nineteenth and early twentieth centuries and, by extension, the incorporation of the West into modern capitalism. The best way to understand the American West and the production of history about the Nez Perce is through an "interpretive framework grounded in the theoretical and empirical world of modern capitalism."[2] Within this framework, this study understands modern capitalism not only as an economic system, but also as "a body of ideas and values that are lived at great depth and that permeate our culture." Capitalism, in this sense, "saturates the consciousness of the societies it has come to influence."[3] In other words, the emergence of modern industrial capitalism in the late nineteenth and early twentieth century influenced and infused the creation of narratives about the Nez Perce, while also shaping the policies and practices of government officials, white settlers and academics who interacted with the Nez Perce.

Within the context of modern industrial capitalism, racial constructs interacted and informed the production of history and influenced the incorporation of silences and uneven historical traces. Anglo Americans used racial constructs as significant sources of power for creating inter-class loyalty based on race rather than social or class positions in Anglo-American communities. This is important since race can be mobilized within the context of modern capitalism as an instrument for creating cultural hegemony. T.J. Jackson Lears used the term "cultural hegemony" to understand "the role of culture in sustaining inequalities of wealth and power." Cultural hegemony then is "the winning of spontaneous loyalty of subordinate groups to a common set of values and attitudes."[4] In the Pacific Northwest, the story of the Nez Perce and the labeling of Indians as "savages" and hindrances to progressive, civilized Anglo-American culture mobilized the power of racial constructs to create a "cultural hegemony" regarding Indians on the Columbia Plateau. In other words, the production of history and the racialization of Native Americans worked together to subordinate Native Americans, solidify the loyalty of different classes within the dominant Anglo-American society, and justify the theft, murder and rape required to consolidate the Pacific Northwest region.

The conquest and colonization of Native American communities focused the power of representation, memory, and forgetting in the mind of the colonizers and created an imagined "Indian" that informed the writing of Native American history. There was a script that "Indians" were to follow, mirrored in film and photographic mediums, leading Native Americans down the "inevitable" path to assimilation and incorporation into American society. This tradition of imagining and defining the "Indian" is an important theoretical concern of this work. The theoretical question that must be addressed is how to represent the "Other," in this case the Nez Perce or any Native American culture, without falling into the narrative modes, myths and stereotypes that perpetuate the imagined "Indian" whose culture was doomed to extinction because of its "inferiority" to Anglo-American culture.

Representing the "Other" is an extremely problematic task. The major problem of writing history about Native Americans is to avoid reinforcing or reinventing preexisting representations from the late nineteenth and early twentieth century. Robert Young, in *White Mythologies: Writing History and the West*, attempted to address this problem. The distinct message of Young's book was that all attempts to solve the problem of representing the "Other" created new problems and failed to develop new knowledge or means of communicating that enabled scholars to escape present power and authority relations. Young emphatically stated, "The analysis of colonialism has shown the extent to which such relations of power and authority are still endemic in current social and institutional practices."[5] The inability to solve the problem of representation has brought about the "important realization, articulated so forcibly by writers such as Michel Foucault and Edward Said, of the deep articulation of knowledge and power."[6]

Recognizing the interrelationship between knowledge and power allows historians to reveal how previous Anglo-American narratives, histories, and memory created the definition and image of a "democratic man" in the United States through myths of cultural superiority that relied on defining and marginalizing groups of people like women, Native Americans, and African Americans. Since the creation and maintenance of the "Other" is so integral to the definition of Anglo-American culture, the key is to escape what Calvin Martin called "the dual metaphysics of Indian-White history." Martin warned that by ignoring the memory and cultural knowledge of the Nez Perce, historians risk "writing about ourselves to ourselves." Through a careful investigation and analysis of Anglo-American representations of the Nez Perce, the opportunity arises to critique past and present forms of knowledge about the Nez Perce, and Native Americans in general, while at the same time allowing for the penetration of Nez Perce history and memory, often relegated to the private and communal level, into public memory discourse.[7]

The Nez Perce were not merely objects to be studied or recorded, but they also actively resisted, critiqued, and created their own historical knowledge that often subverted history produced by Anglo Americans. This work is not looking for some essential, exceptional American West or America, but rather, as Robert Young asserted, the author wants to examine "the representations that Anglo Americans produced for themselves of its Other, against and through which it defines itself, together with the function of such representations in a structure of power in which they are used instrumentally."[8]

SILENCING THE PAST

The investigation of Anglo-American representations of the Nez Perce in the late nineteenth and early twentieth centuries is the main object of this work. While these representations, whether produced by academics, missionaries, government officials or amateur historians, differ somewhat in their structure; they nearly always manage to silence Indians at similar points in their narratives.[9] Most of these narratives also created gaps of silence when they introduced Nez Perce and other Columbia Plateau people into the web of their story. These silences helped historians to analyze and evaluate sources of power and identity within Anglo-American society and culture during the late nineteenth and early twentieth centuries. Michel-Rolph Trouillot noted that "Power does not enter the story once and for all, but at different times and from different angles. It precedes the narrative proper, contributes to its creation, and to its interpretation."[10] Silences contribute to our understanding of power structures in the late nineteenth and early twentieth centuries, because they are an integral part of the process of creating historical narratives. Trouillot asserted that silences "crystallize aspects of historical production that are best exposed when and where power gets into the story." The author believes, with Michel-Rolph Trouillot, that:

> Power is constitutive of the story. Tracking power through various "moments" simply helps emphasize the fundamentally processual character of historical production, to insist that what history is matters less than how history works; that power itself works together with history.[11]

Power is expressed in the production of historical narratives. Trouillot noted that silences, or signifiers of power,

> Enter the process of historical production at four crucial moments: the moment of fact creation (the making of sources); the moment of fact assembly (the making of archives); the moment of fact retrieval (the making of narratives); and the moment of retrospective significance (the making of history in the final instance).[12]

In the creation of historical narratives about the Pacific Northwest from the 1870s to 1940, most Anglo Americans silenced Native Americans in all four steps of the process. In the moments of fact creation and fact assembly, professional and amateur historians disregarded Native American sources. Instead, they focused their energy in these steps on finding and collecting sources from pioneers, settlers, government officials, and missionaries. While these two moments of historical production are very important, this work focuses on the third and fourth steps of the process, the making of narratives and the making of history in the final instance. Anglo-American writers in the Pacific Northwest produced historical narratives that gave significance to their own history and connected them to older and more national narratives. As Yellow Wolf observed, these historical narratives were written to "please themselves," to provide explanatory frameworks and interpretations of "facts" that supported Anglo-American myths of cultural superiority and Manifest Destiny.

In essence, this work itself represents step three of Trouillot's framework of historical production. The author is recreating the narrative of Nez Perce history with an eye to illuminate and critique how Anglo Americans used these narratives in the fourth step of the process, the part that provided meaning and significance or that was told to please themselves. A number of different historical narratives from the 1870s to the 1930s will be examined to understand how Anglo Americans told these stories and how they interpreted the actions and presence of Native Americans. This work will not explore later narratives that sought to remedy some of the silences of the works examined in the following chapters. The author is interested in the early narratives, because they still influence more contemporary attempts to remedy the silencing of the Nez Perce and other Columbia Plateau peoples. In many ways, contemporary historians, particularly historians interested in narrating Native American history, are still trying to escape earlier modes of representation and the silencing of Native Americans.

While recognizing that "historical production occurs in many sites," this work focuses on certain narratives to investigate silences in Anglo-American narratives. Two of the main sources analyzed in the following chapters are works created by Edmond S. Meany and C.J. Brosnan, both professors at land-grant colleges in Washington and Idaho. In order to avoid analyzing academic works exclusively, the author sought to include narratives created by amateur historians like Kate McBeth, a missionary to the Nez Perce, Oliver Otis Howard, commanding officer during the Nez Perce War, and a popular history of North Idaho published by the Western Historical Publishing Company. The author chose these sources because they represent different sites of narrative production. Most of these works also appeared in wide distribution throughout the Pacific Northwest and influenced historical consciousness among many different Anglo-American groups. From the 1870s to the 1940s, these narratives certainly did not represent all Anglo-American historical production. It must be kept in mind that local memory and historical production continued to occur among Anglo-American communities in the Pacific Northwest.

CHAPTER OUTLINE

To investigate the creation of Anglo-American narratives between the 1870s and 1940, this work created its own structure and silences. Some Anglo-American sources were silenced and not included, while more Nez Perce sources and voices took their place to remedy previous exclusion. One of the ways that the author included more Nez Perce voices was to use the Nez Perce story of Coyote and Monster as the narrative framework for the book. The version used here originated from Archie Phinney who related the story told by his mother during oral interviews. I found this version in Phinney's book, *Nez Perce Texts*. Other versions continue to live among Nez Perce people on the Nez Perce and Colville reservations. Each chapter begins with a portion of the story that fits the activities of Monster (Anglo Americans) and Coyote (the Nez Perce) in the Pacific Northwest in the nineteenth and twentieth centuries. This story served as a creation story for the Nez Perce, but it also applies to the production of historical narratives. Monster, in this case Anglo Americans, consumed the people and silenced them in the Pacific Northwest, but Coyote, the Nez Perce, did not accept this silencing and resisted Monster, eventually freeing the people for a re-creation of the narrative. In the spirit of the Coyote and Monster Story, the second chapter spends a great deal of time attempting to provide a brief overview of Nez Perce culture and life before the arrival of Europeans. The length of this chapter contends with the large silence of many of the examined narratives, created when they narrated this period of Nez Perce history. Both Anglo-American and Nez Perce sources were used to create this portrayal of the Nez Perce in a way that avoided the "inevitability" of their defeat and confinement to a reservation evident in earlier Anglo-American narratives.

The meeting of Euro-Americans and Native Americans on the Columbia Plateau is the subject of Chapter Three. The analysis of Anglo-American narratives begins in earnest in this chapter. In particular, the penchant for creating romantic and heroic pictures of Anglo-American exploration and explorers is examined as well as the place of Native Americans within these activities. Chapter Four continues this story with an examination of narratives created about the arrival of missionaries and the treaty period on the Columbia Plateau. The events surrounding the Whitman Mission and the historical controversies that arose in the early twentieth century are explored and deconstructed.

Chapter Five is the linchpin chapter in the analysis of Anglo-American narratives about the Nez Perce. The focus of the chapter is the incursion of whites on the Nez Perce Reservation in the 1860s, new treaty negotiations, the events leading to the Nez Perce War, and the Nez Perce War of 1877 itself. This chapter is especially significant because after this point most Nez Perce disappeared from Anglo-American narratives. Once subdued and exiled, Anglo Americans condensed the experience of the non-treaty Nez Perce into the images and words of Chief Joseph, while Christian treaty Nez Perce on the reservation almost completely disappeared from narratives. These silences, the signifiers of power, neared a totality that expressed the perspective of Anglo Americans, namely that the defeat and confinement of Indians proved the power and superiority of Anglo-American culture.

The sixth chapter once again attempts to remedy the silence of most narratives examined in this work. As Indians disappeared from Anglo-American narratives, one Nez Perce, Chief Joseph, remained in the national consciousness and in the memory of people in the Pacific Northwest. The first part of the chapter examines the cult and myth of Chief Joseph and the reasons for Anglo Americans using his images, actions and words. After the examination of the myth of Joseph, the chapter continues with a brief discussion of how Nez Perce people, both Christian and non-Christian, dealt with confinement to the reservation. In particular, allotment and issues of land ownership are discussed because land played such an important role in Anglo-American narratives. The last part of the chapter discusses the frustration of agency officials, missionaries, and others in dealing with Nez Perce people as Anglo Americans attempted to assimilate them into their culture. While silenced in Anglo-American narratives, Nez Perce people failed to conform to their role as the silent, disappearing Indian and created ways of making Anglo Americans listen to their voices.

The work ends with a brief epilogue that relates the problem of being Nez Perce in the midst of a culture that actively worked to silence their history and culture, briefly discussing the life of Yellow Wolf, relative of Chief Joseph and main narrator in L.V. McWhorter's *Yellow Wolf: His Own Story*. His life showed a possible route taken by some Nez Perce in dealing with Anglo-American assimilation policies and historical narratives. Yellow Wolf provides an example of Nez Perce people who resisted white culture. He is also important because McWhorter's work, *Yellow Wolf: His Own*

Story, attempted to present a view of the Nez Perce War from Yellow Wolf's perspective, a Nez Perce perspective. This book, published in 1940, was the first of its kind in the Pacific Northwest and effectively ended the silencing of the Nez Perce, especially with regard to the Nez Perce War of 1877.

The power of these old narratives has waned, but historians of Native American history still confront powerful structures of producing history that rely on older ways of thinking, valuing sources and narrating the Nez Perce story. The author hopes that this brief foray into the processes of Anglo-American historical production in the Pacific Northwest will cause others to examine thoroughly their own frameworks for understanding Nez Perce history and the history of Native Americans as a whole. While it is important to understand the power behind the creation of these narratives, it is also important to understand how these narratives also supported the "power" of Anglo Americans and their beliefs in cultural superiority, Manifest Destiny, and the racial inferiority of Native Americans. When these power structures are illuminated, it is easier to start filling in the gaps of "silence" and to create narratives that respect and include the voices of Nez Perce people.

Chapter Two
Coyote and the Nez Perce

> Coyote was building a fish-ladder, by tearing down the waterfall at Celilo, so that salmon could go upstream for the people to catch. He was busily engaged at this when someone shouted to him, "Why are you bothering with that? All the people are gone: the monster has done for them." – "Well," said Coyote to himself, "then I'll stop doing this, because I was doing it for the people, and now I'll go along too."
>
> From there he went along upstream, by the way of the Salmon River country. Going along he stepped on the leg of a meadow-lark and broke it. The meadow-lark in a temper shouted, "lima, lima, lima, what a chance of finding the people you have going along!" Coyote then asked, "My Aunt! Please inform me, afterwards I will make for you a leg of brush-wood." So the meadow-lark told him, "Already all the people have been swallowed by the monster." Coyote then replied, "Yes, that is where I, too, am going."[1]

In 1879, Sue McBeth arrived in Lapwai, Idaho, to join the missionary group charged with the conversion and instruction of the Nez Perce Indians. While missionary presence in northern Idaho dated from around 1835, the arrival of McBeth in 1879 marked a new era in Anglo American and Nez Perce relations.[2] The defeat of the non-treaty Nez Perce by the United States Army and their subsequent imprisonment and exile in "Eekish Pah – the hot place" allowed missionaries to concentrate on the "Christian" Nez Perce and bring them closer to the faith.[3] Bringing Indians closer to the faith or converting them to Christianity necessarily implied that that they would not only adopt Christian beliefs, but would also take on the cultural aspects of Protestant Christianity in the late nineteenth century. These cultural expectations principally focused on "heathen" practices that missionaries and church workers believed were rooted in the "former" life and religious beliefs of the Nez

Perce people.[4] The dual nature of reconstructing Nez Perce life and history, as practiced by missionaries and church workers, illustrated the amnesiac traits evident in knowledge created about the Nez Perce. The prevalent idea was to bury or kill former Nez Perce knowledge and beliefs while recreating a "new" person that followed the cultural expectations of Anglo Americans. Nez Perce knowledge, beliefs, and history were used against the Nez Perce themselves as weapons to justify their cultural destruction and to lower their social position in Anglo-American society.

The abuse of Nez Perce knowledge, history and cultural practices by missionaries and church workers also illustrated some of the fundamental traps that writers fall into when attempting to describe another culture or present that culture's beliefs. Talking and writing about the Nez Perce and their relationship to Anglo Americans and the production of history necessitates a description or overview of Nez Perce culture before their contact with Anglo Americans. In many ways, this work faces the same problems as earlier researchers and writers when attempting this reconstruction. While many Anglo Americans earlier in this century recognized the problem of reconstructing Nez Perce culture, they normally solved this problem by relying on the myth of Anglo-American cultural superiority and the inevitable demise of Native Americans in general and the Nez Perce in particular.[5] The use of Nez Perce history and the power to manipulate it fell into the hands of Euro- Americans as spoils of war through the use of military force and relegation of Nez Perce people to the reservation. These "spoils" placed Anglo Americans in a position to tell history or the story "to please themselves," as Yellow Wolf noted in his autobiography.[6]

The problems of reconstructing a culture are myriad, but this work focuses on one specific difficulty that is particularly pertinent to the description of Nez Perce culture and history. The problem of sources lies at the heart of much misunderstanding and many misconceptions surrounding Native American experience and history in the United States. During the late nineteenth and early twentieth centuries, non-Indians created knowledge about Native Americans, most often without context or sensitivity to Native American beliefs and life. Anglo-American anthropologists, historians, missionaries and private individuals gathered, organized, interpreted and wrote about the Nez Perce, sometimes using Nez Perce informants. Other times they relied on research and writing methodologies that failed to substantiate their claims since verifying or even discussing a sense of history for those considered outside of the "civilized" concept of historical knowledge and scientific investigation was impossible.[7]

Often this hierarchical system of knowledge was expressed by touting the virtues and superiority of written culture over more "primitive" forms of knowledge recorded through the oral narratives of Native Americans. For example, in his article on native villages and groupings, Verne Ray noted "the notorious unreliability of native verbal traditions when they refer to history a few generations or more removed."[8] The very nature of Nez Perce knowledge, with its expression in education, history, law, and religion, were relegated to a pile of anachronistic beliefs associated with "primitive" cultures, merely because oral means were used to transmit tribal history, cultural beliefs and practices. Not only were the Nez Perce considered a "conquered" people, but their oral narrative tradition was also not regarded as legitimate by those who were attempting to recreate and reconstruct Nez Perce culture before contact with Europeans and Anglo Americans. These beliefs about the Nez Perce and their knowledge practices affected researchers' vision and limited their ability to portray Nez Perce culture in a sensitive and thorough manner.

The tropes of "savagery and civilization" and "history and nature," as described by Kerwin Klein, shaped a narrative structure that informed the research of academics from all disciplines. These tropes or beliefs limited the scope of investigations and also predestined the outcomes for the Nez Perce in later studies. Since Nez Perce knowledge was suspect, it was easy to create a static vision of Nez Perce culture that was frozen in time or romantic visions of the "noble" Indian, unaffected by time or space. The "eternal" Indian, moving between romantic expressions of nobility and savage primitiveness, as opposed to "civilization" and progress, animated the work of academics, missionaries and "ordinary" people. From the very beginning of this work, the inability of the researcher to completely or accurately describe pre-contact Nez Perce culture and beliefs is assumed and expected. To avoid the traps of earlier writers, the author assumes that the brief overview of Nez Perce culture given in this chapter cannot fully portray the complexity and depth of Nez Perce culture before their contact with Europeans and Anglo Americans. Avoiding the traps of romanticization, whether New Age or old fashioned, and reductionism requires that this work recognize the limitations of talking about cultures or culture in general. A sensitive portrayal of any Native American community or culture is problematic at best, but it is the objective of the following sections.[9]

BOUNDARIES AND BOXES

Why is it important to attempt a description of Nez Perce culture and history before the arrival of Europeans? Since this work seeks to understand how

Anglo Americans used Nez Perce culture and history to their own ends, it is extremely important to attempt an understanding of Nez Perce culture that is not so intimately based on the assumptions of previous Anglo-American perceptions of the Nez Perce and Native Americans in general. One of the greatest dangers in this attempt is to slip into a narrative mode that presents pre-contact Nez Perce culture as static or romanticizes this period with visions of noble Indians communing with nature. The Nez Perce had, and continue to have, a dynamic and changing culture that responds to changes in their environment and pressures from other cultures. The persistence of such static or romantic portrayals is based on the simple need to justify Anglo Americans treatment of Indians. It is easier to use military force and relegate a people to a reservation if their culture is static and non-progressive, if it is a "simplistic" culture incapable of the same achievements as Anglo-American culture in the United States.

The Anglo-American penchant to classify, create boundaries, and manipulate knowledge about Native Americans applied as much to the Nez Perce as to any other native community in the United States. While attempting to preserve knowledge about the Nez Perce, Anglo Americans collected and interpreted this knowledge within the framework and beliefs of their own cultural and historical milieu. Collecting ethnographic materials, whether in the form of oral histories, material culture or descriptions of Native American cultures before contact, occurred within the context of private and public museums and collectors competing for artifacts and cultural material as commodities. Collecting was not purely altruistic or for "pure" scientific knowledge, but was often conducted to generate funds to continue collecting and for fieldwork. For example, Franz Boas often "sold" collected materials to museums like the Peabody and others to fund further expeditions. This commodification of Native American material culture and knowledge existed within a capitalist culture devoted to capturing the realm of Native American knowledge and material culture.[10]

Unfortunately, research and fieldwork by Anglo Americans, especially in the late nineteenth and early twentieth centuries, took on a desperation born from perceptions that Native cultures were disappearing or dying. The material collected by researchers like Herbert Spinden, Franz Boas, and others must be used and interpreted in the light of their belief that Native cultures were dying, assimilating or disappearing from the American historical and ethnographic landscape. The perceived disappearance of Nez Perce and other Native American cultures presented a dilemma for these researchers. While often reinforcing their beliefs of Anglo-American superiority and cultural dominance, the disappearance of native cultures, if completed, threatened to deprive Anglo Americans of the very examples of "primitive" and uncivilized cultures that formed the basis for beliefs in Anglo-American cultural superiority. In essence, concerted efforts to collect and store knowledge about the Nez Perce served the triple purpose of academic research, preservation of models that confirming beliefs of superiority and dominance, and financial support for further collecting and fieldwork through the sale of Native American objects as commodities. Even though "dying," these cultures could serve their purposes as examples of the inexorable progress of Anglo-American culture and history and as the means to romanticize, commodify, and enrich those who participated in this process.

In the 1930s, researchers like Verne Ray and others focused on collecting ethnographic materials that related directly to legal concerns over land and treaty rights. Discovering and mapping the land base boundaries of Nez Perce, Palouse, Walla Walla, Cayuse and other Plateau cultures was a primary concern, motivated largely through the investigative efforts of the Indian Claims Commission. While researchers ventured into the field, questioned and listened to informants, and examined historical sources produced by Anglo Americans, the concern was once again over a commodity, land. The creation and mapping of boundaries was an important exercise for Anglo Americans since property and land possession lie at the very heart of capitalist culture, both in its economic and social aspects. Protection of property rights was a fundamental Constitutional issue, and resolving property disputes is an important part of our legal system. Resolving Indian land claims required the expertise of researchers and academics able to provide detailed boundaries and maps used in the legal system (Indian Claims Commission) to clarify property ownership and treaty rights.[11]

Whether concerned with "dying" native cultures, or issues surrounding property rights, these sources provide a wealth of material often gleaned from Nez Perce informants that shed light on their culture, beliefs, and history before the intrusion of Europeans and Anglo Americans into the Pacific Northwest. While this work will rely on various sources created by Anglo Americans, the author recognizes also the cultural assumptions contained in these sources, whether driven by beliefs of native cultural destruction or through testimony in legal proceedings determining the worth and disposition of land. Careful reading and attention to these texts will clarify the voices of those who truly knew and lived their culture.

Most important, this brief description of Nez Perce culture and history before European contact also assumes that the Nez Perce exercised flexibility and the power to adapt their culture in the face of change or threat. Of any cultural group in the United States, Native Americans have managed to adapt and thrive even in the face of overwhelming odds and attempts to destroy their respective cultures. The resilience, adaptability and strength of their cultures is quite clearly demonstrated by communities of Native Americans, including the Nez Perce, thriving and passing on their culture, history and beliefs at the beginning of the twenty-first century.[12]

LIFEWAYS

Ecology and Land

The Columbia Plateau or Basin, home to the Nez Perce and other Sahaptin speaking communities, is a vast region and is the outstanding feature of the area.[13] The Columbia Plateau "includes the middle portion of the Columbia River and a number of smaller rivers like the Deschutes, John Day, Umatilla, and Grande Ronde Rivers."[14] The northern boundary of the Plateau reaches into upper British Columbia and its southern boundary extends to Nevada. The Plateau is bounded on the west by the Cascade Mountains, on the south by the Blue Mountains and on the east and north by low-lying extensions of the Rocky Mountains. Geologically, the region is characterized by a succession of lava flows, drained by the Columbia River, which has cut canyons hundreds of feet deep into the lava beds.[15] This vast stretch of territory exhibits tremendous variety in climate, geology, and ecology. Eugene Hunn noted that the Plateau area alternates "between the extremes of baked-dry riverside flats and cool mountain forest."[16] According to Donald Meinig, the distinguishing characteristic of the Columbia Plateau is the undulating nature of its surface and its general lack of forests. Meinig noted that the Columbia Plateau was an open country dominated by rolling prairie or sagebrush flats that featured bunch wheat grass as the predominate plant life. While the Plateau contained little or no forested areas, the surrounding highlands and mountains held vast forested regions and formed a sharp boundary on the edge of the Columbia Plateau. Most Nez Perce lived in the highlands just west of the Bitterroot Mountains and traveled extensively in the Plateau in search of food and for trade.

The climate and seasons of the Columbia Plateau varied greatly from surrounding areas, in particular those west of the Cascade Mountain range. The Cascade Range forced storms coming into the Pacific Northwest to deposit precipitation on the western slopes of the mountain range, leaving relatively little moisture available for regions east of the Cascade Mountains. On average, the center of the Plateau received six inches or less of rainfall per annum. According to Meinig, the dramatic contrast between the humid regions west of the Cascades and the dry lands of the Plateau exist in very few places in the world. The relative low precipitation in the Columbia Plateau created a seasonal cycle of "cool moderately rainy and snowy winters, wet springs, hot dry summers and warm predominately dry autumns."[17] These conditions varied area to area in the Columbia Plateau depending on elevation, proximity to rivers or streams, and exposures. Meinig noted that the most variation in climate occurred during winter with some areas remaining barren of snow throughout the whole season while other regions closer to the highlands and mountains surrounding the Plateau might remain covered by snow throughout the winter. Late winter and early spring exhibited the most inconsistent climatic conditions. Many areas experienced continued snowfall, but a "Chinook" wind could melt the snow cover and warm temperatures quickly. Rain showers through June characterized late spring with lower areas experiencing higher temperatures and less precipitation. Summers on the Columbia Plateau are hot and dry with temperatures reaching one hundred degrees or more in the lower elevations. The surrounding highlands seldom experienced such extreme temperatures. Relatively hot and dry conditions could continue well into the autumn, but generally the nights trend toward very cool during the months of September and October.[18]

Meinig asserted that the above patterns of climate, life and landscape shaped the human geography of the Columbia Plateau. Conditions on the Plateau required Native Americans living in the region to adapt to a region that contained "no good animal staple, few usable plants and little material for fire and shelter." Unlike the Great Plains to the east, the Columbia Plateau contained no bison and only seasonal herds of elk, deer and antelope. According to Meinig, a minimal number of small animals like squirrels, rabbits and birds lived on the Plateau, but "the rivers teemed with life," mainly salmon. The one plentiful food source on the Columbia Plateau, salmon, drew Indian peoples to the Plateau River system, the Columbia and Snake Rivers as well as to their tributaries, and provided them with a very important source of food for survival. Indian communities in this region either lived on the rivers or came to them seasonally to catch salmon. The Columbia Plateau was not devoid of human habitation, but Indian peoples like the Nez Perce used the region in a seasonal pattern. They wintered in the canyon bottoms and low country on the periphery of the Plateau where it was warmer and less snow fell. During the spring, summer and fall, the Nez Perce and other Plateau communities moved throughout the Plateau region and the bordering highlands hunting and gathering food supplies for their survival. Fishing for salmon along the streams and rivers of the Columbia Plateau formed an important part of the seasonal round, the subsistence cycle of the Nez Perce and other Plateau communities.[19]

Meinig saw the Columbia Plateau before the arrival of Europeans and Anglo Americans as an "empty" zone that was not truly empty. Indian peoples used the Plateau on a seasonal basis and the region played an important part in shaping the larger cultural region of the Plateau Indian life. The region contributed to the shared cultural characteristics of Native Americans in the inland Pacific Northwest. For example, native peoples developed fishing economies to exploit the abundance of salmon in nearby rivers and streams. Most Plateau cultures also supplemented salmon food sources with hunting and gathering in the surrounding highlands and mountains and used similar tools and knowledge to exploit these resources. Meinig also noted that many Plateau communities shared similar dress, social customs, religious and political order that pointed to a common heritage.[20]

The common heritage and cultural characteristics of Plateau Indian communities sprang from the geography of the region. The Columbia Plateau is like a huge bowl cut through with canyons and lowlands. At its edge the Plateau gives way to highlands and then mountains. For many people familiar with the region, the geography suggested isolation from surrounding areas rather than contact and openness. Meinig suggested that the borderlands, the highlands and mountains, channeled contact and limited it mainly to the Columbia River. As Nez Perce and other Plateau cultures acquired horses in the eighteenth century, contact with native culture groups outside of the Columbia Plateau increased. Many Plateau groups, particularly the Nez Perce, trekked east over the Bitterroot Mountains to hunt buffalo; and their enemies to the south and east, Shoshonean cultures and the Blackfeet, also increased their incursions on the Columbia Plateau.

Within the larger Columbia Plateau region, Nez Perce territory "spanned the Clearwater River and extended to the south and middle forks of the Salmon River drainage basins."[21] The importance of the land in Nez Perce culture and belief is clearly illustrated by the number of oral narratives focusing on Coyote's preparing the land for the coming of the people. For example, Coyote tore down the falls at Celilo to allow salmon to reach the upper portions of the Columbia and Snake Rivers in preparation for the coming of human beings.[22] Coyote also destroyed a dam in the Yakima Country. The land and its preparation are important themes in the corpus of Nez Perce and other Plateau communities' cultural stories and oral narratives.[23] The land, to the Nez Perce and other Plateau groups, was not a commodity to be bought or sold, but rather a mother that provided sustenance (food, water, clothing) and connections to spiritual powers important to both individual and group identity. Coyote and other *Wah Tee Tash* (animal people) prepared the land for the coming of human beings; he sought out plentiful food supplies, water and pleasant surroundings for those (the Nez Perce and others) who were shortly to arrive in the Plateau area. Plateau communities imbued geographic locations with cultural significance because of what happened in a place rather than through ownership or through honoring the exploits of one person or group.

Religion

One of the most controversial areas to consider when attempting to gain insight into any culture concerns describing religious belief and practice. Viewed within the context of the late nineteenth and early twentieth century, Nez Perce religious practices were labeled "heathen," "primitive," "backward," and "uninformed." The cultural lens of Christianity filtered many Anglo-American perceptions and often failed to provide understanding or even interest in practices that directly contradicted the teachings of Protestant Christianity. For Anglo Americans, membership in society was bounded on many levels, but one of the most important was religious belief. As Kerwin Klein perceptively noted, "Significant boundaries between humans derived not from natural or linguistic distinctions but from differences of belief."[24] Since Nez Perce religious values, like many other Native American cultures, centered around the land and the life contained within the natural environment, differences between Nez Perce religion and Christianity were not only contended in "the fields of the Lord" but also on "the fields of capitalist ideology," especially around property ownership.[25]

Christians were not the only ones prepared to label Nez Perce religious practice as "backward" or "primitive." Anthropologists, historians, and other academics readily subscribed "primitiveness" to this part of Nez Perce culture and knowledge. Hunn asserted, "even the familiarity of the modern Indian home life hides a deep division in world view from the Anglo-American norm."[26] As with all terms used to describe, classify or label cultural practices or beliefs, the label of "primitive" was often assigned in the context of cultures meeting and competing, with one culture dominating the other after a period of struggle. "Primitive" as applied by Anglo Americans to Nez Perce religious beliefs was often a comparison of their religious practices with those of Protestant Christianity as practiced in the United States during the late nineteenth and early twentieth century. In light of such assertions of "primitive" religious beliefs, a sensitive portrayal of Nez Perce religious life is important. This work maintains that a culture's religious belief is neither simplistic nor primitive, but lies often at the very core of that people's identity and illustrates the complexity and depth of its worldview. Lack of structure or hierarchy does not denote inferiority or simplicity, but rather reflects differing relationships with the environment and other human beings.

The central aspect of Nez Perce religious belief was a deep connection to the land. This connection was not expressed in a duality with humans at the apex of "creation" contesting and controlling nature; rather, it was a holistic approach that emphasized the integration of humans into the environment. In fact, humans arrived late in Nez Perce oral narratives, and animal and plant people inhabited the land before the arrival of human beings. The land and the natural world were not meant to be possessed, controlled, or manipulated. Seeing little or no separation between themselves and the natural world, the Nez Perce recognized their dependence and interdependence with all living beings and the natural environment. According to Hunn, "The relationship between people and other animate creatures is more personal, conceptualized on the model of familiar social relationships among family, villagers, chiefs, shamans, and strangers."[27] However, this concept of human beings relating to the natural world in terms of personal and social relationship perplexed and confused most Anglo Americans dealing with the Nez Perce.

The centrality of the land to Nez Perce religious beliefs led Anglo Americans to often misrepresent or simplify those beliefs, giving them a two-dimensional quality that denigrated their importance to the Nez Perce. In contrast to these earlier simplifications of Plateau Indian religion, Hunn asserted that "traditional Sahaptin religion may be called animistic; it is also a species of shamanism."[28] Hunn defined this in the following way:

> People, animals, plants, and other forces of nature – sun, earth, wind, and rock – are animated by spirit. As such they share with humankind intelligence and will, and thus have moral rights and obligations as PERSONS.[29]

Hunn also maintained that Anglo-American academics often used the term "animism" without understanding "the theological essence of animism."[30] According to Hunn, the heart of animistic belief revolved around a moral principle. The moral principle of animism "extends the moral benefits of human society to the entire local ecosystem."[31] For the Nez Perce and other Plateau Indian cultures, humans and the local environment shared the same spiritual privileges, obligations and equalities. The separation of humans and nature so entrenched in Anglo-American thought was not evident in this arena.

Rooted in the land, Nez Perce religious belief expressed itself through relationships with the spirit or spirits animating the natural environment.

These relationships were based on the concept of power. Gregory Dowd noted, "Nothing was more important for life than power."[32] Spiritual beings, often in the form of animals or other environmental entities, shared their spiritual powers and gifts with selected individuals. This symbiotic relationship between human and guardian spirit lasted a lifetime and was jealously guarded. Power, in this case, was not a simple matter of a spiritual being providing power to a human recipient, but implied obligation for both parties, a relationship based on respect and duty toward other beings that inhabited the land. Allen Slickpoo, Sr., noted that a guardian spirit could punish a person if he broke a law or failed to perform required rituals connected to the relationship that imbued the recipient with power. For example, Nez Perce men prepared for hunting through ritual cleansing that must be done correctly to ensure success.[33]

How did a Nez Perce man or woman enter into this spiritual relationship? Nez Perce youth established a relationship with a "guardian spirit" through a quest that culminated in visions.[34] The quest functioned as the vehicle through which the *"wyakin"* established a relationship with a Nez Perce youth. Deward Walker maintained that *wyakin* referred to both the guardian spirit and the power that was transferred to the human being in the association. Slickpoo noted that for Nez Perce youth to approach a guardian spirit without preparation and proper respect was a serious mistake. Improper actions could result in illness, accident, weakness, bad luck or sometimes even death. Families and the community prepared children by means of oral narrative and by witnessing of dances, songs and rituals associated with the acquisition of a guardian spirit. Preparing a child for the quest also included fasting, exercise, meditation, and the sweat bath. According to Slickpoo, parents instructed their children for years and accompanied them when they left on the quest. The quest involved seclusion in an isolated area with little food and water. Generally, locations chosen for the vigil possessed spiritual significance for the family or community. One of the most commonly used locations was a mountain called *Tuhm-lo-yeets-mekhs* (Pilot Knob Peak) about 30 miles east of Granger, Idaho.[35]

In order for the quest to be successful, a guardian spirit appeared to the youth. For example, the spirit could manifest itself as a cloud, thunder, water bugs, birds, deer, bear, or any number of animate or inanimate objects. The spirit taught the youth about the nature of the power to be given and proper maintenance of the relationship. The guardian spirit also taught the youth a "special power song" which was used later on ritual occasions or when they needed supernatural aid.[36] Individuals rarely discussed their vision in public since disclosure of the vision could result in the weakening of the spiritual power. When asked about his power, Yellow Wolf remarked that "Therefore no one must ever tell anywhere outside of the war, only when war happens. I will not tell just how I obtained that Power. I should not express it. I can not, I must not tell."[37] When the youth returned to the community, the shaman reintroduced the youth into the community and helped with manifestations of power that occurred after the quest.

Public discussion of the vision was not permitted but, at the "Medicine Dance" or winter dances, people sang songs learned from guardian spirits. Youth sang their newly learned songs and danced in representation of the spirit while members of the community attempted to discern their special powers. Shamans, in particular, assisted young people in understanding and discerning their power. Young people sometimes sang until they entered a trance and later the shaman revived them. At times, a person might express his power without using words, either through dance or some other form of nonverbal communication. The Nez Perce and other Plateau peoples treated matters surrounding power and guardian spirits with the utmost care and shamans played a key role in the community by helping to understand and contain these new powers.[38]

Yellow Wolf's experience of receiving his *wyakin* (spirit power) was particularly interesting since he related only the visitation of the spirit that gave him the name Hemene Moxmox or Yellow Wolf and not the other vision that imparted his "real" name, Heinmot Hihhih or White Thunder. Yellow Wolf noted that the Yellow Wolf name was his nickname, a name used by whites. He related his acquisition of wolf power but kept the other power to himself, hiding his true name and power. The sacredness of this relationship prevented Yellow Wolf from revealing the source of his power and abilities. Nez Perce elders, Horace Axtell and Allen Slickpoo, Sr., also mentioned the sacredness of these beliefs and their importance for identity.[39]

As Hunn noted, Nez Perce religious belief, like other Plateau cultures, was shamanistic in nature. Shamans or medicine men and women (*tiewets* or *tooats*) held important positions within the Nez Perce community and provided vital services. Only a handful of people achieved this position. On their quest as youths, they received the power necessary for the responsibilities of this role in the community. Slickpoo noted that individual Nez Perce, in the Winter Dance, often challenged the spirit or power of each other to see whose spirit was strongest. The person with the strongest *wyakin*, as demonstrated over a number of years, would "graduate" into becoming a medicine man or woman. The primary activity or responsibility of the shaman, according to Slickpoo, centered on curing individuals who were "threatened or hurt by the evil thoughts of envious or hateful people."[40] Intervention by a shaman in such instances occurred only after other methods like herbs, sweat baths, or unsuccessful requests for help from the sick person's guardian spirit had failed.

Shamans relied on the same spiritual guardians that other Nez Perce appealed to for power and guidance, but shamans were necessary when spiritual power was directed malevolently toward another person or a person offended the spiritual guardian and lost some of his power or *wyakin*. Either occurrence could lead to "spirit" sickness and required the intervention of shamans to correct the misuse of power. Sometimes "spirit" sickness originated from the power itself, the manifestation of too much spiritual power. This type of spirit sickness also required the intervention of shamans to "bring out" the power and restore the person to balance. The containment of spiritual forces was essential to the survival of the Nez Perce and required a person with great spiritual knowledge and ability to deal with these forces. In particular, shamans acted as important guides for youth experiencing and attempting to understand the nature of their own relationship with their guardian spirit for the first time. This role was essential because it was crucial to help the younger person successfully understand this relationship or it could have significant consequences for the individual and the community.[41]

Hunn noted that animism and shamanism, as practiced by the Nez Perce and other Plateau cultures, "suggests a rather different view of the world of nature and of the human place in it than does mainstream Anglo-American culture."[42] This difference led many researchers like Herbert Spinden and, even more recently, Deward Walker, to highlight the simplicity of Nez Perce religion and religious practice. For example, in 1908 Herbert Spinden remarked, "The religious beliefs of the Nez Perces were marked by simplicity, rationality, and freedom from ceremonial restraint. They seemed to realize the paucity of their religious traditions and from the first eagerly seconded the efforts of missionaries to instruct them in the Christian faith."[43] Similarly, Walker noted, "We may conclude, therefore, that the absence of centralized tendencies in aboriginal Nez Perce religion reflected the decentralization and pronounced social and political simplicity typical of aboriginal Nez Perce society."[44] These "simplistic" conclusions illustrated the continuation of Anglo-American misconceptions about the lack of sophisticated and complex beliefs and systems in Native American cultures. Difference, in this case, demonstrated the perceived superiority of one culture's religious practices over another. Nez Perce religion did not stand on its own coherence or success but was researched, recorded, and judged as simplistic compared with a completely different set of religious experiences and beliefs. The efficacy of Nez Perce religion for its participants should stand on its own merits.

Shortly before the arrival of Anglo Americans on the Columbia Plateau, many Plateau Indian communities dealt with the stresses and disruptions created by outside forces. Religious practice and forms began a process that eventually altered Plateau Indian religious practices rooted in the past, but also sought to deal with problems of the early nineteenth century. The Washani religion or Washat, the ancient Nez Perce religion that was revised in the 1850s and 1860s, will be discussed in Chapter Three within the context of forces initiated by initial contact with Europeans and Anglo Americans. However, it is important to understand that the Washani religion existed first within the traditional context of beliefs present in Plateau Indian culture and signified a change in form rather than in the substance of those religious beliefs. For example, native people in the Pacific Northwest continued to seek power from spiritual beings and people still honored gifts offered by guardian spirits present in the environment.[45]

Social and Political Life

Social life and relationships flowed from Nez Perce religious beliefs about their relationship to the land. The gifts of spiritual power by guardian spirits served the community in various ways and gave each person with such powers various responsibilities and positions in the community. Verne Ray noted, "the peoples of the Plateau were unreceptive to notions of caste."[46] Instead, most Plateau cultures, including the Nez Perce, based their social relations on a form of egalitarianism that stressed equality and freedom of action. While recognizing the fluidity and freedom of Nez Perce social relations, it is also important to avoid slipping into a romanticization of the Nez Perce by portraying their social and political relations as a type of proto-democratic society. Nez Perce social relations exhibited hierarchy, definite gender roles, and family structures that placed individuals in positions of power over others, but the level of coercion and institutions to carry out programs of social conformity did not exist to the same extent as in European and Anglo-American societies.[47] Before contact with Europeans and Anglo Americans, virtually all Nez Perce lived in small villages located principally along streams and rivers. Herbert Spinden noted that the most favorable locations for villages were the Wallowa and Clearwater Valleys and the tributaries that flowed into these areas; however, he also asserted that the Nez Perce never built permanent settlements or villages and that, as part of the seasonal round, the semi-permanent villages often stood empty for long periods of time during the year.[48] Generally, villages consisted of a body of relatives or kin. Membership in a village was not limited to relatives since villages interacted with one another and often encouraged intermarriage and social interaction. Social divisions among villages largely revolved around geographic location.[49]

Nez Perce political structure was based in the village. According to Verne Ray, every man and woman of the village comprised the general assembly of the village. A headman led the village. Since the position of headman was not hereditary, residents either chose the leader through "election" or a son was chosen to succeed a father.[50] This process of selecting a leader was more like selection through consensus. Nez Perce villagers chose leaders based on the abilities of the individuals conferred through their relationships with the guardian spirits. Nez Perce people recognized persuasion and oratory as powerful spiritual gifts and the community regarded these skills as essential for maintaining social relationships and leading the village.[51] Slickpoo noted that the duties of the headman included correct behavior and required him to "act as spokesman for the village, mediate disputes, and attend to the general welfare of village members."[52] A council of village elders helped the headman and met to discuss matters of justice, intervillage relations, and affairs of war and peace.[53]

One of the major misconceptions of Nez Perce culture rested in the perceptions and observations of Anglo Americans concerning community leadership and positions of power. Headmen led individual villages, but the concept of an overall headman for the Nez Perce tribe did not exist in their political practice before contact with Euro-Americans. The designation of an overall chief for many Native American cultures, particularly in the western United States, was instituted most frequently through the efforts of Anglo Americans because of their desire to deal with one person in authority who told the entire community what to do. Anglo-American conceptions of leadership contradicted well-established traditional channels of authority based on consensus and unanimity. The closest leadership position to an overall chief was the person designated to lead during times of war. The war leader held almost absolute authority during times of conflict, but while treated with honor during peacetime, he rarely exercised significant power in day-to-day decisions in the village. Considerable amounts of frustration and conflict arose from Anglo-American misperceptions and expectations of Nez Perce leadership, particularly in treaty negotiations involving numerous villages and differing cultural groups.

Life in over 300 different Nez Perce settlements revolved in great part around relationships with relatives and the seasonal round. From birth, grandparents and other members of the extended family involved themselves in the lives of children, providing a crucial link to the past and also serving as the educators for children in the family. Often, grandfathers took male children on their first hunting and fishing trips and also taught them to ride horses. Grandmothers served in a similar role for female children, teaching them about plant resources, childcare, cooking, camp making and other duties performed by women. Grandparents also introduced children to the oral narratives that formed the core of Nez Perce knowledge. For example, the story of Coyote and Monster helped children understand the origins of their community and the origins of other communities in the area. The narratives also reinforced lessons about important social behaviors and characteristics necessary for communal living. While grandparents taught many important skills and lessons to the children, aunts and uncles also took on the roles of teaching and enforcing correct social behavior. Children were disciplined, but often by a "whipper," who administered corporal punishment for disobedience or misbehavior.[54]

Nez Perce youth also spent a great deal of time with siblings and cousins who were all regarded as brothers and sisters. Kinship and family relationships operated under different social assumptions, for, as Hunn astutely asserted, "the same categories of kin are not everywhere recognized in the same way."[55] For example, three English terms for brother, sister and cousin require seven terms in the Sahaptin language. Family membership shifted and tended toward inclusion at the village level, where friends or allies could become part of a family network or kin relationship.[56] At age three, both boys and girls assisted in the subsistence activities of the family. Hunting, fishing, root digging, and berrying ensured the survival of the family, and the efforts of children and adolescents increased the family's productivity. Other family members assisted children in these activities and also taught them rituals and ceremonies when the children successfully completed their first subsistence activity.

Adolescence brought great change as young Nez Perce prepared for the quest that they hoped would culminate in the acquisition of *wyakin*. Both males and females participated in the quest and often "went out numerous times before receiving a vision."[57] The successful completion of the quest signified one of the most important steps to maturity. As adolescents learned more about their spiritual power and the relationship to their spiritual guardian, they entered more deeply into the adult world and accepted more responsibility in their family and kin network.

After entrance into the adult world, young Nez Perce continued on to the next important milestone in Nez Perce social life, marriage. According to Slickpoo, Nez Perce people regarded marriage as a serious matter with much consideration given by the family and kin network in selecting an appropriate mate for eligible men and women. Slickpoo also noted that family heads arranged most marriages and negotiated betrothals for young children in the family. Frequently, the male's female relations observed the girl to see if she fit the mold of a good mate and to review family histories to ensure that the families were not related. If the female elders deemed her to be acceptable and the families proved compatible, then the families set a time for the ceremony of exchanging gifts.[58] The negotiations and observations of families were very important because, as Hunn observed, familial and kin relationships established through marriage remained even after the death of one or both spouses.[59] Spinden, Slickpoo, and Hunn all noted that divorce and separation occurred infrequently among the Nez Perce and Plateau Indian cultures in general. Most likely, the close familial and kin relationships discouraged such actions because of the repercussions to kinship ties.[60]

During the course of married life, Nez Perce men and women worked and performed tasks based on gender. Hunn noted that the Plateau Indian culture's "economy involved a division of labor nearly universal among known hunting-and-gathering peoples."[61] In this organizational system of labor, "men fished and hunted large game while women gathered roots and berries and had primary responsibility for processing all kinds of food."[62] While it is tempting or even culturally fashionable to label this division as "sexual exploitation," Hunn asserted that labels of exploitation assumed that these roles were unfair and that somehow in Plateau cultures men imposed on women tasks considered monotonous, while reserving the more exciting tasks like hunting and fishing for themselves.[63] These assumptions were based on cultural biases and predispositions carried by Anglo Americans about which type of labor reflected greater cultural significance or power in relationships. Hunn observed that Indians did not view the economic contribution of women in Plateau cultures as less valuable than that of men. During Plateau Indian thanksgiving feasts, most of the sacred foods were plant-based, provided to the community through female labor, with salmon standing out as the exception.[64] Anglo Americans frequently regarded gathering as requiring little or no skill, but quite the contrary is true. Hunn noted that gathering required "detailed knowledge of the land and of the plant habitat associations and life cycles."[65] Nez Perce people needed this knowledge to ensure their safety because some poisonous roots resembled camas, one of the principal sources of plant food, and could cause death if ingested. In essence, gathering called upon vast knowledge and the development and application of technology (tools, preparation and storage of food materials) in order to foster the survival of the entire family unit. Hunn's Plateau Indian informant, James Selam, regarded all food as important and failed to single out one food in particular as giving the producer some sort of special status.

Hunn concluded "there is no rational basis for judging the economic contributions of one sex as more important than that of the other."[66] Nez Perce people spent a great deal of their adulthood moving about gathering, fishing, and hunting, but the people understood at an early age that their lives upon the earth were limited by time. Like all living things, they had to face death, a law created at the beginning of time and reaffirmed when Coyote tried to change the law to have continuous life on earth, a plan which he thwarted himself by opening a bag of souls before the assigned time.[67]

Death ends life's journey, and the Nez Perce marked death with special ritual and ceremony. Slickpoo noted that, as soon as a death occurred, the village crier or herald announced the death to the entire village. The female relatives of the deceased immediately began a grieving wail, and other relatives and friends joined in mourning as news reached them. Relatives and friends cleansed the body through a ritual bath, dressed the deceased in fine clothing and favorite adornments, combed the hair and painted the face red.[68] Family and friends prepared graves within sight of the village. The funeral ceremony consisted mainly of the shaman giving a brief speech extolling the virtues and achievements of the deceased. As Spinden noted, the main duty of the shaman was to "lay the ghost" or ensure that the deceased spirit remained at rest. After the funeral ceremony, relatives dismantled and moved the deceased's house to a new location to prevent the spirit from returning to live in the house and bringing madness to those living there. Relatives also sponsored a funeral feast where they distributed the personal possessions of the deceased to friends and family. In the late eighteenth and early nineteenth centuries, the practice of distributing the deceased possessions contributed to the spread of contagious diseases like smallpox, tuberculosis, and other contagion. After the completion of these ceremonies, relatives who had attended the funeral, and particularly those who had handled the body, purified themselves through sweatbath cleansing that lasted approximately a week.

Making a Living — The Seasonal Round

The rhythms of life and relationships intertwined with the work of survival and subsistence. Families and villages worked together to provide enough food and other materials for survival throughout the year. Hunting, fishing, and gathering were often portrayed by the Anglo-American imagination, in academic writing, and popular culture as "primitive" activities that existed below agriculture and more "civilized" subsistence activities. Such beliefs assumed that these activities required little forethought, planning, knowledge, or technology. These assumptions failed to seriously consider the depth of knowledge required and the technological innovation necessary to survive on the Columbia Plateau. Nez Perce families taught this information and technology to their young people, which ensured survival through the active participation of all family members in the collection of food.

When Anglo Americans used words like "hunters-gatherers," they generally focused on the hunting part of this type of subsistence culture. The notion of hunting, in Anglo-American culture, somehow signified greater freedom, superiority of males, excitement, and competition against nature. It is also a very gendered term that focused on the efforts of males procuring food in these cultures. Hunn noted that hunting, in Plateau Indian cultures, actually contributed only a small portion of the overall food energy budget, approximately 10 percent.[69] Gathering and fishing provided ninety percent of food calories in the Nez Perce diet. Since Plateau cultures regarded all foods equally and viewed them all as necessary for survival, it is imperative that researchers, and Anglo Americans in general, abandon their penchant for placing their own values on the modes of production practiced by the Nez Perce and other Native American cultures. Hunting, gathering, and fishing existed and Indians practiced them in a cooperative effort to ensure survival; clearly the Nez Perce did not categorize work activities in the same way as Anglo Americans.[70]

Anglo-American assumptions about Nez Perce subsistence practices that viewed them as unplanned or spontaneous efforts driven by hunger or need contradicted the complexity exhibited by the Nez Perce seasonal round. The Nez Perce and most Plateau Indian cultures relied on the seasonal round for survival, and they carefully planned and executed the seasonal round to maximize the acquisition of food materials. Hunn, in his work with Mid-Columbia Indians, detailed the activities and rhythms of the seasonal round. Hunn's interest in the seasonal round stemmed from his training as an ethnobiologist and his experience with the depth and precision of Plateau people's knowledge about plants and animals. Nez Perce and other Plateau Indian cultures based the seasonal round on extensive and detailed understanding of the natural environment and created a body of information, passed on to each generation, crucial for survival and maintenance of these resources. This knowledge was even more impressive since it passed from generation to generation through oral tradition and teachings.

Each season required a set of activities and movements to access and exploit food resources. Timing and planning were crucial activities and constant awareness of changes in the environment was required in order for the seasonal round to be successful. Women, in particular, played an important role, often determining where and when the village or family moved, depending on various plant and animal resources and their readiness for harvest. It is important to stress that the Nez Perce and other Plateau cultures viewed gender and the division of labor differently from Anglo Americans. All activities that contributed to the survival of the family and village were honored and considered important. Non-Nez Perce must continually remind themselves of these distinctions when attempting to understand Nez Perce culture before contact.

Hunn described the seasonal round by a thorough discussion of the various activities performed during each season. All Nez Perce villages participated in the seasonal round with many families or villages gathering in certain geographic areas known for their rich plant or animal resources. The observations of researchers like Spinden and Ray stressing the lack of contact between tribes during peaceful times failed to take into account the movement and interaction that occurred during the seasonal round. During the round, Indians played games, raced horses, gambled, danced and conducted other communal activities among villagers from diverse places. While villages often moved and worked together, families and individuals maintained extensive freedom of movement and could move in and out of contact with other families and villages. Generally, the Nez Perce and other Plateau Indian cultures used land and resources in common, while they allowed visitors and strangers access to and use of these resources. The only restriction on this practice concerned areas traditionally used by one family and village. Visitors needed permission to use these lands.

The seasonal round required specific tasks and movements according to the seasons and location of food resources. Hunn first described the activities occurring during winter.[71] Winter functioned as a time to construct and maintain tools, tell stories, relate historical memory and educate children since ample time was available. Visiting relatives and other families also occurred during the winter. Visiting which gave time to renew and strengthen relationships was often focused on storytelling and also connected to the winter shamanistic performances of the winter or Guardian Spirit Dance. Hunn also noted that visiting served a broader purpose beyond social interaction. He asserted that plans and information were shared for the next cycle of harvest. Families and villages shared and redistributed food surpluses during visiting since visits often were occasions for feasting (Figure 1).[72]

Change from winter to spring centered on warming and unpredictable weather conditions and the return or emergence of food resources after winter dormancy. Hunn emphasized that many traditional accounts mark the end of winter and the beginning of spring with the arrival of the spring Chinook salmon run that normally occurred in early June. While the run may

Figure 1 The Stick Game played by Columbia Plateau people in the early twentieth century. Courtesy of Manuscripts, Archives, and Special Collections, Washington State University Libraries, Lucullus Virgil McWhorter Collection, 70-0419

have officially marked the end of winter, Hunn maintained that women, in particular, actively worked to stockpile food resources before the arrival of the Chinook salmon, providing over fifty percent of the total food supply for the family and village through their gathering efforts. As Hunn persuasively argued, anthropologists in the past vastly underrated these efforts and dismissed them as being barely removed from the foraging of animals for their food. Hunn asserted again that women organized gathering expeditions that relied on complex planning, effort, and knowledge. These efforts required knowledge of when certain plants could be harvested, when salmon runs occurred, and the location of these resources. Tasks varied according to which resource was available at any particular time. For example, when the spring Chinook run began, women attended to the cleaning and drying of the catch. However, in May when the spring flood covered fishing sites, they would then pack up and set off for camas meadows located in nearby mountains.

Nez Perce and other Plateau cultures harvested a number of different plants during the spring and summer seasons. Slickpoo listed basic foods of the Nez Perce, including *kehm-mes* (camas), *thlee-than* (bitterroot), khouse, *tsa-weetkh* (wild carrot), and *keh-kheet* (wild onion). Of the plants listed, Hunn observed that camas, khouse, and bitterroot provided the bulk of plant foods.[73] The importance of these plants was readily observed through the names the Nez Perce gave to months of the year since many centered on the activities of the seasonal round and were names based on the type of plant harvested or prepared during a particular month.[74] Indians used large concentrations of camas in places like Weippe and around present-day Kamiah, Idaho.[75] The gathering of these plant foods and their concentration in certain locations created socializing opportunities, inter-village connections like matchmaking, and the business of inter-tribal politics. Again, the process of gathering was enmeshed in larger cultural activities and was not merely a simple or "primitive" means of survival.

Gatherings were not limited to plant harvests, but also occurred during salmon runs and fishing efforts. Hunn noted that by late June or early July, the Columbia dropped enough to expose summer runs of salmon. At this point, the Nez Perce and other Plateau communities put aside root harvesting and focused on fishing. Runs lasted only a few days or maybe a week with some time in between each run. During salmon runs, ceaseless activity occurred as families and villages took advantage of this crucial resource. Men conducted most, but not all, fishing, as elders, children, and women split and cleaned the fish, hanging them on racks to dry for future use. When the salmon runs slackened, women returned to gathering plant resources like currants, gooseberries, serviceberries, and chokeberries while men hunted small game. During the late summer, around mid-August, families moved to high country camps and worked the productive black mountain huckleberry fields, sometimes staying in the mountains until the beginning of October. At the same time, men hunted bear and deer, laying in stores of meat that women dried into jerky. During the late fall, Plateau communities reoccupied winter villages and conducted last minute hunting and gathering in preparation for winter. Women processed spawned-out salmon and gathered most plant foods while men hunted for larger game. They spent a great deal of time preparing the village for winter and ensuring that they gathered enough wood or other combustible material for fires.

The seasonal round changed somewhat with the arrival and domestication of the horse by the Nez Perce during the eighteenth century. Horses eased the burden of moving from place to place and also considerably lightened the load of carrying food resources from one place to another. The arrival of the horse also enabled the Nez Perce and other Plateau cultures to expand hunting expeditions across the Bitterroot Mountains and to hunt buffalo to a greater extent in territories to the east of the mountains. Earlier expeditions had relied on foot travel and were more difficult than those following the introduction of the horse. The Nez Perce were familiar with Plains Indian cultures and adopted some aspects of this culture, particularly in dress, songs and the use of buffalo hide tipis. Expeditions of the Nez Perce to the Great Plains could last anywhere from six months to two years.[76]

The seasonal round, encompassing gathering, fishing, and hunting, was a crucial aspect of Nez Perce culture and of other Plateau Indian cultures. The seasonal round connected families and villages with one another, gave larger tribal entities an opportunity to meet, and provided the necessary food resources for survival. The seasonal round was more than subsistence and was connected to the other cycles and aspects of Nez Perce life. For example, gifts from guardian spirits enabled individual Nez Perce to find, either through hunting or gathering, abundant supplies of food. While an important source of food, the Nez Perce considered salmon and other animals as spiritual beings with moral rights that obligated proper respect and treatment from the Nez Perce in order to ensure an abundant hunting and fishing season. Both men and women ritually purified themselves before participating in gathering, harvesting, and fishing. This purification was part of the deep relationship that existed between the Nez Perce and their natural world. Far from the picture of "simple" and "primitive" means of producing the necessities of survival, the seasonal round required a great deal of knowledge and preparation as well as cooperation between families and communities to ensure the necessary food materials for survival.

Language and Interrelationships

Anglo Americans often portrayed Nez Perce and Plateau Indian cultures through a lens of simplicity and "primitiveness," marginalizing activities like the seasonal round or religious practices. Portraying Nez Perce culture in this way eased the task of cultural dominance and also justified actions taken by Anglo Americans to possess Nez Perce land, resources and knowledge. Anglo Americans simplified Nez Perce culture and stressed the atomistic or isolated nature of their culture while consistently denying the Nez Perce and other Plateau cultures depth and complexity to inter-family, inter-village, inter-environmental and inter-tribal relations as well as the spiritual nature of their lifeway. For example, Verne Ray contended that villages were isolated except during times of war.[77] However, in actuality, social interaction with other Nez Perce villages and with other Plateau Indian groups happened at various times throughout the year. In addition, marriage of Nez Perce people with other Indians also promoted interactions as people traveled to visit relatives. While keeping in mind that distance served as a hindrance to contact, the Nez Perce and other Plateau groups like the Palouse, Cayuse and Umatilla not only gathered for the Winter or Guardian Spirit dance, but they also visited other villages during the winter and saw one another consistently during the seasonal round, either when fishing or at common root or plant gathering areas. Far from being isolated, it appears that the Nez Perce and other Plateau Indian cultures enjoyed rich contact with neighbors and often cooperated with each other outside of the context of war or time of crisis.

The Nez Perce relied upon and maintained relationships with other neighboring Plateau Indian groups not only for the purposes of defense but also for social reasons (Figure 2). Winter dances brought different groups together like the Nez Perce, Palouse, and Cayuse. Also, intermarriage between different peoples occurred and often served as an important bond to neighboring Sahaptin-speaking groups. For example, Chief Joseph's mother was a Umatilla, thereby creating a link between families and different tribal groups important during times of peace and war. These interrelationships most frequently existed between the Nez Perce and neighbors like the Cayuse, Walla Walla, Palouse, and Umatilla, but they were not limited to these Sahaptin-speaking groups. Other Sahaptin-speakers like the Yakama and Wanapum participated in these types of relationships, but not to the same degree of the other groups mainly as a result of distance. Sahaptin communities also intermarried with Salish-speaking communities and established important links with Salish groups like the Coeur d'Alene, the Spokans, the Flatheads and Salish Columbia River communities.

Figure 2 A Sweathouse used for ritual cleansing by Columbia Plateau people. Courtesy of Manuscripts, Archives, and Special Collections, Washington State University Libraries, Lucullus Virgil McWhorter Collection, 82-025.

One of the principal bonds between these groups was the Sahaptin language. While each of the groups mentioned, like the Palouse and Umatilla, spoke their own dialect or form of Sahaptin, interactions and intermarriage supplied enough translators and also encouraged learning different dialects to enhance general understanding. Other more distantly related languages like Cayuse could also be understood in the same way. As an alternative, diverse groups also used sign language or trade jargons like the Chinook Jargon to make themselves understood. Many people spoke multiple languages that included Chinook Jargon, Sahaptin, Salish and sign language.

Trade and interaction, including warfare, also existed between Salish speaking communities to the north as well as with groups on western side of the Cascade Mountains. After the introduction of the horse, the Nez Perce and other Plateau Indian cultures interacted with Plains Indian culture communities, sometimes peacefully and at other times as enemies. To the south, the Nez Perce and their allies consistently entered into hostilities with Shoshonean groups from the Great Basin. While hostile in nature, these conflicts highlight the fact that Plateau Indian cultures were interconnected with other Native American groups. This contact intensified and increased with the introduction of the horse and stimulated adoption of cultural practices from other groups. The amount and breadth of interaction between the Nez Perce and other groups argue against the simplicity and isolation mentioned earlier.

This brief discussion of some of the broader outlines of Nez Perce and Plateau culture serves as a reminder that describing a culture and attempting to understand their way of life is an arduous task requiring a great deal of patience and tolerance. The Nez Perce and their neighbors created cultures and belief systems that explained their existence and maintained their communities in an environment that constantly changed even before the arrival of Europeans and Anglo Americans. Only within the past two or three decades have academics consistently attempted to understand and respectfully portray Nez Perce culture in ways other than the predetermined exercise of describing a "primitive" society, unaware of the dynamic forces that would destroy them and their culture. With the arrival of Europeans on the Plateau in the late eighteenth and early nineteenth centuries, Nez Perce and Plateau cultures attempted to deal with this outside influence through interactive strategies that had worked for them for centuries.

Coyote and Monster

The Coyote and Monster narrative is a pivotal story in Nez Perce oral education and belief. Grandparents told this story to children as an important part of their education and socialization into Nez Perce belief and practice.

Not only does it feature Coyote, a central character in Plateau oral narratives, but it also explains the Nez Perce view of how different native peoples in the Northwest came to live in their respective geographic areas. For the Nez Perce, the story concretely explained the position of the Nez Perce in Plateau culture and their creation from the heart blood of the monster. The "Heart of Monster" is not an intangible object or symbol, but it is instead a place near Kamiah, Idaho, that continues as a sacred site for members of the Nez Perce community. It is the heart of the community, of being Nez Perce, a reminder of who they are. The story is how they know, how they were made whole and consummate as a people.[78]

At the beginning of this chapter, the author provided a portion of this story and connected it to the narrative structure of this work. For the Nez Perce, Coyote and Monster are not mythical creatures in some distant past, but historical and living entities connected to the present. The version provided here is just one of many, a version preserved by Archie Phinney and used here as a creative force in presenting aspects of Nez Perce culture that many accounts ignore, forgetting its central position in Nez Perce history. Allen Slickpoo, Sr., mentioned that Coyote continues to intervene in the present, inventing things and helping human beings just like he did at the beginning of the Coyote and Monster narrative. For example, Slickpoo noted that oral tradition gave credit to Coyote for the invention of the television, going to the moon, and other important milestones in the twentieth century.[79]

Just as the Nez Perce place Coyote in the present, this work seeks to use the Coyote and Monster narrative as a framework for understanding the relationship of Nez Perce and Anglo-American historical constructs. As the portion of the narrative at the beginning of the chapter suggests, Coyote worked to prepare the land for the coming of human beings, and in the present he also works to maintain the land for the Nez Perce and others. Coyote continues his creative actions, reclaiming the Nez Perce estate and resources in accordance with the old laws. In the ancient story, Coyote worked to complete the early creation when he heard of a monster that swallowed all the people.

The first chapter related how the Nez Perce, Coyote and other beings coexisted on the land in an interdependent relationship. However, this relationship was disturbed by the entrance of a new being, Monster, who will attempt to "swallow" all the people and make the land its own (Figure 3). This first chapter will end with Coyote traveling to meet the monster. The next chapter relates the meeting of Coyote and Monster. While the monster in the narrative appeared before humans arrived in the Pacific Northwest, the monster that Coyote must wrestle in the next chapter is different; it is a

Figure 3 Heart of the Monster near Kamiah, Idaho. Photographer – L.V. McWhorter. Courtesy of Manuscripts, Archives, and Special Collections, Washington State University Libraries, Lucullus Virgil McWhorter Collection, PC 87-7-98-043.

monster that does not appear as a large, all-consuming beast, but rather conceals itself in many different guises. In the end, this "monster," the land-and culture-hungry Anglo-American "monster," devours the people and Coyote, forcing them to search for ways to survive in the belly of the beast and possibly escape the bonds of Monster's hold.

Chapter Three
Coyote Meets Monster

> From there he traveled on. Along the way he took a good bath saying to himself, "Lest I make myself repulsive to his taste," and then he dressed himself all up, "Lest he will vomit me up or spit me out." There he tied himself with rope to three mountains. For there he came along up and over ridges. Suddenly, behold, he saw a great head. He quickly hid himself in the grass and gazed at it. Never before in his life had he seen anything like it: never such a large thing – away off somewhere melting into the horizon was its gigantic body.[1]

Coyote and Monster are familiar people to the Nez Perce, and their story is central to Nez Perce culture. The use of Coyote and Monster in this work is not a Nez Perce understanding, but an application by the author. In the nineteenth and twentieth centuries, Anglo-American historians recreated and reshaped Pacific Northwest history, emphasizing such topics as the Lewis and Clark Expedition and the Whitman Massacre. As an alternative presentation, the story of Coyote and Monster might be used as a narrative device to emplot and understand the contact and conflict experienced between Nez Perce and Anglo-American communities in a way that does not depend on frameworks established by Anglo-American academics or popular imaginations.[2]

In Chapter Two, Coyote prepared the land for the people and the people used Coyote's gifts to live and sustain themselves. Chapter Three begins an investigation into the meeting of Coyote and the Monster. In this work's use of the narrative, Coyote represents Nez Perce and other Plateau Indian cultures, while Monster represents Europeans and Anglo Americans. Coyote remarked that he had never seen anything like it (Monster) before. Just as Coyote had never seen the likes of Monster before, so the Nez Perce and other Plateau cultures encountered something new and strange in Europeans and Anglo Americans. Coyote was not only seeing something completely

43

new, but he also prepared himself to be swallowed by the Monster. There is a bit of prophetic knowledge in the story since Coyote seems to know intuitively the outcome of his encounter with Monster. Monster will swallow him, but Coyote had prepared for this and eventually rescued the people from the bowels of Monster.[3] Just as the rescue of the people required forethought on the part of Coyote and the Nez Perce, encountering Europeans and Anglo Americans demanded innovation, planning and preparation on the part of Plateau groups.

Using Coyote and Monster as a narrative foil, the author seeks to fulfill two purposes in Chapter Three. The first is to relate the experience of contact between the Nez Perce and Europeans/Anglo Americans. Coyote viewed Monster from afar, fearful of Monster's enormity. However, he was not devoured but was brave and he willingly faced Monster. Anglo Americans created and narrated this cultural encounter countless times in textbooks, monographs, speeches, and through other means but failed to incorporate Coyote's perspective. This chapter discusses the narrative devices and emplotment of the contact story used by Anglo-American historians and popular writers to tell the story of the meeting of two very different cultures. The second overall objective of this chapter is to deconstruct Anglo-American historical production surrounding this early contact of Plateau cultures and Euro-Americans.

Coyote's actions foreshadowed his fate when he finally met Monster. On the surface, the plausible interpretation, as narrated by many Anglo-American sources, related to the inevitability of Monster swallowing Coyote. The production of Anglo-American historical knowledge reiterated the inevitability of Native American defeat, eventual relegation to reservations, and their final assimilation into Anglo-American society. But this was only part of the story. Anglo-American historical imagination perceived the swallowing of the Nez Perce as a quick occurrence. In many non-native narratives, Indians played peripheral roles unless non-native narration required Indians to step onto the stage as counter-images to demonstrate Anglo-American cultural superiority and the inevitability of Native American physical and cultural disappearance.

The assault on Nez Perce society, land and culture, often narrated in a very physical, military and spatial way, reached deeper and took longer than the mere "swallowing of Coyote." Monster also sought to swallow Nez Perce history, culture, belief and knowledge. The physical "swallowing" took only a relatively short time while the other "swallowing," the ingestion of culture and history, took longer.

HORSES, GUNS, AND DISEASE: PRE-CONTACT NON-NATIVE INFLUENCES ON PLATEAU CULTURE

Life on the Columbia Plateau, prior to white contact, should not be romanticized or idealized in any way. As with all human societies, Nez Perce and other Plateau Indian communities dealt with challenges from the environment, other communities outside the Plateau, and people within their own communities. These challenges encouraged change and adaptation, but also reinforced the social, political and cultural institutions most useful for insuring survival. Hunn noted that archaeological evidence suggested, "the Plateau Indian way of life had remained fundamentally the same for ten thousand years prior to the first Euro-American influences of the eighteenth century."[4] According to Hunn, two fundamental factors, climatic change and innovations in resource harvest strategies and techniques, affected life on the Plateau before contact with Euro-Americans. As most people who live in the trans-Mississippi West understand, climate determines activity and livelihood in this region. Weather does not remain static and cycles of abundance and scarcity characterize this region's propensity for drought. Nez Perce and other Plateau communities attempted to deal with climatic change by expanding the scope of the seasonal round and harvesting other sources of plants and animals that may not have been used in more abundant times. One of the great strengths of Plateau culture sprang from communal values that emphasized sharing food and joint use of areas and resources during periods of scarcity. The community worked together to support and help one another.

Christopher Miller, in *Prophetic Worlds: Indians and Whites on the Columbia Plateau*, asserted that one of these climatic cycles occurred about 250 years before the arrival of Euro-Americans on the Columbia Plateau.[5] He postulated that a three-hundred-year cold spell, a direct result of the "Little Ice Age," created conditions on the Plateau that may have stretched the limits of Plateau subsistence culture.[6] A change in temperature and precipitation, as described by Miller, might have significantly reduced the supply of both plant and animal foods available to Plateau communities. The lack of food supplies might have impacted population and food resources while also creating the opportunity for inter-and intra-community relationships to strengthen and to expand as communities attempted to pool resources to survive these environmental challenges.

As Nez Perce communities dealt with environmental changes, the most important and radical influences on their culture resulted from pressures and forces set in motion by Europeans and Euro-Americans during the sixteenth, seventeenth and eighteenth centuries. One of the misconceptions of Native Americans shared by many Anglo Americans was that native communities isolated themselves from one another and that population shifts and forces acting on one group did not affect other communities in different geographical regions. This belief helped Anglo Americans to cope psychologically with the consequences of their own presence and destruction of native communities and groups. Rather than dealing with these consequences on a national or world-historical level, Anglo Americans preferred to see the impact of Manifest Destiny in terms of small communities of hundreds, not the hundreds of thousands or millions affected by the arrival of Europeans.

The occupation of Mexico by Spain, the incursion of Europeans along the eastern seaboard of North America, and the exploration of the Pacific Coast set in motion many different indirect forces that influenced Nez Perce and Plateau culture. Three of the most significant were the domestication of the horse, the introduction of firearms and steel weapons, and the devastation of diseases. These three forces interacted to alter population distribution, technologies used for gathering food supplies, and military and political relationships of Native American communities.[7] Hunn noted that these outside forces produced important demographic, epidemiological and cultural changes occurring shortly before the arrival of Euro-Americans.[8]

The domestication and integration of the horse into Plateau culture initiated rapid change and adaptation of Nez Perce culture. This change was so central to Plateau culture that James Selam, Hunn's collaborator and informant, believed Plateau Indians always possessed horses.[9] The spread of horse culture and its profound impact on the Nez Perce started with the importation and use of horses in Spanish colonial possessions in North America. Spanish soldiers, settlers, and later colonial administrators closely regulated the possession and use of horses to the point that Hunn mentioned that horses represented "the Spaniards' colonial domination."[10] Spanish colonists brought horses with them as they moved north into New Mexico and when Indian Pueblos revolted in 1680, Indians liberated many horses and others escaped, spreading north up both sides of the Rocky Mountains.[11] Alvin M. Joesphy Jr. argued that sometime between 1700 and 1730 Plateau cultures acquired horses from their neighbors, most likely through trade.[12] By 1700, Bannock groups south of Nez Perce and Plateau territory possessed horses, and Nez Perce tradition related that a trading expedition purchased stock to start their own herds. The interesting point was that Plateau and Bannock cultures fought almost continually after 1700, especially after the horse gave Bannock communities a distinct advantage in raiding for captives or for vengeance.

The introduction of horse culture in the eighteenth century significantly impacted the daily life of Nez Perce people. For example, seasonal round movement eased as horses carried greater loads and traveled greater distances in less time. Hunn asserted that horses "did not radically change Plateau life so much as it accelerated existing patterns by enhancing this mobility."[13] Greater mobility also allowed the Nez Perce, Cayuse, Palouse, and other Plateau communities to travel east of the Rocky Mountains to hunt for buffalo and to move farther south on expeditions against Shoshonean, Blackfeet and Bannock groups. The trek east to hunt buffalo brought the Nez Perce into greater contact with other Native American groups east of the mountains, especially the Blackfeet and Lakotas. Josephy noted that Flathead territory possessed some of the finest buffalo hunting grounds between the Bitterroot Valley and the Rockies. Nez Perce hunting groups often attached themselves to Salish-speaking Flathead groups since these two communities shared many cultural traits and practices.

Trade also occurred between Nez Perce and Plains groups like the Blackfeet and Shoshonis, even though they were usually enemies. Nez Perce expeditions transported trade articles such as buffalo-related materials, Plains-style clothing, tipis, and cultural practices like songs, dances and pow wows back to the Plateau. Josephy observed that Plains articles and practices enriched Nez Perce and Plateau cultures. As with the horse, the Nez Perce integrated and adapted cultural influences of other communities like the tipi, pow wow, songs and dances while still retaining the integrity of their own cultural practices.[14] Hunn asserted that the impact of Plains culture was limited to eastern groups along the Columbia Plateau. Nez Perce, Cayuse, and Palouse communities took advantage of the opportunity to enrich their diet and resources through hunting buffalo. These communities used buffalo-related articles for trade with groups on the Plateau with little or no access to buffalo hunting areas east of the Bitterroot Mountains. According to Robert Boyd, mid-Columbia Indians continued to rely on salmon as the mainstay of their diets and mostly wanted robes or blankets made from buffalo skins.[15]

Horse culture and its accompanying influences were only one force set in motion by Europeans and Euro-Americans. Population shifts, conflict, and the introduction of guns and other weapons also significantly impacted Plateau cultures. As Europeans forced communities out of their homelands mostly through military force or uninvited intrusions on Indian land, native groups moved west, placing pressure on other Native American communities or integrating with them to form new groups. The displacement created by Euro-Americans indirectly affected the Nez Perce and other Plateau cultures. As eastern Native American communities moved into the Plains region, their movement created tension and conflict over territory and resources. Some communities moved to other regions, resisted the encroachment of other Indian communities or attempted to form alliances or confederations to resist the encroachment of Euro-Americans and other Native American groups.

One of the most direct impacts of these demographic shifts was the introduction of the gun. As fur traders penetrated deeper into the North American continent, they traded guns, ammunition, and other goods for pelts acquired by Native Americans. Guns gave certain groups distinct advantages over other groups and also influenced how Native American communities greeted their first contact with Euro-Americans. By the end of the eighteenth century, Alexander Mackenzie of the Northwest Company crossed the Continental Divide, trading with Native Americans along the way and distributing guns and ammunition to those Native Americans who brought furs. As Hunn asserted, the introduction of the gun set in motion repercussions for Native American communities west of groups possessing guns. As native peoples acquired guns, they used them for hunting and fur-trapping efforts and used them against their neighbors to the west. Suffering from raids and other forms of violence, western Native American groups attempted to obtain guns for their own protection and use.[16] For the Nez Perce, great challenges arose as a direct result of traditional enemy communities possessing firearms. To the south, Shoshones raided north into Nez Perce and Plateau territories, while to the west and north, Nez Perce, Cayuse, Flathead, and other Salish-speaking groups constantly fought with Blackfeet and other Plains groups. Nez Perce and other Plateau communities fiercely defended their territorial boundaries, acting in self-defense and attacking for retribution and revenge, while at the same time seeking to obtain firearms to better defend themselves.

Most early Anglo-American historical writing failed to recognize this cycle of raiding and defense created by forces set in motion through the workings of Euro-Americans. As Europeans and later Anglo Americans came into contact with Plateau cultures, they observed and interacted with cultures already deeply affected by forces set in motion centuries earlier. For example, the integration of some Plains culture dress and articles by Nez Perce groups was a fairly recent event. European observers failed to recognize the continuity that remained in Plateau culture and often based their observations or evaluations on misinformation or superficial appearance.[17] One of the greatest misconceptions stemmed from the incessant simplistic description of all Native American cultures as "primitive" or "backward," affirming the Anglo-American myth of cultural superiority that placed Native Americans at the base of a hierarchal system that essentially legitimated the conquests of Anglo Americans.

The indirect impact of Euro-Americans on Nez Perce and Plateau cultures was not limited to the introduction of the horse, guns or the inception of population shifts, but also occurred through the introduction of diseases like smallpox that devastated many Native American communities throughout North and South America. Even before the arrival of the first Euro-Americans on the Columbia Plateau, disease raged across the Plateau through contact with other Native American communities infected by Euro-Americans. Boyd asserted that the first smallpox epidemic arrived in the Pacific Northwest between 1775 and 1781 and started as a result of Euro-American exploration and trade along the North Pacific coast.[18] Boyd noted that this epidemic most likely emerged from contact with Spanish ships and their crews in 1774. Disease transference intensified during this period since the purpose of most of these expeditions in the late eighteenth century was to obtain furs and the exchange of goods and foods probably enhanced the chances of Native Americans contracting deadly diseases. Diseases like smallpox, tuberculosis, venereal diseases, and others spread inland as Plateau communities interacted with mid-Columbia Indians and Chinookan groups along the Columbia River. According to Boyd, another smallpox epidemic occurred in 1801-1802, four years before the Lewis and Clark expedition arrived on the Plateau. Hunn noted that approximately fifty percent of the population perished in these two epidemics.[19] While the impact of these epidemics is impossible to determine, it seems reasonable to assume that the death of fifty percent of any community's population would create profound problems. Such a demographic holocaust created a great deal of distress for Plateau communities and held the potential for altering social, political, economic and religious relationships on the Plateau. Disease and its consequences continued to disrupt and threaten Plateau communities into the nineteenth century. As more and more Anglo Americans traveled to the Columbia Plateau, a plethora of new diseases afflicted the Nez Perce and their neighbors. Boyd asserted that the great migrations occurring in the early 1840s contributed to new outbreaks of dysentery and whooping cough.[20] The Whitman Massacre, in particular, was an example of Plateau peoples dealing with these diseases and increased pressure on their land and resources.[21]

The previous section demonstrates that Nez Perce and other Plateau communities experienced indirect influences from Euro-Americans and Anglo Americans before actually seeing a white person in their homeland. The combination of these three major indirect forces, the introduction of horses, guns and the devastation of disease, created new conditions that required Nez Perce adaptation. In addition, Plateau communities heard about and met Europeans and Anglo Americans before the Lewis and Clark expedition arrived in 1805. They greeted the arrival of Anglo Americans and Europeans with the same adaptability and ingenuity applied to the introduction of the horse, and gun, and encroachment of other Native American communities. Contact between Euro-Americans and Plateau cultures must be seen within the context of the flow of time and history. Europeans and Anglo Americans did not surprise isolated Nez Perce communities, but Nez Perce people greeted non-natives within the context of 150 years of experience in dealing with diseases, trade encounters, and hearing prophetic utterances about Europeans. Nez Perce culture and communities, both adaptable and flexible, ably dealt with many challenges and opportunities arising out of the above forces and the arrival of Anglo Americans on the Columbia Plateau. Many Anglo Americans already possessed opinions of Native Americans formed through contact and conflict with other groups to the east and did not recognize the adaptability of Plateau Indians. Anglo Americans, who generally lacked interest in learning about Native American cultures, focused primarily on the goal at hand, the increase of trade and acquisition of land. They viewed Native American cultures in a skewed and lop-sided manner that neglected to address the profound cultural forces shaping the Nez Perce world just prior to Anglo-American arrival on the Columbia Plateau.

A NEW RELIGION?

Many historians and anthropologists believed that the forces described above radically changed the nature of Plateau religious practice and experience. Recently, scholars have created two frameworks that attempted to explain the impact of these forces on Nez Perce and Plateau religion. Historians like Christopher Miller asserted that the combination of disease, pressures from outside the Plateau, environmental changes, and the introduction of the horse and gun reshaped the religious world of Plateau Indians.[22] Miller argued for a substantive change in Indian religion and postulated that this change inaugurated new religious beliefs and practices. However, this perspective placed too much emphasis on the disruptive impact of the above forces on religious practice and thought since the changes described by many white observers at the beginning of the nineteenth century related more to form than to substance.[23] Miller noted that around the turn of the century, prophets emerged claiming a death experience, including communication with the "Chief" or Creator and a return to the world of the living to relay messages from this spiritual entity.[24] While this may seem a new perspective, it is directly related to previous religious practice and thought.

The greatest impact on religious thought emerged out of the epidemics that arrived on the Columbia Plateau starting around 1775 and continuing through the mid-nineteenth century. It is not hard to imagine the disruption and despair that accompanied the death of one of every three people in the first epidemic and a combined fifty percent loss of population by the beginning of the nineteenth century. As Hunn noted, the impact of death reached deeper into Plateau and Mid-Columbian cultures than is generally realized.[25] Such death not only affected the ability of families to procure enough foodstuffs to maintain a viable diet, but the death and absence of elders also disrupted the transmission of cultural knowledge and severed well-established links to other villages and communities on the Columbia Plateau.

According to Hunn, disease epidemics created "a spiritual apocalypse."[26] Before the arrival of Euro-Americans, Plateau cultures generally explained sickness and death as the direct results of the misuse of spiritual power, witchcraft, and regular physical ailments.[27] The epidemics assaulted the concepts of moral imbalance or "power struggles in the society of animate beings" and created a unique situation that required explanation.[28] Boyd also noted that mid-Columbian and Plateau communities required new systems and rituals "that would help explain and cope with the unprecedented effects of White contact."[29] Remember that the initial waves of smallpox crested and broke on Plateau cultures before the arrival of Euro-Americans and left Native Americans on the Columbia Plateau to wrestle with the moral and spiritual consequences of the epidemics without knowing their true origins.

What religious changes occurred during the stressful times associated with disease, epidemics and death? Clifford Trafzer and Eugene Hunn both described the shifts in religious practice and ritual in their most recent books. Both emphasized that the religious practices of the early nineteenth century were not a break with the past, but rather a continuation of previous beliefs. What changed was the number of spirit encounters experienced by Plateau peoples and a marked withdrawal inward to define and cope with disease epidemics and the impact of the Anglo-American intrusions on the Columbia Plateau. One of the changes that emerged during this period was an increased emphasis on prophecy and the accompanying "death" and return to life by most prophets. Prophecy and the "death" and return to life motifs associated with prophets existed before the arrival of Europeans. These practices were not breaks with the past, but they continued and amplified existing practices and beliefs. However, the increased frequency of experiences like spirit encounters, death and resurrection, and prophecy arose as ways to define and cope with the enormous consequences of disease and death. Indian people on the Plateau turned inward and used their own religious knowledge and practice to deal with disease and death. The disruption of the relationship between the people and the spirit realm and the moral imbalance created by epidemics and constant violence resulting from the introduction of the horse and gun produced an atmosphere requiring an explanation and a way to deal with the holocaust facing their communities. Hunn asserted that shamans and healers were powerless against smallpox and that elders who appeared to die and then returned to life brought back from the spirit realm new songs, rituals and messages that directly dealt with the stress and uncertainty created by the spread of such disease epidemics.[30]

Community members listened to these elders and integrated their visions and experiences into their previous religious thought and practice. Dancing was an integral part of the prophecies, and people danced to understand and deal with epidemics. Along with dancing and new songs, prophets also preached that the world, as known by Plateau communities, was coming to an end. At the end of the world, families and friends would be reunited and the Creator would establish a new world. Prophets also predicted the coming of the white man.[31] Hunn asserted, "The persuasive power of these revelations clearly derives from the fact that they held out one last hope that the apocalypse the white man brought might be reversed and the world restored to its former harmony."[32] The theme of restoring harmony to the Columbia Plateau also tied in with the story of Monster and Coyote. Coyote helped the community by fighting the Monster and recreating the environment after Monster's death. Plateau peoples hoped for Coyote and other spirit beings to intervene on their behalf and to restore their societies and environment to the balance that existed before the arrival of Euro-Americans. At its root, the religious innovation described by many Anglo Americans was really a recreation or regeneration of previous belief. Native American spiritual leaders in the Pacific Northwest never intended their prophecies, new songs and dances to separate Plateau peoples from their traditional religious practices, but their messages were actually designed to restore order and the former relationship to their environment and the spirit realm.

Far from representing the emergence of new religious thinking, the prophets calling the Plateau peoples to a renewed spiritual relationship rooted their calls in practices and beliefs present before the epidemics of the late eighteenth and early nineteenth centuries. They offered access to the strongest power known to Plateau peoples and encouraged people to appeal to these powers to understand the stress and uncertainty of these crises. The epidemics necessitated the reevaluation of spiritual relationships and encouraged a renewal that fostered hope in the face of disease and death. As noted earlier, many writers and researchers explained this religious transformation as a reaction to outside forces and disruptions initiated by Euro-Americans in North America. Outside forces affected Nez Perce and Plateau cultures, but the responses of Indian people to these forces must be analyzed and evaluated in the light of their own historical struggles and not through the lens of Anglo-American influences or goals. The Nez Perce acted and believed in ways consistent with their own institutions and religious practices even in the face of the desperate situation created by disease and epidemic. Nez Perce responses came from their own communities or through relationships with other Plateau communities. As Anglo Americans arrived on the scene, the new rituals, songs, dances, and prophecies served as powerful weapons and sources of resistance for Plateau communities.

The travails of the Nez Perce and other Plateau communities during the late eighteenth and early nineteenth century illustrate the enormity of Monster and also the beginning of the physical devouring of the people. The epidemics and their devouring of half of the population represent Monster's first steps in consuming Coyote and Plateau culture. Monster was multi-faceted and devoured people on both a physical and cultural level. The death of many elders and other leaders tested the endurance of Nez Perce culture and religion to the extreme. Elders represented the wealth of religious, political, and historical knowledge and their absence left many communities with fewer people to teach and guide younger people, inculcate cultural values, and lead communities in their initial contact with Euro-Americans. Disease and the general invasion of the Pacific Northwest worked to swallow Nez Perce culture and to destroy them as a people, but the survival and continuance of Washani religion into the twentieth century testifies to the power of these rituals and their connections to older ways of life.

FIRST CONTACT

In a way, Nez Perce and other Plateau Indian communities met Euro-Americans many years before they physically stepped onto the Columbia Plateau. Many outside forces affected Nez Perce life, some the result of Euro-American influences and others related to the environment surrounding Plateau communities. Nez Perce people, traveling on expeditions east of the Bitterroot and Rocky Mountains, heard stories about Euro-Americans and recognized their influence when confronted with new weapons like the gun. Trading encounters spread goods such as pots, pans, beads, pipes, knives and other articles slowly onto the Great Plains, the Rocky Mountains and the Columbia Plateau from coastal areas and also formed the core for stories and narratives about Euro-Americans. Nez Perce and Plateau peoples probably met whites on the Columbia River or the Pacific Coast prior to 1805. While the arrival of Lewis and Clark marked the first official contact with Anglo Americans on the Columbia Plateau, many Nez Perce had already prepared themselves, at least through religious prophecy and stories, for their appearance in 1805. Far from being unprepared for these strangers, Nez Perce communities recognized the importance of Euro-Americans on a material, political and social level.[33]

While the Nez Perce had somehow divined the enormity of Monster through the epidemics and rumors of Euro-Americans, their first contact with whites belied and contradicted what came later when Anglo Americans began to stream into the Pacific Northwest. Today much fanfare and activity has surrounded the 195th anniversary of the Lewis and Clark expedition. A documentary on PBS, an accompanying website, re-creations of the expedition's journey, and a few books all extolled the accomplishments of Lewis and Clark and the importance of their expedition in the history of the United States. Generally, Lewis and Clark related well to most Native Americans along the expedition's route and fulfilled their mission requirements by attempting to negotiate with many of the groups they contacted. Nez Perce remembered the expedition favorably and with hope, no doubt as a result of prophecy and the belief that Anglo Americans might be powerful allies or friends capable of helping the Nez Perce and other Plateau communities against their enemies.

The purchase of the Louisiana territory in 1803, an international transaction directly affecting numerous Native American communities, had nearly doubled the landmass of the United States. It also fell within the grand tradition of European colonialism since neither Napoleon nor Jefferson consulted or informed the native inhabitants of the region of their supposed transference from France's legal jurisdiction to that of the United States. The act of purchasing someone else's land without their consent was a European act of arrogance that completely disregarded Indian claims to the land encompassed by the Louisiana Purchase. The Purchase thrust the Nez Perce and other Plateau communities into the midst of international diplomacy and international trade. Fur, land and natural resources existed in abundance in the Louisiana Territory and in the Oregon Territory. The United States, Britain, Spain and France all hoped to exploit these riches and integrate these regions into their own economies. On a geopolitical level, the Nez Perce and other Plateau communities occupied a strategic area rich in resources and claimed by these various international players. As with most land acquisition by the United States, economic interests and activities were foremost in the minds of those involved in the purchase.[34]

Recognizing the importance of actually knowing what the United States had purchased, Jefferson decided to send an expedition to explore the route of the Missouri River and also to determine the strength and intentions of Native American inhabitants in the newly acquired region. Captains Meriwether Lewis and William Clark departed St. Louis on May 14, 1804, with twenty-nine others, traveling northwest along the Missouri River. The expedition spent their first winter with the Mandan along the Missouri River, building Fort Mandan and meeting various Native American groups. One of the principal objectives of the Corps of Discovery was "to gather, record, and analyze a vast amount of information about the Indians in the West and Pacific Northwest."[35] While not trained as ethnographers, Lewis and Clark compiled a great deal of information about Native Americans and also attempted to intervene in affairs between different Indian groups. For example, while at Fort Mandan during the winter of 1804, the expedition made extensive observations of the Mandans and attempted to mediate between the Mandans and the Arikara in their disputes over raids and territory.

After their winter stay with the Mandan, the expedition continued up the Missouri River in the spring of 1805. Before leaving their winter camp with the Mandans, Lewis and Clark formulated goals for the expedition. Among the most important of these goals was to find the Shoshoni Indians, to procure horses for the trip over the Continental Divide, and to avoid Assiniboin bands that Lewis and Clark viewed as potential threats to the expedition. Traveling during the spring and summer of 1805, the expedition reached the Great Falls of the Missouri River on June 13, 1805, and began the grueling portage around the Falls. As the summer wore on, the expedition faced the potential danger of being trapped on the eastern slopes of the Continental Divide if they did not find friendly Shoshoni Indians and trade for horses. Their search ended on August 13, 1805, when an advance party, led by Meriwether Lewis, confronted "a band of some sixty mounted warriors riding at full speed."[36] The Corps of Discovery had finally found the Northern Shoshoni Indians. After spending six days at Camp Fortunate with Cameahwait, the leader of the band of Shoshoni Indians that Lewis had encountered, the expedition set out to cross the Continental Divide at Lemhi Pass and to trade for horses. As James Rhonda pointed out, Lewis was forced to pay dearly for the horses as the Indians understood the expedition's desperate situation and took advantage of the situation.

Following the Nez Perce trail, the Corps of Discovery entered the Bitterroot Valley on September 4, 1805, and encountered a Flathead camp. These Salish-speaking people often hunted buffalo with the Shoshonis and the Nez Perce. After resting for a few days and trading horses, the expedition began its assault of the Lolo Trail, probably one of the most difficult portions of the journey. Confronted with snow and steep slopes, Clark pressed ahead with a small group of men. After struggling for two days, Clark and his men reached the end of the Lolo Trail and emerged on a small plain known now as the Weippe Prairie, where many Nez Perce people gathered to dig roots, hunt and fish. The advance party met the inhabitants of two small villages and received some supplies of camas root and dried salmon as well as a positive welcome from the people. This may have been a very comforting respite since the Corps of Discovery nearly starved on its passage over the Continental Divide and the Bitterroot Mountains. After spending two days with these Nez Perce, the advance party moved further up the Clearwater River to the camp of Twisted Hair, an important Nez Perce leader in the area.[37]

The pleasant reception of the expedition by Nez Perce people probably arose from two very different sources. Among the people at Twisted Hair's camp was a woman named Watkuweis, a Nez Perce woman who had been taken captive, traded to a white man, and lived in Canada among white people for several years. During her captivity, Watkuweis was treated well and she continued to hold whites in high regard. According to Rhonda, Watkuweis played an instrumental role in securing the favorable treatment of the expedition during their stay with the Nez Perce. Allen Slickpoo Sr. also noted the importance of Watkuweis and mentioned that her entreaties to not hurt Clark and his men probably smoothed the way for their reception. Not only Watkuweis' words, but also Nez Perce hopes affected the reception of the expedition. While curious about the expedition, the Nez Perce also perceived them as potential allies and, perhaps more importantly, as suppliers of guns and ammunition to help in their own self-defense. James Rhonda commented that as traditional Nez Perce enemies like the Blackfeet gained firearms from Canadian traders, the Nez Perce desperately wanted to obtain guns for protection and military expeditions against their enemies.[38]

After staying with the Nez Perce for nearly two weeks, the Corps of Discovery left their horses in Nez Perce keeping and, during early October, proceeded with their journey down the Clearwater, Snake and Columbia Rivers to the Pacific Ocean. Accompanying them were two Nez Perce chiefs, Twisted Hair and Tetoharsky, who promised to serve as guides and interpreters on the journey. As the expedition traveled down the Snake River and into the Columbia, Twisted Hair and Tetoharsky moved ahead of the group to prepare the way. Near the confluence of the Snake and Columbia Rivers, Lewis and Clark met a large delegation of Yakama and Wanapam people, but they had difficulty understanding one another because of translation problems. Moving down the Columbia River, the expedition encountered Walla Walla people and received a warm welcome based partly on Twisted Hair and Tetoharsky's preparations and on the desire of the Walla Wallas to procure European goods, especially firearms. The friendly welcomes subsided as Lewis and Clark paddled further down the Columbia River. By the time they reached the confluence of the John Day and Columbia Rivers, the expedition encountered Indian communities deeply involved in trade with Europeans. On October 22, 1805, the party reached Celilo Falls, a large set of falls that offered the first obstacle to the Corps of Discovery on their journey down the Columbia River. Two days later Twisted Hair and Tetoharsky left the expedition because they feared for their lives; they had reached the boundary between Sahaptian and Chinookan cultures.[39] After a short stay at the Dalles with the Wishram people, the Corps of Discovery continued on toward the Pacific Ocean. They reached the mouth of the Columbia on November 14, 1805, and built their winter lodgings, which they called Fort Clatsop. On the return trip, the expedition traveled overland through Umatilla, Cayuse, Walla Walla and Nez Perce country to the Bitterroot Mountains and then split up, Lewis proceeding to the Great Falls and Clark exploring the Yellowstone River. They reunited on August 12, 1806, and returned to St. Louis on September 23, 1806. In twenty-eight months, the Lewis and Clark expedition covered more than 4,000 miles and lost only one member of the corps.[40]

What was the impact of the Lewis and Clark expedition? According to historian Carlos Schwantes, the expedition revealed the wealth of fur-bearing animals in the interior West, bolstered United States claims to the Oregon country, and added much knowledge of the peoples and environment of the West. In a broader sense, the Corps of Discovery also captured the imaginations of contemporaries and fired the historical imaginations of future generations of historians and the general population. The expedition has been mythologized and reconstructed into the national story. Schwantes recognized the import of the expedition and noted that Lewis and Clark represented one of many chapters in the imperial and commercial story unfolding as a result of competition between various commercial enterprises and nations in the western portion of North America.[41]

The success of the Lewis and Clark expedition encouraged others to follow in their footsteps, especially those willing to endure the risks involved in exploiting the region's resources, particularly fur-bearing animals. After the expedition, fur trappers and traders penetrated deeper and deeper into the interior of the continent, trading with Native Americans and establishing claims for Britain and the United States. First the North West Company, then John Astor's American Fur Company and, finally, the Hudson's Bay Company acted as the first commercial enterprises to travel into the Columbia Plateau. From 1789 onward, Alexander Mackenzie and the North West Company attempted to explore and exploit the richness of the interior West and the Columbia Plateau. Both Simon Fraser and David Thompson followed in Mackenzie's footsteps, exploring and opening up posts for the North West Company within British Columbia and the Pacific Northwest.[42]

American presence in the Pacific Northwest started with the establishment of a trading post at the mouth of the Columbia River by the John Astor's American Fur Company. While Fort Astoria was being built in 1811, Astor sent out expeditions to find furs and compete with British fur traders. The presence of the post and American trappers came to its end with the start of hostilities between the United States and Great Britain during the War of 1812. Operating at a loss, the Americans sold their assets to their British competitors, and Fort Astoria, renamed Fort George, fell under British control shortly after the departure of the American Fur Company's personnel.[43]

Astor did not return to the Pacific Northwest and left the Columbia Plateau to his competitor, the North West Company. After the war, the North West Company attempted to open new areas for fur exploitation. By 1821, the British government forced the North West Company to merge with the Hudson's Bay Company out of concern that violence between the two companies might hinder profits. Hudson's Bay Company exercised de facto control of the Pacific Northwest and continued the exploitation of fur-bearing animals in the region.[44] From 1823 to 1832, the Company maintained outposts throughout the region with the main post, Fort Vancouver, located at the present-day site of Vancouver, Washington. John McLoughlin, the chief factor for the Company in the region from 1824 to 1846, encouraged the development of other economic activities, particularly those helpful in supplying Company ventures. The treaty ending the War of 1812 allowed Americans free entry into the Oregon Country, but most Americans stayed away from the area. Many independent trappers who entered the region were not successful, and the Hudson's Bay Company maintained its hold over the region until the 1840s.[45]

While the exploits of mountain men and fur trappers figured large in the imagination of many narratives about the opening of the Pacific Northwest, the sixty years of their presence in the region marked them as transitory and often contradictory entities in the life of Plateau Indians. As with any commercial enterprise, the fur business was interested in profits. These profits often involved the use of Native American labor and expertise to procure the commodity, fur-bearing animals, desired by these companies. The impact of these companies and their activities was manifest in two areas. The North West Company and later the Hudson's Bay Company were instrumental in exploring the interior west and establishing relationships with Native Americans. The knowledge of the employees of these firms formed the basis for bringing many other people into the Columbia Plateau and other regions of the West.

Fur trapping and trading also affected Columbia Plateau Native Americans by integrating them into a global network of trade. While Nez Perce and other Plateau cultures rarely worked for wages, the traders and trappers associated with the fur companies exploited existing trade networks developed over time by Columbia Plateau Indians, distributing trade items in exchange for furs. For the first time, Euro-Americans enticed Plateau Indians into a relationship with the natural environment that contradicted their beliefs and teachings. Europeans asked the Nez Perce and others to participate in a system that fundamentally worked against the seasonal round practiced by most Columbia Plateau cultures. Schwantes perceptively maintained that fur trading companies and their activities "revealed economic attitudes and patterns that were to be replicated in the future and with far greater impact upon the region's natural environment."[46] Trappers and their economic activity foreshadowed the radically different relationship that Europeans and Anglo Americans maintained with the natural environment. This relationship with the natural environment encouraged and fostered misunderstandings of Native American perspectives and often lay at the root of conflict and struggle with Columbia Plateau Indians.

The history of Nez Perce and Plateau cultural contact with Europeans and Anglo Americans started before the arrival of whites on the Columbia Plateau. The horse, guns, trade articles, and diseases brought change to Nez Perce life and even threatened their existence and their ability to transmit cultural and historical knowledge. The arrival of Europeans and Anglo Americans, whether Lewis and Clark, David Thompson, Alexander Mackenzie or others, merely affirmed what the Nez Perce already knew or heard through contact with other Native American communities and their own religious prophets. While this contact and its consequences had great meaning for both Nez Perce and Anglo-American communities, the way this contact was narrated in the late nineteenth and early twentieth centuries established a way of understanding this period that privileged the knowledge and historical imagination of Anglo Americans. The narratives created and codified by American historians could also be called a sort of contact story, a knowledge contact story, since the way Anglo-American historians contacted the knowledge of Columbia Plateau Indians continued the experience of contact initiated through earlier forces started by Europeans and Anglo Americans.

Monster was a consumer, eating up every competitor and creating a situation advantageous only to its existence. The fur trade and distribution of European and Anglo-American trade goods intruded into well-established Columbia Plateau economic relationships, changing and consuming them and integrating the Indians into a world market and economy. Monster's consuming the people began with the first contact, a contact felt even before the physical arrival of whites. Monster's consuming of the Nez Perce and other Plateau cultures began long before and continued well after the conquest of the Nez Perce in 1877-78 in ways far more subtle and powerful than the guns, sabers and artillery used to defeat them on the battlefield. The central questions that must be asked in this contact and consumption of knowledge are: how did Anglo-American historians and observers contact and react to Native American knowledge about this period? What events or people were privileged in this narrative? The answers to these questions lie in an investigation and understanding of some of the major creators and narrators of Pacific Northwest History. While many included Pacific Northwest history in their narratives, the job of creating a lasting regional history fell to Edmond Meany, Cornelius J. Brosnan, and other historians rooted in the institutions and region of the Pacific Northwest.

THE MEETING OF COYOTE AND MONSTER AS TOLD BY MONSTER

On the national stage, historians like Hubert Howe Bancroft and later Frederick Jackson Turner attempted to narrate the expansion of Europeans and then Anglo Americans in North America. While differing in approach, both men sought to construct a narrative that helped citizens of the United States to understand their place in a new land and their place on the world stage. Much of this narrative focused on the swallowing of Native American cultures through direct military force, disease, or assimilation into the new American nation. Others, on a more local or regional level, sought to understand the particularities of their region within the context of the national narrative produced by more influential historians. Edmond Meany played a significant role in the creation, construction and early interpretation of Pacific Northwest history. Influenced and trained by Frederick Jackson Turner, professor at the University of Wisconsin, and other well-known historians of the late nineteenth and early twentieth century, Meany adopted the perspective of a profession struggling to create itself and produce a codex of history explaining the nation's past. Meany spent most of his life in pursuit of a unique story that encompassed those he regarded as the important people and events that shaped the region he called home.[47]

The author intends to use Meany as an example of the spirit or practice of history, particularly in the Pacific Northwest, on a professional and non-professional level. While seeing Meany as representative of Anglo-American historical thought, the reader must remember that narratives, even those created by Meany, are not one-dimensional, static texts, but are dynamic. They change over time and incorporate different cues and landmarks as they evolve in interaction with other texts and narratives. Meany's narratives also changed over time, but they also remained the same. Meany, Cornelius J. Brosnan and others used the same cues, events, and landmarks in their narratives, but they changed their emphasis or their interpretation to encompass present concerns and societal needs.

Why use Edmond Meany's writings as a foil to understand the creation and construction of historical narratives and imagination in the Pacific Northwest? During his life, Meany filled many different roles as booster, politician, businessman, and academic, each deeply embedding him in the life of his home region. These experiences also granted him access to the memories of an earlier generation of Anglo Americans responsible for the invasion and settlement of Washington State and the Pacific Northwest. As a major professor of history at the University of Washington, Meany wrote history about this area, but he also collected and archived the documentary and material culture of those he so admired and respected and he created texts and institutions necessary for the propagation of historical knowledge among Anglo Americans in the Pacific Northwest. While Meany's texts were not hegemonic, the state sanctioned his creation of historical narratives through his university employment and the broader social groups of Washington State and the Pacific Northwest listened and consumed his narratives through countless speeches, textbook purchases, memorial and statue commemorations, and other activities connected to Meany's position as historian and archivist.

Meany's texts competed and interacted with many different narratives and memories of events in the Pacific Northwest. While popular and academic narratives diverged in their versions, they often relied on the same narrative cues and structure to assemble a story about the history of the Pacific Northwest. The value of examining Meany's work lies in his proximity to local and popular memory. Through his devotion to pioneer life and lore, Meany created a narrative framework and structure that integrated these perspectives into his work while he attempted to maintain a professional devotion to the historical practices and methods of the late nineteenth and early twentieth centuries.

Meany's work is also valuable since he worked directly under Frederick Jackson Turner, one of the most influential historians in the late nineteenth and early twentieth centuries. Meany not only devoted himself to local historical memory, but he also trained under the man responsible for one of the most enduring interpretive frameworks in the American historical profession. Meany's narratives moved between two competing and cooperating fields: local or popular memory and professional historical practice and methods; but these fields existed in a very white world and were predicated on not listening to Indians. Meany created texts about Native Americans and the Pacific Northwest that were connected to the broader narratives and interpretative frameworks of Turner, Bancroft and others and that represented the penetration of national historical imagination into the creation of regional and local historical texts and narratives.[48]

Throughout his career, Meany remained fairly consistent in his emplotment of Pacific Northwest history. After publication of *History of the State of Washington*, his narrative structures solidified and remained intact throughout the rest of his career.[49] This is not meant to suggest that Meany failed to grow in his academic career, add new material to his presentations when available, or change the flow of the narrative. Indeed, Meany created and sustained a framework that survived the addition of new material and the assaults of interpretive debate. The major point here is that non-professional and professional historians disagreed sometimes on the material to be included, but they remained true to a structure that shaped and modeled the narrative into a cohesive story.

The following analysis seeks to deconstruct Meany's main narrative about initial contact between Columbia Plateau Native Americans and Euro-Americans. Through an examination of the *History of the State of Washington*, Meany's course syllabi, and some of Meany's speeches, it is possible to discover how "Monster" swallowed the Nez Perce, ingested them, and, for a brief time, made them disappear from the historical landscape.[50] While Meany represents one voice or actor in this "swallowing," his work and writings are indicative of broader societal endeavors to consume Native Americans, their history, and their culture.

How was this accomplished? How did Monster swallow Coyote and then narrate the encounter? As with most historical writing, particularly general histories intended to narrate and instruct, Meany's first chapter of the *History of the State of Washington* introduced the region and its early inhabitants. This practice still exists to a large degree in most high school and college level textbooks. Authors must start their narratives somewhere, and most historians of the Western United States begin their narratives at the beginning, the time before "civilization" arrived in a particular region.[51] Meany also started his narrative at the "beginning," pre-historic or "pre-civilization" time. The first chapter of Meany's history occupied only eight short pages, but it contained a wealth of material about the place of the Nez Perce within the broader historical narrative of the Pacific Northwest.

Most of the first chapter provided a description of the physical environment of Washington State and the Pacific Northwest. Using the work of Thomas Condon, a geologist specializing in the Pacific Northwest, Meany sought to describe the rich variation present in the physical environment of Pacific Northwest. Unfortunately, he failed to consult with the Nez Perce and other Columbia Plateau Indians for information regarding the land, a territory that they had inhabited for thousands of years prior to the arrival of Europeans. The land and topography, according to Meany, shaped the history of the region and created the avenues available for European and Anglo-American activities. While the land determined the routes "civilization" would take into the Pacific Northwest, Meany asserted that the environment "developed the aborigines while wresting from the wilderness a rude dominion."[52] In Meany's mind, not only were Native Americans natural men and women, connected to the land through their activities and culture, but they also stood powerless to shape their own destinies or a civilization. The environment controlled the activities and lives of Native Americans and destined their level of cultural development. In this first chapter, Meany quickly placed Indians into the box of nature. Once there, their script was already provided for them by Meany's devotion to the progressive view of history which held that the environment determined the Indians' place in this historical hierarchy. As Meany confidently asserted, "They had not reached the culture plain of barbarians, but were all in the bow-and-arrow plane of savagery."[53]

What does their placement in this hierarchy mean for the Nez Perce and other Plateau Indian communities? In the historical imagination of Anglo Americans in the late nineteenth and early twentieth centuries, this view relegated Native Americans and their cultures to destruction and disappearance as the direct result of historical forces that Anglo Americans believed worked in all situations. Anglo-American belief in the progressive nature of history meant that "lower" or "inferior" societies must yield to "higher" more "civilized" societies. Kerwin Klein observed that historians like Turner and Meany situated the central conflict of the "frontier" story in the struggle between "savagery" (nature) and "civilization" and that the outcome of this conflict was predetermined since history's progressive nature allowed no room for returns to nature or wildness.[54] Readers of Meany's work in 1909 or 1910 required little knowledge or explanation of Native American culture or history since the ultimate fate of these cultures was predestined to vanish before a superior culture. They considered Native cultures and peoples inconsequential. Meany therefore provided only the briefest of passages about Native American cultures of the Pacific Northwest because most whites viewed the fate of Native Americans as already sealed, in large part because of native dependence on nature.

Meany ended the first chapter with another interpretive structure meant to help his readers understand the nature of Pacific Northwest life before the arrival of Europeans. He noted that "in the prehistoric period the native races might be classed as Horse Indians on the east and Canoe Indians on the west of the Cascade Mountains."[55] Again, Meany created a simplistic structure, an imaginary distinction, which enabled his readers to clearly grasp the condition of Native Americans before the arrival of Europeans. Meany believed that this "rough classification" helped the reader understand subsequent events since the "Horse" Indians were "more virile" than the Canoe Indians, thus explaining why interior Columbia Plateau Indian communities resisted disease and white encroachment to a greater extent than did coastal communities.

After this cursory description of Pacific Northwest geography and native peoples, Meany entered into the central drama of his narrative, the arrival of "civilization" in the form of Europeans. In the first paragraph of chapter two, "Lure of the Pacific," Meany declared the theory behind his narrative: the past revealed the unity of history. For Meany and many Anglo Americans, the written word of history was the unfolding of the modern, the expansion of "civilization" through European influence in the "New World," new only to Europeans and Anglo Americans. The exploits of explorers, regardless of origin or nationality, heralded this arrival of civilization in the New World and specifically in the Pacific Northwest. Meany described in detail the activities and "discoveries" of Sir Francis Drake, Captain James Cook, Russian explorers and American captains/explorers like Robert Gray. Klein noted that this type of narration slipped into the "romantic" as historians like Meany elevated a "transcendent hero over vanquished foe."[56] Even though in most cases, the explorers maintained a discrete distance from Native Americans, they occupied the position of heroes in this portion of the narrative. Their persistence, ingenuity and bravery and their role as representatives of "civilization" marked them as the victor even before conflict erupted on the Columbia Plateau between Native Americans and Euro-Americans. Meany and other historians of the early twentieth century relegated Native American history and experience to a few lines in an introductory paragraph because the reader already knew the outcome of the conflict between "civilization" and "savagery." The immortal transcendent Anglo-American heroes already possessed the kernel of victory in the all-powerful Euro-American "civilization," when they arrived on the shores of the Pacific Northwest.

This interpretation of Meany's introductory chapters on the "Period of Discovery" is reinforced by a brief look at a non-professional historical text published four years before Meany's *History of the State of Washington*. Published by the Western Historical Publishing Company in 1903, the authors of *An Illustrated History of North Idaho embracing Nez Perces, Idaho, Latah, Kootenai, and Shoshone Counties, State of Idaho*, attempted to furnish an exhaustive account of the history of several northern Idaho counties.[57] The introductory chapter neglected even the kind of brief discussion of Native Americans in Meany's first chapter, and launched directly into recounting various explorers and expeditions pertinent to the history of northern Idaho. Again, the authors of this history assumed the narrative structures evident in Meany's later work. Native American history need not be mentioned since there was only one possible outcome to the work begun by the heroic explorers. This sentiment is clearly stated later in the text when the authors noted:

> When the indomitable Anglo-Saxon race began following the course of destiny to the westward the doom of the thriftless aboriginal peoples was sealed. The time had arrived in the progress of the world when the dusky, nomadic savage had become a cumberer of the soil. The day of a grander development for this vast prodigious west, teeming with the crude elements of wealth production, had at last dawned. The night of savagery was over. The red man must himself become a factor in pushing forward the cause of Progress or be crushed beneath its wheels. Poor child of the darkness and night! Without knowing it he was face to face with the harshest, most inexorable law of life, the law of the survival of the fittest. He must lay aside at once his ancestral habits and adopt those of another and superior race or he must perish and perish miserably.[58]

The audience for this history and Meany's more professional work understood the emplotment of the story. They required little information about "the thriftless aboriginal peoples" because their fate was sealed with the arrival of Europeans, most notably the "Anglo Saxon" races of Great Britain and the United States. While Meany avoided the cruder language of the above passage, his words still placed him in harmony with the above sentiments.

Meany's course syllabi and outlines of Pacific Northwest History also reflected the same narrative cues and structure as *History of the State of Washington* and *History of Northern Idaho*.[59] All three outlines failed to mention Native American cultures or civilizations before the arrival of Europeans. They began with Spanish explorations and moved quickly into a detailed discussion of explorations by other European nations. This story of exploration or "Period of Discovery" also followed a progressive cadence, ending again at the pinnacle of "civilization," namely British and American explorations. Meany organized his narratives around men or explorers, describing their activities and importance to the great move of civilization to the Pacific Northwest.

After narrating the "discovery" of the Pacific Northwest, Meany and the authors of *History of North Idaho* moved into a detailed story of exploration. The markers on the narrative road Meany and others created generally began with Alexander Mackenzie, moved into a detailed discussion of the Lewis and Clark Expedition, and ended with discussions of Hall Jackson Kelley, Captain Bonneville, Nathaniel Wyeth, William Slacum, and the Charles Wilkes expedition.[60] As the narrative progressed, Mackenzie was the trailblazer, Lewis and Clark formed the pinnacle of American efforts to explore the American West, and the other expeditions supported or enhanced the achievements of Lewis and Clark. The "romance" of these stories appealed to Anglo-American sensibilities and to their desire to attach significance and importance to their own acquisition of the Pacific Northwest.

The narrative shifted after the initial "period of exploration" to the struggle between the United States and Great Britain, two English-speaking countries attempting to control the Pacific Northwest. Meany and others generally narrated this struggle through the economic activities of various fur-trading companies. The importance of the fur trade extended in two distinct directions. First, the fur trade represented the introduction of commodity based economic activity into the lives of Native Americans. This type of economic activity symbolized the next level of "civilization" entering into the Pacific Northwest. Two of the characteristics differentiating Native Americans and Euro-Americans were their economic activity and their use of natural resources. According to the

Anglo-American narrative framework, the fur trade integrated this region into a larger world economy and represented a step ahead in the region's ascent to "civilization."

Klein asserted that this difference in economic activity formed one of the main ways that Anglo Americans relegated Native Americans to "savagery" or "barbarism." According to Klein, Turner, Meany and other historians of the late nineteenth and early twentieth centuries equated "savagery" and "barbarism" with lack of economic activity. "Savages/barbarians do not engage in commerce, they do not command the concept of private property, they do not have a cash economy, and they did not exhibit the typical features of nineteenth century capitalism."[61] Narratives created by Anglo Americans relegated Native Americans to the level of "savagery" and justified their integration into global markets and, eventually, the invasion and confiscation of their land. For Turner and Meany, not only did civilization triumph over savagery, but the conflict between the two also created a new American form of "civilization," a distinct American culture forged in the crucible of the "frontier."

The fur trade also represented the advance of "civilization" in other ways. Just as Turner narrated, Meany and others saw the fur trade in terms of the next stage of Anglo Saxon "civilization" struggling to gain control of the Pacific Northwest. The clash of "nature" and "civilization" played itself out initially in the crude economic exploitation of fur-bearing animals in the American West and, particularly, in the Pacific Northwest. Again, Meany combined heroism and romanticism to narrate this period. The following passage from Meany's *History of the State of Washington* clearly exemplified the combination of these narrative structures:

> Jedediah S. Smith was one of the most remarkable men that ever engaged in the American Fur Trade. He was like that distinguished character of later years, Stonewall Jackson, in combining with the most ardent belief in, and practice of, the Christian religion, an undaunted courage, fierce and impetuous nature, and untiring energy. His deeds are unfortunately much veiled in obscurity, but enough has survived to show that he was a true knight errant, a lover of that kind of adventure which the unexplored West afforded in such ample degree.[62]

Meany connected Jedediah Smith to the larger national mythos by comparing him to the contemporary Stonewall Jackson and emphasizing his devotion to Christianity. For Meany, the exploration of the West loomed as an adventure, ripe for those men to pick and taste, just as "knights errant" pursued glory in medieval Europe. Meany believed that the "true knight errant" was a wielder of Anglo-American civilization, struggling on the rugged borders between savagery and civilization to bring about the transformation of this region. No matter what the name, Jedediah Smith, Alexander Mackenzie, Lewis and Clark, Bonneville or Nathaniel Wyeth, these men ventured forth in a valiant quest for civilization.

This brief foray into Meany's narrative sets the stage for the unfolding and deconstruction of his framework and the work of others. The exploits of explorers, discoverers and fur trappers/traders figured large in the historical imagination of Anglo Americans. Their place in the narrative was crucial since they were the first to subject themselves to the struggle between "nature" and "civilization," the first to confront Native Americans. As Klein perceptively noted, "Native America spurred the development of white America's historical consciousness."[63] These "knights errant" charged through the land; their foes were Native Americans, ready to engulf them in the abyss of "savagery" and "barbarism." Klein also maintained that the development of Anglo-American historical consciousness deprived Native Americans of agency through a shrewd use of language since Indians appeared in Turner and Meany's narratives but they "own no verbs of their own."[64]

For example, in Meany's first chapter of *History of the State of Washington*, the environment developed or worked on Indians, not the other way around. The active characters in Meany's story were all Europeans or Anglo Americans ready to advance the cause of civilization. To introduce Indians as dynamic participants would have subverted the plot of the narrative and created too much dissonance for the reader. Placing agency into the hands of Native Americans would have eroded the "knight errant" trope and relegated Euro-Americans and Indians to the same level with competing narratives and actions, but it would have also not given a clear direction to the narrative. For Turner and Meany, there could only be one hero and one vanquished foe. The plot was set and the characters acted accordingly.

The thread of this plot continues into the next "phase" or part of the Coyote and Monster narrative. As missionaries and settlers moved into the Pacific Northwest, they reenacted a story played out in many other regions of North America. While the plot for Anglo Americans focused on romanticism and heroism, Native Americans faced conflict, competition for resources, and assaults on their history and culture. In Chapter Four, Coyote and Monster compete with one another, attempting to swallow each other. For the Nez Perce and other Plateau communities, the struggle intensified.

Chapter Four
Words and Boundaries: Missionaries, Settlers, and Treaties

> Now then Coyote shouted to him, "Oh Monster, we are going to inhale each other!" The big eyes of the monster roved around looking all over for Coyote but did not find him, because Coyote's body was painted with clay to achieve a perfect protective coloring in the grass. Coyote had on his back a pack consisting of five stone knives, some pure pitch, and a flint fire making set. Presently Coyote shook the grass to and fro and shouted again, "Monster! We are going to inhale each other." Suddenly the monster saw the swaying grass and replied, "Oh you Coyote, you swallow me first then; you inhale first." Now Coyote tried. Powerfully and noisily he drew his breath and the great monster just swayed and quivered. Then Coyote said, "Now you inhale me, for already you have swallowed all the people, so swallow me too lest I become lonely." Now the Monster inhaled like a mighty wind.[1]

The struggle between Coyote and Monster symbolizes the struggle between the Nez Perce and Anglo Americans that intensified during the early part of the nineteenth century. Coyote prepared for the struggle by gathering five stone knives and he attempted to defend himself by his attempts at swallowing Monster. Initially, Nez Perce and other Plateau Indian communities met and matched Anglo Americans on an equal footing. They prepared by gaining knowledge about Monster, learning as they went. White missionaries and early settlers recognized the powerful position of the Nez Perce but they actively worked to erode their sovereignty and to limit their power, possessions, and land holdings. Coyote kept a low profile in his initial meeting with Monster just as the Nez Perce attempted to maintain friendly and non-confrontational relationships with those who would later seek to consume their culture.

A deconstruction of the narrative concerning the arrival of missionaries, settlers, and American policy on the Columbia Plateau occupies the central focus of the fourth chapter. Edmond Meany, C.J. Brosnan, Kate McBeth, the editors of Western Historical Publishing and many others created numerous narratives about the Nez Perce and their history. Most of these narratives, on some level, shared a similar cadence in their writing. Meany focused his work on heroes, explorers, and "great men" preparing the way for settlers and civilization. The struggle of "great men," according to most of these writers, was against "nature" and "savagery," most often represented by Indians, their land and their way of life. These works called into question the validity and value of native culture, history, literature, and religion. By surviving their prolonged exposure to nature and the threat of Indian savagery, explorers, fur trappers and traders marked the initial steps toward "civilizing" the region. In this struggle, history was always on the side of Anglo Americans, and Meany, like most authors of his era, clearly stated that these struggles would end with the inevitable victory of civilization and the possession of the land by the United States and its citizens. In essence, Meany's narrative and its structure took on the trappings of a liturgy, a scripted narrative easily recognizable and recited by those familiar with the story, repeated many times since the nineteenth century.

The next part of this liturgy, practiced by many authors and recited in the popular imagination, narrated the positive exploits of missionaries, soldiers, and settlers and the constructive establishment of treaties to protect the possessors of "civilization" and limit the property and influence of Native Americans, its opponents. This part of the narrative focused on the theme of "civilization" versus "savagery." For the authors of the *An Illustrated History of North Idaho*, the arrival of missionaries signaled the next stage in the story of civilization's move to the west. The heroism of missionaries and settlers resided in a different realm than that of the explorer or adventurer. The romance remained, but the authors portraying this period wove a story that focused on the hard work of establishing in the Pacific Northwest a settled way of life that recreated the institutions and values of the national community.

"THE MISSIONARY EPOCH" AND THE WHITMAN MASSACRE

Fur trappers and traders entered the Pacific Northwest in the late eighteenth century and continued their operations through the late 1840s. Once a lucrative occupation, the fur industry fell on hard times during the 1840s due to changes in fashion, over-trapping, and the beginnings of white settlement in the Pacific Northwest and other regions in the West. As trappers and traders shifted their activities or even became farmers, a new wave of settlement loomed on the horizon. The forerunners of this new immigration came in the guise of Protestant missionaries and their accompanying support staff. Well-meaning and devoted to their cause, these missionaries provided valuable experience and expertise for other Anglo Americans who wished to follow them into the Pacific Northwest.

Conflict among trappers, traders, those interested in exploiting furs and Native Americans had existed but failed to reach the level of tension and violence that occurred between 1840 and the late 1870s. While the period of fur exploitation cannot be characterized as a peaceful period, it certainly took on a more settled feel once more and more settlers began arriving in the 1840s. The resulting intensified conflict signaled the end of a precarious coexistence and illustrated the misunderstandings, problems and motivations of both the Anglo American and Native American sides. The narrative cues and devices used to tell the story of transition from fur exploitation to the "missionary epoch" remained in the realm of heroism, sacrifice, martyrdom, and other tropes of civilization and Manifest Destiny. Meany and others remained attached to the same language in their depictions of missionaries but relied more heavily on a Christian subtext that reinforced the mission and purpose of the people involved with bringing "civilization" and "light" to the wilderness.

For historians like Meany and even Kate McBeth, the story of the "missionary epoch" often began with a discussion of the Nez Perce delegation sent to St. Louis to learn "the truth about the white man's religion."[2] This episode served as a crucial link between the previous period of fur trapping and trading and the arrival of missionaries in the Pacific Northwest. Through their contact with Euro Americans from varying fur trading companies, the Nez Perce and other Plateau communities learned about Christian religious practices. Meany even noted that this knowledge may have come from a group of Iroquois from Canada who received religious instruction from Catholic missionaries. Some communities, like the Flathead and Spokans, sent sons of influential leaders to mission schools in Canada.[3] As interest in Christianity increased, the Nez Perce and Flatheads decided to send delegations to St. Louis to find out about this new religion.

For Edmond Meany, a devout Christian and member of the Congregational Church, the delegations sent to St. Louis represented an attempt by Native Americans to acquire the spiritual advantages they witnessed in their interactions with Euro Americans. Meany and others, most notably, Kate McBeth, assumed the superiority of Christianity. McBeth's book, *The Nez Perces Since Lewis and Clark*, even went so far as to contend that Lewis and

Clark were instrumental in changing Nez Perce religion and practice through their gestures and actions. According to McBeth, the Nez Perce worshipped the sun after contact with Lewis and Clark but soon realized that this worship was unsatisfying because of their acquaintance with Christianity and their own misgivings about sun worship.[4]

The story of the Nez Perce delegation began rather innocently with various Native American communities relating stories about Anglo Americans. The Nez Perce and Flathead often hunted buffalo together and attended the annual fur trapper rendezvous on the Green River. They traded, talked, and built relationships with Americans, Canadians, and Native Americans from the east and attempted to understand the lives and ways of these newcomers to the Pacific Northwest. At the rendezvous, Nez Perce people observed the lifestyle and possessions of Europeans and Anglo Americans. In particular, the Nez Perce were very interested in discerning the source of spiritual power that Anglo Americans possessed. During 1831, a delegation of Nez Perce and Flatheads accompanied fur traders of the American Fur Company to St. Louis. There they met William Clark, of Lewis and Clark fame, who had become Superintendent of Indian Affairs for the vast West. Clark introduced them to Catholic Bishop Joseph Rosati and hosted them while in St Louis. Two of the delegation members died in St. Louis, one died on the return trip, and only one of the four-man delegation returned to the Pacific Northwest.[5]

Trafzer and Scheuerman noted that the arrival of the Nez Perce/Flathead delegation coincided with the presence of William Walker, a Wyandot chief and devout Methodist, in St. Louis. Walker corresponded with G.P. Disoway, a Christian friend, who wrote an essay for the *Christian Advocate and Journal and Zion's Herald*. In the essay, Disoway appealed for missionaries to answer "the call" to the Pacific Northwest brought by the Flathead and Nez Perce delegation.[6] As Meany quoted in his chapter on missionaries, Christian workers referred to the delegation as a "Macedonian cry," in reference to the Apostle Paul's vision of a Macedonian beckoning him to bring the Gospel to his homeland.[7] Disoway's appeal for missionaries bore immediate fruit in Jason Lee, who headed to the Pacific Northwest in 1834 and eventually settled in the Willamette Valley at the suggestion of Dr. John McLoughlin, the Hudson's Bay Company factor.

Lee's mission served Indians and Euro Americans in the Willamette but failed to reach the Nez Perce or other Plateau Indian communities. Mission work among the Nez Perce, Cayuse, Palouse, Walla Wallas and other Plateau communities began in earnest with the arrival of Dr. Marcus Whitman and Henry Spalding, their wives, and others on the Columbia Plateau.

Whitman and Samuel Parker traveled west in 1835 and met Nez Perce at the annual rendezvous at Green River. Whitman returned to the eastern United States to recruit more people, and Parker proceeded to the Oregon Country to explore possible locations and peoples for the missions. Whitman recruited Spalding and others to return to the Northwest and arrived on the Great Columbia Plain in September 1836.[8]

The Whitmans and Spaldings chose different locations for their missions. The missionaries located the Whitman mission at Waiilatpu, "The Place of Rye Grass," along the Walla Walla River in Cayuse country, and the Spaldings started a mission for the Nez Perce along the Clearwater River, close to the Nez Perce village of Lapwai, "The Place of the Butterfly."[9] Nez Perce elder and historian Allen Slickpoo, Sr. noted that the missions succeeded and made some converts in their early years. He also maintained that initially the Nez Perce welcomed the missionaries since the Nez Perce were a very religious people and wanted to know more about Christianity. This early success soon changed as the missionaries moved from preaching the gospel to persuading the Nez Perce to leave their traditional ways of living and adopt Anglo-American culture.[10] The "civilizing" aspect of missions was also clearly stated in the *Illustrated History of North Idaho*. The authors noted that while fur trappers and traders had introduced the first aspects of "civilization," it was the entrance of the Methodist missionary, Jason Lee who truly brought a new level of "civilization" into the Pacific Northwest. They stated that "an element of civilization was introduced of a vastly higher nature than any which accompanied the inroad of the Hudson's Bay Company's employees and of trappers and traders."[11] According to these authors, real "civilization" arrived with missionaries who encouraged Native Americans to become Christians and fur traders, trappers, and new settlers to hold onto, embrace and expand their Christian and Anglo-American values on the "frontier."

The drive to "civilize" Native Americans also expressed itself at the Waiilatpu and Lapwai missions. Slickpoo noted the Lapwai mission was soon joined by a United States government agency with an Indian agent in 1842.[12] The agent and Henry Spalding wanted the Nez Perce to give up their way of life and take up farming, a more settled way of life. The Nez Perces particularly resented a set of laws introduced by Spalding and Indian Agent Dr. Elijah White in 1840.[13] Slickpoo noted that, at first, the Nez Perce received the missionaries because they believed they posed no threats, took little land, and required very little from the Nez Perce. Attitudes changed as the Indian Agent and Spalding worked to change Nez Perce life and impose Anglo American and Christian values on Nez Perce communities.

The mission at Waiilatpu faced similar but different challenges. Whitman's mission was near the trading post at Walla Walla, and white settlers, traders, and trappers frequented the area. The Whitmans failed to recognize the legitimate claims of a Cayuse headman to the land and did not pay him for the use of the site.[14] Due to this insult, many Cayuse showed no interest in Whitman's mission and did not help the Whitmans, either materially or psychologically. Hostility from surrounding Native American communities was not the only trouble the missions suffered, as infighting and dissent arose among their ranks. Strong personalities, differing visions of mission work, and the strain of attempting to recreate their culture in an isolated area contributed to strife among Whitman, Spalding, Gray and other missionaries present in the Inland Northwest.

In 1840, the Protestant mission movement on the Great Columbia Plain suffered another blow with news of the arrival of the first Catholic missionary among Plateau communities. Jesuit Father Pierre Jean De Smet crossed the Rockies, attended the rendezvous at Green River and met a group of Flatheads who desired to have religious instruction of their own. Josephy contended that De Smet's arrival coincided with the collapse of the fur trade in the inland West and set in motion a cycle of violence and disillusionment that led many trappers and traders to settle in the Willamette Valley, to turn to providing guide services for settlers seeking land in the Oregon Country and other places, or to return to the eastern United States.[15] The arrival of Catholic missionaries and the end of the fur trade introduced strife among two Christian sects on the Columbia Plateau and eroded an economic arrangement established over the past sixty years that supported both Indians and Euro Americans.

In 1842, shortly after the arrival of Catholic missionaries and the demise of the fur trade, the Protestant missionaries received word from the American Board of Foreign Missions requiring the closing of both missions and their return east. The conflicts among the missionaries themselves and their problems with the Nez Perce, Cayuse, Palouse and others had reached the board through letters from various factions, with the Board finally recognizing the potential for failure and disaster at the missions. The recall letter stunned the missionaries at Waiilatpu and Lapwai, and Whitman immediately planned a trip East to appeal the Board's decision. Whitman and the other missionaries also hoped to recruit settlers and workers to help them at the missions with their task of "civilizing" surrounding Native American communities. While the trip started late in the season, Whitman safely returned to the East and persuaded the Board to reverse its decision. He was also able to recruit settlers to help the mission.

Unknown to Whitman, the letters from him, Jason Lee, and other missionaries describing the Oregon Country fueled the desire of many to attempt the trip and set in motion a wave of emigration that would shift power relationships in the Pacific Northwest.

In May 1843, Whitman prepared to return to the Pacific Northwest with a wagon train of over 1,000 settlers, which gathered in St. Louis to organize the trip. Whitman accompanied the train and aided their progress. Josephy asserted that this train of settlers was "a momentous event for the Northwest,"[16] since the arrival of so many American settlers upset Native Americans and raised fears among British administrators.[17] Indians around the Waiilatpu mission particularly focused their anger toward Whitman because they understood his role in guiding the wagon train to the Columbia Plateau. Whitman hoped that some of the settlers would remain at Waiilatpu or in the vicinity but was disappointed when they traveled on to the Willamette Valley. The missionaries hoped that more settlers would arrive each year and that some would eventually settle in the area.

Tensions and conflict continued after Whitman's return and intensified as more settlers arrived in the Pacific Northwest. Trafzer and Scheuerman asserted that Whitman's emphasis changed after the mission failed to attract Indians to Christianity, to promoting settlement and development while aiding emigration when possible. After 1843, tensions mounted at Waiilatpu and Lapwai, with the Nez Perce, Cayuse, Palouse, and other Native American communities increasingly sensing the potential danger associated with emigration and white settlement. The Nez Perce ordered Spalding to stay out of their affairs, destroyed some property, and literally wrestled with him when he attempted to stop their singing and dancing. The Cayuse and Walla Wallas also connected Whitman and the mission with settlement and attacked a few wagon trains in 1847, hoping to scare settlers from the region.[18]

The tensions experienced at the missions came to a head in 1847. Trafzer and Scheuerman noted that American emigrants brought measles with them during this year, and many Native Americans died from the ensuing epidemic. While understanding the relationship between whites and the emergence of disease in their communities, the Nez Perce, Cayuse and other Plateau communities also recognized the role of the missions in the distribution of disease. Marcus Whitman, in particular, stood out in these epidemics since he administered medicine to Native Americans and attempted to help the sick, but rarely succeeded in curing anyone. Since the Cayuse and Nez Perce often perceived Whitman and Spalding as "medicine men," their failure to stop disease and their role in bringing settlers discredited them and stoked the anger among the Native Americans on the Plateau.

This anger expressed itself on November 29, 1847, with the murders of Marcus and Narcissa Whitman and eleven other whites at Waiilatpu. After the murders, the Indians involved burned the mission and then planned an attack on Henry Spalding, who was visiting nearby. Spalding reached Lapwai, where William Craig, a long time foe of Spalding's, saved him and the mission.[19] While the murders and burning of the mission were conducted by a small number of Cayuse, the sentiments of most Cayuse and many other Plateau communities sympathized with these actions. They felt threatened not only by disease and the loss of land, but many Plateau Indian communities also saw missionaries as threats to their way of life and their religious practice. The call of Smohalla to return to older beliefs and practices had influenced many Native American communities on the Columbia Plateau. This call served as an important source of resistance to the efforts of Christian missionaries and as a source of renewal and hope for these communities.[20]

Settlers in the Willamette Valley responded to news of the Whitman murders with cries to assemble an army to punish those responsible and also to strike at Indians in general. Even though many Native communities did not support the actions at Waiilatpu and even refused the proposals of the Cayuse to broaden the conflict against all whites, for many white settlers, the attack on the Whitmans represented the specter of a larger Indian war, and they believed that they could not let the murders go unanswered. The intercession of Hudson's Bay traders eased some of the tension, but Americans organized a volunteer army under the command of Colonel Cornelius Gilliam and marched to the Columbia Plateau to avenge the death of the Whitmans. Peace commissions accompanied the volunteer army and secured the cooperation of the Nez Perce. However, Colonel Gilliam refused to accept a peaceful solution to the situation and set out to punish all Indians on the Great Columbia Plain. Gilliam rounded up horse herds belonging to the Palouse, suffered severe counter-attacks, released the herds and then retreated. After Gilliam's accidental death, the volunteer army continued its search for those responsible but never successfully captured the Cayuse accused of murdering the Whitmans. Plateau Indian communities actually resolved the tension when Nez Perce delegations persuaded the Cayuse to hand over five men reportedly involved in the murders. These men were given up to the Americans, who tried and executed them in June 1850.[21]

MYTH AND MOTIVE: "WHITMAN SAVES OREGON" AND THE "MASSACRE"

Anglo-American historians and Native Americans narrated and interpreted the arrival of missionaries on the Columbia Plateau from very different perspectives. For Edmond Meany and C.J. Brosnan, the presence of missionaries signaled a new stage in the march of "civilization."[22] The romance and tragedy surrounding the narration of Marcus Whitman and the missions on the Columbia Plateau followed in the footsteps of the romantic portrayal of explorers and fur traders. The themes of sacrifice and martyrdom accompanied the story of missionaries and made sense to an audience familiar with stories of Christian martyrs and who held beliefs of Anglo-American cultural superiority. These themes resided in the words of historians like Edmond Meany and C.J. Brosnan, but they also echoed in more "popular" authors like Kate McBeth and the authors of the *Illustrated History of North Idaho*.[23]

The shared narrative cues of the story surrounding missionary presence in the Pacific Northwest remained consistent throughout the early twentieth century. From Meany's *History of the State of Washington* (1908) through C.J. Brosnan's *History of the State of Idaho* (1926), the narrative began with an introductory note explaining the transition from fur trapper/trader to missionary work in the Pacific Northwest, but failed to mention Native Americans. Meany explained that the "Indians of the Northwest became known through the reports of explorers. Promptly, the fur traders began to exploit them by land and sea. Among the explorers and fur traders were men who informed the Indians that the white men had a religion superior to their forms of worship."[24] Anglo Americans believed that Christianity was a "higher" form of religion, organized around intricate institutions and rituals that denoted civilization and superiority. For Meany, the progression of civilization began with explorers, proceeded through the rudimentary efforts of fur traders, and reached a new level with missionary activity and their attempts to convert Indians in the Pacific Northwest. C.J. Brosnan reproduced this narrative cadence nearly eighteen years later in his *History of the State of Idaho*. Brosnan developed a clearer progression and began chapter eight of his history of Idaho with the following sentence: "The Missionary Follows the Explorer and the Fur-Trader."[25] He continued with the exposition of a "general plan of development that is usually followed in the opening of new countries."[26] This plan started with explorers, continued with fur-traders exploiting the natural resources of the region, and then followed with missionaries. This progression was echoed both by Meany and Frederick Jackson Turner. Meany quoted Turner in his chapter on the Missionary Epoch to support his argument that missionaries played an important role in the possession of the Oregon Country by the United States. Turner had asserted that Whitman, Spalding and other missionaries to the Pacific Northwest followed the "old story of the sequence of fur trader, missionary, and settler."[27] All three of these historians agreed on the cadence of the narrative. Without these narrative cues, the story became unintelligible and undecipherable for Anglo Americans. The power of Turner's "frontier" thesis, and its adoption by regional historians like Meany and Brosnan, resided in its simplicity and comprehensibility by a broad sweep of the Anglo-American populace.[28]

The inevitability of this progression and the ultimate victory of "civilization" were even more starkly laid out by the authors of the *An Illustrated History of North Idaho* (1908). For these authors:

> Another struggle for possession followed hard upon that with Great Britain, the final struggle in the great race war as a result of which our national domain was wrested from the hands of its aboriginal inhabitants. This struggle could have but one termination. The inferior race must yield to the superior. The Cayuse war, growing out of the Whitman massacre at Waiilatpu in 1847, and the Indian wars of the 'fifties resulted favorably to the whites and though the red man was a power in the land for many years, he could not withstand the steady oncoming tide of thrifty gold hunters and homeseekers.[29]

The progression of explorers, fur traders, and missionaries fit neatly into the dogma of Social Darwinism evident in the above passage. Anglo Americans knew the end of the story, but the characters and events in the narrative provided examples and instruction in the cultural superiority of Anglo Americans. Native American perspectives and history were not required or even desired because they contributed very little to the overall narrative structure of non-native presentations. Their lives and history represented the fate of those relegated to destruction and disappearance and were unwelcome visitors in the story unless clothed in the garb of "noble savage" or "blood-thirsty savage." In fact, Native Americans are so superfluous to the narrative that the authors of *An Illustrated History of North Idaho* generally focused their discussion on the diplomatic history surrounding the acquisition of the Oregon Country by the United States in 1846, without mention of the native inhabitants who already possessed the land.

Another important aspect of the narrative surrounding Whitman and the arrival of missionaries was the list of "firsts" that both Edmond Meany and C.J. Brosnan recounted in their manuscripts. The romantic adventure of the "missionary epoch" required the portrayal of Whitman, Spalding and their wives in ways that raised them to near mythical levels. For example, both Meany and Brosnan asserted that Narcissa Whitman and Eliza Spalding were the first women to cross the Rockies into the Oregon Country.

Meany noted that their journey served as an example for women settlers who would come later in the 1840s. Other "achievements" followed like the first printing press in the Northwest, the first white child born in Idaho, and the first missionaries to reside on the Columbia Plateau. The litany of firsts reinforced the place of Jason Lee, Marcus Whitman, and Henry Spalding in the pantheon of "civilizers" who arrived in the Oregon Country to help procure the region for the United States. The romantic nature of this type of language created a heroic portrait of missionaries and placed them on an equal footing with the explorers and fur traders who prepared the way for Christian workers.

In particular, Edmond Meany created a portrait of Marcus Whitman firmly rooted in the romantic hero who sacrificed himself for the cause, in this case "civilization" and the procurement of the Oregon Country. Whitman's life created a perfect example for Meany of the Christian "savior" and "civilizer" bent on bringing the light of Christianity and the benefits of Anglo-American culture to Native Americans on the Columbia Plateau. Not only interested in Indians, Whitman also fulfilled a crucial role as an encourager of settlement by Anglo Americans. For Meany, "Doctor Whitman was a man of tireless energy and of inflexible firmness" who was also instrumental in the extension of a wagon road to the Oregon Country.[30] The missionary's home building activities were also crucial harbingers of civilization and proved their courage in the face of great odds created by living in the "wilderness" or wild-ness of the frontier. Whitman also served his fellow Anglo Americans by guiding them to the Oregon Country in 1843, providing crucial information and medical services along the way. In many ways, Whitman followed the model set out for scouts like Davy Crockett, Daniel Boone, Natty Bumppo, Hawkeye of Cooper's *Last of the Mohicans*, Kit Carson, and many others.

The role of Whitman in Pacific Northwest history reached a crescendo of narrative importance through the interpretative battles surrounding Marcus Whitman's return to the eastern United States during 1843 to ask the Board of Foreign Missions to reconsider their decision to close the missions and to recall the missionaries. Henry Harmon Spalding, in 1865, created a myth about Whitman during battles with the government about reopening the mission at Lapwai, Idaho. Spalding asserted that Whitman rode east not to save the missions but to warn the United States government about British settlers and the threat to retaining Oregon for the American Republic. According to Spalding's version of the myth, Whitman rushed to Washington, D.C., persuaded the government to postpone negotiations with the British to turn over the Oregon Territory and then recruited a large number of settlers to return to the Oregon Country to secure it for the United States.[31]

According to Cornelius J. Brosnan, professor of history at the University of Idaho specializing in Idaho and Western history, the first version of the myth appeared in the *Sacramento Union* with other journalists and papers using this article as reference for their own reporting. Historians and other writers accepted the myth and included this version in their manuscripts and publications.[32] By the time Edmond Meany produced *History of the State of Washington*, professional historians had already questioned the Whitman-Saved-Oregon myth and were debating the origins and correctness of the story. Brosnan noted that by 1900-1901, historian E.G. Bourne of Yale University and W.I. Marshall of Chicago attacked the validity of the myth and sparked a spirited debate on Whitman's role in the acquisition of the Oregon Country. Bourne and Marshall assaulted the myth because of the lack of documentary evidence surrounding the incident. Their own evidence contradicted earlier versions based on Spalding's story. By 1910, Edmond Meany, who idolized Whitman, committed a large section in *History of the State of Washington* to the debate. Meany found himself in a difficult position. While he idolized Whitman, he also represented an emerging historical profession devoted to distancing themselves from the anecdotal and reminiscence-based history popular among many people.[33]

Meany solved this dilemma diplomatically by discussing both versions and leaving the final verdict up to his readers. For example, Meany prefaced his discussion of the debate by using the metaphor of a pendulum swinging back and forth, not allowing readers a place to put Whitman and his actions.[34] Meany instead chose a middle ground that allowed him to stand in the professional historical community while recognizing the power and popularity of popular historical imagination. For Meany, the truth of Whitman's role resided somewhere in between the two sides of the debate. Whitman did not save Oregon, but Meany refused to negate completely the role Whitman may have played in the acquisition and settlement of the Oregon Country. He both agreed and disagreed with the two sides. The discussion in the text of Meany's history shifted back and forth along the evidentiary trail of Whitman's ride to the eastern United States and attempted to salvage Whitman and his role in Pacific Northwest history. In the end, Meany agreed with his colleagues but rescued popular historical imagination by re-romanticizing Whitman. According to Meany, while the Whitman myth failed to stand up to professional historical criticism, Whitman himself remained an important figure in Pacific Northwest history because "Doctor Whitman did a man's full share." Meany concluded the debate by stating, "In spite of the ridicule of myths and legends justly hurled upon their insistent presumptions, Marcus Whitman is a hero. He wrought faithfully and well. He bravely died at his post for the cause he loved."[35] For Meany, the myth matters little because

Whitman continued to represent the larger themes of the expansion of civilization and Christianity into the realm of "savagery" and "wildness." Despite the critiques of the myth, Whitman died supporting the causes he held dear, the settlement and expansion of the Pacific Northwest by Christian Anglo Americans and bringing "light" to Indians.

The depth and popularity of the Whitman myth remained an issue that Cornelius Brosnan addressed in the 1920s. In a paper written for a history course at University of California, Berkeley, Brosnan reviewed the debate and firmly stood with the historical profession that had already debunked the myth 20 years earlier. The notes in his bibliography revealed the underlying motivation for his paper. Brosnan described the works of the proponents of the "Whitman-Saved-Oregon" myth as lacking in scholarly method, failing to recognize the distinction between recollection and reminiscence (memory) and documentary evidence, and as being too partisan.[36] Brosnan's paper clearly indicated that popular imagination continued to embrace the "Whitman-Saved-Oregon" myth into the 1920s. While serving as an exercise in historical criticism, Brosnan later wrote a book about Jason Lee, the Methodist missionary who preceded Whitman and Spalding to the Pacific Northwest, maintaining that Lee deserved greater credit for populating Oregon than the other missionaries, including Whitman.

Despite the arguments over Whitman's role in the Anglo-American acquisition of Oregon, the rhythm of the narratives, starting with Spalding's of the 1850s and running through Brosnan's in the late 1920s, remained intact and thereby intelligible to the broader populace. Historians like Meany and Brosnan argued about the myth, but both included Whitman in their narratives. In a broader sense, the actors in the narrative, whether Jason Lee, Henry Spalding, Marcus Whitman, in and of themselves were not important, but they were included because they fit the broader sweep of progressive history that required explorers to come first, then fur traders/trappers, and then missionaries. The narrative built around their activities reinforced ideas about the progressive nature of civilization and the eventual victory of Anglo-American culture over the "Other" present in North America. In the end, it mattered not whether Marcus Whitman or Jason Lee contributed more to the annexation of Oregon, but that their activities reinforced the narrative cues of romanticism, adventure, heroism and civilizing that made the narrative understandable. The ability of this narrative to homogenize and contain disparate interpretations and constructs sustained its hold on Anglo-American imagination and historical consciousness throughout the twentieth century and allowed both scholars and lay people to debate the merits and achievements of the players without tearing apart the narrative structure.[37]

The killing of the Whitmans and the subsequent burning of the mission at Waiilatpu effectively ended the Protestant missionary period on the Columbia Plateau. Missionaries returned to this region in later years, but they mainly worked within the confines of treaty and executive order reservations. The narrative structure of progressive historical development and the civilizing of the region remained intact for historians and non-historians alike, even in the face of the destruction of the missionary effort and the death of missionaries. At the very moment that Native perceptions of the missionaries, their activities, and views of the civilizing task threatened to enter into the narrative, the weavers of the story worked to minimize and to contain the threat to the framework. The inclusion of Nez Perce, Cayuse, Walla Walla or Palouse voices would have eroded the tropes of "civilization" and "savagery" and simultaneously blurred the shining, heroic vision of Whitman, Lee, Spalding and others, who were portrayed as workers for the Lord and for Anglo-American civilization. In the narrative framework created by historian and non-historian alike, the possibility of understanding the anger and fear experienced by the Cayuse and other Plateau communities could only be allowed to enter the narrative in the guise of ungrateful superstition. For example, Meany recounted a list of grievances and problems that the Cayuse and other communities experienced at the mission and with the Whitmans.

These grievances or causes of the "massacre" were not rooted in an understanding of the cultural, social, political and historical understanding of the Cayuse but were instead attributed to forces acting on the Cayuse that contributed to their unrest and discontent. The destruction of the mission and the deaths of Whitman and the others were considered the result of impersonal forces like disease, fear of land loss, and the novelty of the missionaries wearing off, rather than a rational response by the Cayuse to these pressures. For Meany, the episode served as another marker of the struggle between "civilization" and "savagery." Ungrateful, unrepentant and superstitious natives struck out against the Whitmans as representatives of civilization, evidenced by Whitman's tireless work among both Indians and Anglo Americans. For Meany, in the larger scheme of the narrative, the "massacre" and its explanations pale in importance to the debate surrounding Whitman's role in the acquisition of the Oregon Country by the United States. Meany took Whitman's death out of the local Native context and subordinated it to the struggle to acquire the last piece of land required to fulfill the nation's destiny.

In his narrative, Meany rescued Whitman through his death and martyrdom. The importance of the killings resided not in the motivations, rationale

Words and Boundaries 83

or fears of the Cayuse and other Native communities, but in the example provided by Whitman for other Anglo Americans. Meany noted, "He bravely died at his post for the cause he loved." Marcus Whitman was a hero because he fulfilled his purpose as a defender and propagator of Christianity and civilization.[38] He also narrated the aftermath of the murders in a straightforward and succinct manner, but he ignored Native Americans whom he made absent from the stage except in the guise of "hostiles" and "murderers." The bulk of the paragraph focused on the "reasoned" response by the provisional government and the determined action against "hostile" Indians. Gilliam's bloodlust, the stealing of Palouse horses, and the desire for revenge failed to appear in Meany's account as did the fact that the Cayuse themselves handed over five men, including leaders who sacrificed themselves, believed to have participated in the murders. The main concern of the paragraph revolved around the efforts of Peter Skeen Ogden to secure the release of hostages taken at the mission. This fit into the narrative because Ogden possessed all the requisite hero qualifications. He was white and intimately connected with the "advance of civilization" in the Pacific Northwest. Meany shifted the narrative to these efforts to comfort his readers and remind them that "civilization" could be rescued from the "vile" clutches of "savagery."

Brosnan mentioned the murder of the Whitmans but did not narrate the ensuing military action. The silences in both of these narratives were particularly glaring. Michel-Rolph Trouillot asserted, "any historical narrative is a particular bundle of silences."[39] Both Meany and Brosnan minimized the actions that occurred after the murders, one using one paragraph to narrate the military action and release of hostages and the other completely ignoring the incursions of United States military on the Columbia Plateau in 1847-48. Brosnan left the narrative out because of his focus on Idaho history and his interest in "larger" Indian wars narrated in chapter twelve of *History of the State of Idaho*. The narrowness of their narratives also arose from the creation of their own boundaries dictated by Anglo Americans and not by the geography or a native view of the region.

THE TREATY OF 1855 AND THE YAKAMA WAR

The end of the "missionary epoch" overlapped with the division of the Oregon Country between the United States and Great Britain in June 1846. The Whitman "Massacre" in 1847 and the military expeditions that followed hinted at things to come. Congress created the Territory of Oregon in August 1848 and appointed Joseph Lane territorial governor. The territory, which included the present states of Oregon, Washington, Idaho and portions of Wyoming and Montana, was never unified, and various communities throughout the territory resented the power of Willamette Valley residents and farmers in the territorial government.[40] This resentment came to a head from 1851 to 1853, as settlers in the northern parts of the territory organized and petitioned Congress to grant a separate territory. On May 2, 1853 Congress created Washington Territory, named after the first President, with fewer than four thousand non-Indian residents.[41]

With territorial status, Congress appointed the first territorial governor, Isaac I. Stevens.[42] Stevens combined his role as territorial governor with Superintendent of Indian Affairs, head of the Pacific Railroad Survey and active booster and encourager of Manifest Destiny and the expansion of the United States.[43] Trafzer and Scheuerman noted that Stevens was qualified for the positions of governor and surveyor but not for the role of chief Indian Agent for Washington Territory.[44] As Superintendent of Indian Affairs, Stevens presided over treaty negotiations and councils without knowledge of or concern for the peoples involved in the discussions. According to Trafzer and Scheuerman, Steven's principal aim, voiced by himself, centered on extinguishing Indian title to lands in the Pacific Northwest in order to promote the settlement of the region.[45] His role as lead surveyor for the Pacific Railroad Survey enhanced his devotion to territorial and capitalist development.

Before the treaty councils of 1854 and 1855, survey parties sent out to scout and survey possible routes for a northern transcontinental railroad created tension among Native American communities on the Columbia Plateau. The anxiety over the incursions of these survey parties added to the high emotions already created by yearly influxes of settlers into the new territories. During the summer of 1853, one party led by Captain George B. McClellan surveyed east from Fort Vancouver while Governor Stevens and his party surveyed west from St. Paul, Minnesota. Most Plateau Indian communities and their leaders desired to know the intentions of the survey parties and the possible effects of their activities on their homeland. Kamiakin, an important leader among the Yakama, mistrusted the motivations and activities of the survey parties. Many Indian people on the Columbia Plateau shared his misgivings, as they learned that whites hoped to "buy" their land and open it to white settlement.[46] Both survey parties attempted to reassure various communities that they would receive a fair price for their land and also retain large portions of land for their exclusive use. These reassurances failed to quell the uneasiness of Native Americans since they already knew much about the history of United States Indian policy through relationships with the Iroquois and others who had lived through the effects of war, land pressures, and reservation negotiations. Native Americans on the Columbia Plateau also owned all the land and saw no reason to "sell" it to whites.

There was no advantage in such a transaction and "selling" land violated native law. Religious leaders like Smohalla and Toohoolhoolzote spoke against giving up land for any reason and denounced the commodity-based logic of Anglo-American relationships to the land and environment.[47]

After completion of the surveys in late 1853 and early 1854, Stevens turned to extinguishing title to every acre of ground on the Columbia Plateau and along the Pacific Coast. Stevens continued to assure Indians that he intended to protect their property and holdings while at the same time allowing more whites into the region and providing land for them. Late in 1854 and early in 1855, Stevens rapidly negotiated treaties with native communities surrounding the Puget Sound, and several Indian people in the interior Pacific Northwest heard about these treaties and the conditions imposed on Native Americans on Washington's Pacific Coast. Some leaders refused to sign, but American negotiators forged their signatures. Kamiakin and other leaders among Columbia Plateau groups who had relatives among Puget Sound communities, understood the implications of Steven's drive to complete treaties with all Native American communities in Washington Territory.[48]

During March 1855, envoys from Governor Stevens approached Plateau communities about the possibility of a treaty council. While most leaders distrusted white men and did not want to relinquish land to the United States government, they agreed to meet in order to hear what Governor Stevens wanted to say to them. Kamiakin, in particular, distrusted Steven's representatives and refused to accept gifts offered to entice his involvement. Kamiakin constantly reiterated his unwillingness to sell land at any price.[49] The negotiators set the council for spring 1855, and participants started arriving in the Walla Walla Valley in May of that year. Governor Stevens arrived on May 21, 1855 and the Council started on May 29, 1855.[50]

The council and the treaty that came out of it were watershed events for the Nez Perce and their Columbia Plateau neighbors. Faced with increasing pressure to relinquish land and resources, the Nez Perce and their neighbors attempted to find a way to avoid conflict while retaining their land and way of life. From the very beginning, the Walla Walla Council of 1855 was rife with misunderstandings, coercion, and language problems that contributed to the conflict that followed in the years to come. Three problems stand out in an analysis of the council and treaty negotiations. The first, and perhaps greatest, problem centered on the issue of language. Translation problems arose early for Governor Stevens in his treaty negotiations with the native communities around the Puget Sound. In 1854 and 1855, Stevens and his staff used the Chinook jargon, a trade dialect, to explain the details and implications of the treaties. No one read the entire treaty to the Indians present, but only "explained" or interpreted for them the terms and results of the treaties. The Chinook jargon was an imprecise language and could not relate the nuances of either native languages or English.[51] As the oft-quoted phrase so aptly states, much was indeed "lost in translation." The leaders of the Plateau communities knew of the problems experienced by Puget Sound communities and wished to appoint interpreters capable of speaking the languages of those communities present. They also wanted the appointment of more than one interpreter to ensure the veracity of speeches and documents involved in the council.

Even with interpreters, the task of communicating with numerous Plateau groups and Stevens's party was daunting and virtually impossible from the very beginning. Slickpoo noted, "It is very hard for two peoples who speak different languages to really understand each other."[52] The presence of many different groups speaking diverse Sahaptin dialects and also the presence of some Salish speakers compounded the troubles arising out of the Walla Walla Council. According to Slickpoo, the Nez Perce believed that the interpreters translated too literally and did not convey the sense of Indian statements, often misinterpreting since the Sahaptin languages had multiple meanings for words that depended on context and tone for accuracy of meaning. As Slickpoo asserted, "Both sides were probably speaking by each other rather than to each other."[53]

Isaac Stevens and his party also exacerbated the language problems through a misunderstanding of Plateau political organization and structures. From the beginning, Stevens adopted United States policy and bias by arbitrarily appointing "chiefs" or leaders to represent and sign for their communities. Thus, United States representatives failed to comprehend the decentralized nature of many Native American communities and attempted to satisfy their own desires to deal with only one or a few representatives rather than a whole community. In the instance of the Walla Walla Council, Slickpoo maintained that Stevens and Palmer falsely appointed Aleiya (Lawyer) as head chief of the Nez Perce without consulting the Nez Perce themselves or their hereditary leaders. According to Slickpoo and Nez Perce educator Patty Murphy, Lawyer was not a chief, but a camp crier responsible for informing the Nez Perce of important events and news.[54] Problems like this arose in Steven's dealings with other communities as well. For example, Stevens and Palmer falsely believed that Kamiakin represented the Palouse at the Walla Walla Council. As Trafzer and Scheuerman noted, Kamiakin was related to Palouse people, but he never claimed to be a Palouse chief at the time of the Council.[55]

The third and last problem centered on the lofty attitude and condescending expressions used by Stevens and Palmer during the Council. Stevens constantly insulted the Indian participants by referring to them as "my children." Slickpoo noted, "Many of the chiefs were older than the whites who were present."[56] Stevens's use of this phrase betrayed his egocentric attitude toward native communities on the Columbia Plateau and aroused suspicions from the beginning that the terms of the treaty might be forced on them without due consideration. Schwantes noted that to Stevens "Washington's seventeen thousand Indians were children whose culture was of little value."[57] These attitudes were not lost on Native American participants whose children still view the council as one of many instances of betrayal and deception perpetuated by the United States government and its representatives.

The above problems reflected the lack of understanding inherent in most treaty negotiations with Native Americans in the nineteenth century. From the outset, problems of language, lack of cultural understanding, and Anglo-American attitudes of cultural superiority contributed to much resentment, disappointment and anger among Native American groups. Columbia Plateau anger heightened as Anglo Americans often pitted various native groups against one another in the negotiation process, creating divisions and tensions between friends and families. Treaty negotiations also did not take place in historical vacuums, and many Columbia Plateau Indian people had heard from other people about their experiences with Europeans and Anglo Americans. In the midst of all these language and cultural problems, the United States and Native Americans of the Columbia Plateau set out to negotiate the sensitive issue of land and its ownership.

Governor Isaac Stevens and Oregon's Superintendent of Indian Affairs, Joel Palmer, negotiated for the United States and began the council with lengthy remarks designed to explain the government's position and historical position of the United States. The speeches wandered from point to point, mentioning various historical figures in United States history, previous treaties and treatment of Native Americans, and, most obviously, the desire of the government to obtain land and transform the lives of the Nez Perce and other Plateau communities.[58] On the third day of the proceedings, Stevens impatiently explained his and the government's position:

> We want you to agree to live on tracts of land, which shall be your own and your children's; we want you to sell the land you do not need to your Great Father; we want to agree with us upon the payments for these lands; we want you to have schools and mills and shops and farms; we want your people to learn to read and write; your men and boys to be

farmers or millwrights or mechanics, or to be of some profession as a lawyer or doctor. We want your wives and daughters to learn to spin and to weave and to make clothes and all the labor of the house; this is for a number of years as we may agree.[59]

While the Nez Perce and others suspected that this was what the government intended to do, the speed with which the Governor laid out the government's position alarmed many present and created anger since Stevens and Palmer failed to listen to Indian concerns before articulating their position. Walla Walla leader Peo Peo Mox Mox constantly asked for time to present the Indian position and to think about the speeches and proposals of Stevens and Palmer.[60] They wanted to adjourn, go home and talk in councils about the Anglo-American proposals. Most Indian participants remained quiet until the third day of the council and were surprised by Stevens's statement and proposal.

According to Trafzer and Scheuerman, anger surfaced after Stevens's statements and many leaders of various Plateau communities voiced their difficulties with relinquishing land through sale to the United States government. Leaders like Five Crows (Cayuse), Owhi (Yakama), Young Chief (Cayuse) and Peo Peo Mox Mox (Walla Walla) expressed their spiritual views about the land and their relationship to their homelands. Trafzer and Scheuerman noted that Sahaptin religious beliefs prohibited the sale of land and considered any sale of land as a sin.[61] Stevens and Palmer completely misunderstood this view of the land and its relationship to human beings. As Trafzer and Scheuerman asserted, both men did not understand Indian concepts of the land "as spiritual partner" but instead viewed the land as a commodity, something "to be tamed and manipulated."[62] In fact Stevens and Palmer became impatient as Plateau leaders attempted to explain their position and its implications for their communities and the treaty negotiations.

The lack of Nez Perce participation in these debates rested not on disagreements with their neighbors, but rather can be explained by the fact that Lawyer and his followers agreed to the terms of the treaty (Figure 4). A significant number of the Nez Perce present supported the treaty since their homeland largely remained intact, requiring them to relinquish little of their traditional homeland. This was not the case for most of the other groups and communities. Peo Peo Mox Mox and others suspected that the Nez Perce or at least Lawyer's followers had already agreed to the terms of the treaty before the council started and were angry about this apparent breach of trust. The convenience of recognizing Lawyer as the leader of all Nez Perce allowed Stevens and Palmer to play various groups against one another, using threats of violence, and complete loss of land to coerce leaders to agree to the treaty.

Figure 4 Chief Lawyer, circa 1861. Courtesy of Manuscripts, Special Collections, University Archives, University of Washington Libraries, NA 627.

Anger and discontent ruled the negotiations and heightened on June 8 when Looking Glass, an important Nez Perce leader, arrived in camp and, in an angry speech, passionately argued against giving up any land. That night many of the communities met to discuss the treaties and the various speeches given by the participants.[63] The next day, the issue of reservation borders and land reached a peak as Looking Glass drew new boundaries for the proposed reservations and Stevens, in exasperation, ended the meeting. During the next two days, several leaders "signed" the treaty, often after meetings among themselves and with Stevens.[64] A controversy arose surrounding the circumstances of Kamiakin's mark that would later lead to armed conflict and Anglo-American military intervention.[65] The Walla Walla, Umatilla, Cayuse and Nez Perce signed the treaty, including Looking Glass and Old Joseph, who initially opposed the treaty. In his diary, Stevens wrote, "Thus ended in the most satisfactory manner this great council." He left Walla Walla Valley on June 16, 1855, forwarding messages to the press that he had opened the Pacific Northwest to white settlement.[66]

The treaty created three reservations of varying sizes while ceding more than 60,000 square miles to the United States government.[67] Slickpoo remarked that Indians expressed considerable opposition to the treaty, particularly among the various communities in attendance. The resentment and opposition continued after the council ended and later erupted in violence as a result of violations largely perpetrated by Anglo-American settlers and miners.[68] Slickpoo also noted that leaders signed the treaty as a result of threats spoken by Governor Stevens and General Palmer. Most of these statements threatened that white settlers would overrun their land if they did not sign. However, the single-minded goal of extinguishing Indian land title led directly to the conflict and war that Stevens and Palmer hoped to avoid. Misunderstandings of Nez Perce and Plateau Indian cultures set the stage for many of the conflicts experienced during the next twenty-three years.

One of the first large scale conflicts resulting from the council and treaty erupted during the same year as the treaty negotiations themselves. Kamiakin, one of the main Yakama leaders, deeply resented the proceedings at Walla Walla and almost immediately started organizing and recruiting allies to oppose the United States and removal to a reservation. In particular, many Plateau people resented the way that both Palmer and Stevens treated them as children and forced communities and leaders to decide about their futures and interests quickly.[69]

The cultural slights and haste of the treaty only exacerbated ill feelings during the summer of 1855 as Plateau communities dealt with the opening of their land to white settlement and the rush of miners and prospectors when whites discovered gold near Fort Colville in northeastern Washington Territory. Miners and settlers trespassed on native land throughout the Inland Northwest, and conflict and violence erupted when Indians attempted to maintain the integrity of their territorial borders. Most, if not all, of the territorial violations directly disregarded the terms of the Walla Walla treaty and created deep misgivings about the treaty and the trustworthiness of Anglo Americans.

In September 1855, Yakama leader Qualchin and his followers attacked and killed a party of six miners. Shortly thereafter, a party of Yakamas murdered Andrew Jackson Bolon, Indian Agent to the Yakamas.[70] Widely reviled and distrusted by the Yakama, Bolon ignored warnings about traveling alone in the growing climate of anger and resentment. According to Trafzer and Scheuerman, the murder of Agent Bolon served as the most immediate cause of the war fought on the Columbia Plateau from 1855 to 1858. The reaction to Bolon's murder mirrored the reaction to the earlier deaths of the Whitmans and elicited calls for vengeance and retribution against Native Americans. The murder struck a nerve among Anglo Americans who were constantly concerned by and afraid of attacks by Native Americans. As Trafzer and Scheuerman noted, "Whites believed that the Indians planned a war of extermination and that Kamiakin was single-handedly responsible."[71] The murder tapped into deep racial hatreds and stereotypes ingrained in Anglo-American psyches. In the minds of most Anglo Americans in the Pacific Northwest, Native Americans again revealed their savagery and barbarism. The murder of Bolon provided a just cause for whites to attack Indians and to inflict punishment on Indians for hindering the extension of civilization into the Pacific Northwest.

In response to the murder of Agent Bolon, the territorial governor and legislature authorized an expedition of territorial volunteers and regular army under the command of Major Granville O. Haller to punish the Indians and to counter the perceived threat of a general Indian uprising against whites in the Pacific Northwest. The military invasion of the Columbia Plateau started in October 1855 and continued intermittently until 1858. Josephy noted that the presence of these volunteer and regular military forces on the Columbia Plateau betrayed the very treaty signed, but not ratified, by many Native Americans in May 1855 and confirmed the misgivings many Plateau groups had expressed about the viability of the treaty.[72]

The initial Anglo-American military incursion, led by Major Haller, met defeat in October 1855 and retreated back to The Dalles. Unfortunately, the defeat coincided with news that Puget Sound and Rouge River native communities in Oregon had started troubles, convincing many people that a general Indian uprising was imminent and that Kamiakin was the main organizer. After Haller's defeat in Yakama Country, Major Gabriel Rains, commander of Fort Vancouver, immediately organized another force to march north into Yakama country to quell the perceived threat. While finding very few Indians, Rains' men burned a Catholic mission on Ahtanum Creek and found a letter by Kamiakin offering an explanation of the war and a proposal for peace. Rains rejected Kamiakin's explanation and offer, preferring to continue the war and threatening the Indians with extermination. At the same time, a volunteer force under the command of Colonel Thomas Kelly defeated a force of Walla Wallas, Palouse, Umatilla and Cayuses and moved to punish Indian communities in southeast Washington and northeast Oregon. While negotiating with Peo Peo Mox Mox, he kidnapped the Walla Walla leader and used him and his companions as hostages. Skirmishes broke out between the volunteers and Indians, with heavy casualties among the volunteers. During the battle, guards murdered Peo Peo Mox Mox and his companions. This incident illustrated the unpredictable and undisciplined nature of volunteer forces used by American territorial governments to quell Indian "uprisings." Generally, volunteers, who regarded their mission as vengeance and raiding to steal booty, openly spoke for the extermination of Indians on the Columbia Plateau. Their reaction was often based on fear generated from exaggerated press reports or rumors hyping the danger of a large scale Indian uprising. Volunteer forces, as in the instance of Peo Peo Mox Mox's murder, often took matters in their own hands since they lacked the discipline of regular army units.

Volunteer forces remained in the field during 1856 but failed to engage Indian forces. A major regular army campaign was organized by Colonel George Wright in March 1856 and set out to engage the Yakama. While the campaign failed to produce the desired results, Trafzer and Scheuerman asserted that the constant campaigns on the Columbia Plateau not only disrupted the lives of many Plateau communities through food shortages and dislocation, but they also created divisions among different groups over blame for the war.[73] While many people, even Kamiakin, realized the futility of fighting United States forces, many others were also afraid to surrender or negotiate with Anglo Americans since they mistrusted whites and feared a fate like Peo Peo Mox Mox.

According to Trafzer and Scheuerman, Wright "determined to occupy and secure the inland Northwest with the regular troops, stationed only at The Dalles and the Cascades."[74] Wright ordered the construction of Forts Walla Walla and Simcoe and ordered Colonel Edward Steptoe to relieve volunteers in the Walla Walla Valley. Skirmishes continued throughout 1856 and 1857 as both Wright and Steptoe attempted to engage and subdue Indian activities. During spring 1858, Palouse raided the horse herds at Fort Walla Walla and two miners were killed as they traveled through Palouse country. Once again, miners and settlers demanded military action against Indians, and Colonel Steptoe organized an expedition to defeat the Palouse in May 1858. Steptoe's campaign resulted in defeat as Native Americans from many different communities organized and resisted his invasion of their territory. The running battle and the retreat of Steptoe's command was a bitter blow to Anglo-American military aspirations, but military commanders in the Pacific Northwest immediately planned a campaign to end the conflict on the Columbia Plateau.

Using a multi-pronged campaign issuing from Fort Simcoe and Fort Walla Walla and moving through the region, Wright and his troops pursued Indian groups to the Spokane Plain and engaged a large number of Indians in the Battles of Four Lakes and the Spokane Plains. These battles did not go well for the Palouse, Yakama, Walla Wallas and others who were part of the united front opposing American military invasion of their homeland. Trafzer and Scheuerman maintained that the defeats on the Spokane Plain created dissension among Indian allies. As Wright moved northeast, his forces captured a herd of 900 horses belonging to the Palouse; they kept about 130 and killed the rest. The killings remain in the Palouse historical memory to this day. The killings confused and saddened the Native Americans because they simply could not believe other human beings were capable of such slaughter and they believed that they were next. As Wright's forces moved with impunity throughout western Idaho and eastern Washington, many Native American communities hoped to make peace. Wright's campaign ended with the capture and execution of Qualchin and Owhi, both important Yakama leaders. The Palouse hoped to make peace, but five men were identified as murderers and Wright's men hanged them.

Wright's campaign defeated the major military force organized by those opposing the treaty of 1855 and the military invasion by the United States of the Columbia Plateau. In essence, the United States military unilaterally abrogated the treaty negotiated in 1855 and invaded the Inland Northwest for the express purpose of punishing Indians who were merely protecting their lands and resources according to the terms of the treaty. At the end of the war, the United States military permanently occupied various areas of the Inland Northwest and maintained military outposts specifically to blunt a perceived Indian threat to Anglo-American settlers and miners. For the Nez Perce, the war was an ambivalent experience. Some Nez Perce actively helped United States military forces as scouts, ferry operators or negotiators, but others most likely aided their relatives and friends during the conflict. Others watched the conflict closely, noting the hypocrisy of Anglo-American treatment of many Plateau communities. Nez Perce communities observed the war from the relative isolation of their homeland and did not feel the same pressure from white intruders that their friends to the west experienced. This situation would change, however, with the discovery of gold near present day Orofino, in the middle of the Nez Perce traditional homeland.

"THE ONLY REAL FRIENDS AT THE COUNCIL"[75]

Both Edmond Meany and C.J. Brosnan included discussions of the Walla Walla Council, the Treaty of 1855, and the so-called Yakama War, but the length of the narrative and the depth of interpretive text varied in their narratives. These differences highlight the regional nature of their texts that required them to focus on Washington and Idaho, respectively. While differing in length and interpretive depth, the narrative cadence remained true to form since both authors placed the council and treaty in the context of "Indian Wars." There is a "natural" progression to the narrative in their chapters that followed in the footsteps of explorer, fur trapper/trader and missionary. In order for settlers, the next wave of Anglo-American "civilization," to occupy the Pacific Northwest, title to the land had to be clarified, and Indian title extinguished. Meany clearly stated this sentiment when he asserted, "One effect of these treaties was to quiet the Indian title to one hundred thousand square miles of land, making it possible for white settlers to acquire homes without a bargain or a quarrel with "savage" owners or claimants."[76] Brosnan also ended a paragraph discussing the Treaty of 1855 with the statement, "they signed the treaty consenting to the sale of Indian lands to the whites."[77] Both authors recognized the importance of these proceedings in the progression of Anglo-American "civilization" into the Pacific Northwest.

Meany focused his treaty narrative on the efforts of Governor Stevens to secure the Columbia Plateau for the United States. Meany disputed the claims that Stevens' treaty negotiations caused the wars immediately after the councils. While the treaties led to the war, according to Meany the real cause of the war rested in the last desperate but futile efforts of Indians "to make one more stand against the wave of civilization thus threatening to engulf their old ways of living."[78] Governor Stevens served as the purveyor of "civilization" and reasonableness and, in Meany's narrative, Stevens acted in the best interests of the Indians and sought to insure that they understood the implications of treaties by securing interpreters agreeable to the leaders present at the councils. For Meany, Stevens created the treaties with Native Americans in the Pacific Northwest with care and patience.

The role of the Nez Perce at the Walla Walla Council occupied an interesting position in Meany's narrative. At one point, Meany asserted that the Nez Perce were the only real friends of the governor and whites at the council. Their role ranged from thwarting plots against Governor Stevens to serving as the "reasonable" Native American participants at the council. Meany set up an interesting comparison between the Cayuse and the Nez Perce. The Cayuse were presented as the murderous Indians who had perpetrated the killing of the Whitmans and plotted to kill the white negotiators and wipe out the military garrison at The Dalles. The "noble" Nez Perce "Head Chief" Lawyer found out about the plot, warned the whites and even moved the American negotiating party under the protection of the Nez Perce delegation. According to Meany, the steadfastness of the Nez Perce resulted in special consideration and favorable treaty terms.[79]

All of the treaty negotiations mentioned by Meany in his chapter on Indian treaties were narrated in the context of Governor Stevens' heroic attempts to "arrange, on a permanent basis, the future of the Indians of this Territory."[80] Stevens followed in the narrative footsteps of those heroes concerned with the expansion of civilization into the Pacific Northwest. According to Meany, Stevens' efforts opened the Columbia Plateau to American settlers and miners. While the treaties resulted in an atmosphere of conflict and war, Meany encouraged his readers to remember that the people at the time regarded the treaties as essential. The essential nature of the treaties rested on the underlying beliefs of Anglo Americans that Indian populations were relatively small and that they failed to use the land productively. Meany echoed Frederick Jackson Turner when he stated, "It was inevitable that there should be a clash when civilization and savagery met."[81] According to Turner, the frontier was that space where American civilization was forged in the confrontation of "civilized" European and Anglo-American institutions and the wildness of nature that included Native Americans and their culture. To Meany, Anglo Americans were coming with their institutions to occupy the land and the best Indian policy sought negotiation, payment for land, relocation to reservations, and provision of the necessary resources for assimilation of Indians into Anglo-American society.

C.J. Brosnan's narrative also mentioned the treaty of 1855, but tied the results of the treaty and the tensions created to the Nez Perce War of 1877. The regional nature of his history of Idaho dictated this narrative flow. While chiefly concerned with the Nez Perce, Brosnan connected Idaho history with the national narrative and claimed that Idaho "like other States, had her era of Indian wars."[82] These wars and the treaties associated with them, occurred during the initial periods of emigration and mining. For

Brosnan, the root of conflict lay in the "numerous murderous and thieving raids perpetrated by lawless bands of roving Indians."[83] This simple sentence contained some, if not all, of the same sentiments expressed by Meany nearly seventeen years earlier. Native Americans represented the savagery that threatened the "civilizers" and their property. Their "savagery" was embedded in their "roving" or unsettled lifestyle that encouraged lawlessness, especially theft and murder. While Brosnan attributed most of the "outrages" to mere criminal behavior, he also recognized that some of the conflict emerged from the "bitter resentment over the enforced surrender of what he considered his God-given inheritance of stream, lake, camas-meadow, and hunting-ground."[84] In the midst of this recognition, however, Brosnan still characterized the struggle as one between those of nature, Native Americans, and those of civilization, Anglo-American emigrants and miners.

In the end, for both Meany and Brosnan, the Yakama War that followed on the heels of the Treaty of 1855 resulted from the "misguided" acts of Native Americans, whether "criminal" or in defense of their homeland. While the incursion of white settlers, miners and United States military forces was mentioned, both authors portrayed Native Americans, the Nez Perce, Yakama, Palouse or other Plateau peoples, as the root cause for the conflict. Meany boldly asserted "Even though they signed the treaties to sell the lands, they changed their minds and would try to kill the invaders and keep white people away from their lands."[85] Recognizing some of the legitimate grievances of Plateau communities could have posed a problem for both authors, but this narrative structure rescued Anglo Americans from the guilt associated with issues of breaking treaties, military occupation, and the theft of native land. Both Brosnan and Meany rescued their readers from an ambivalent situation by tapping into themes already familiar to their Anglo-American audience. Meany constantly reminded his readers about the progressive and civilizing nature of the struggle in the Inland Northwest and reassured his readers that history had already determined the outcome and that heroic men like Isaac Stevens worked for the triumph of Anglo-American civilization.[86]

Following the narrative structure, the Yakama War resulted from the confrontation of "civilization" and "savagery," as represented by Anglo Americans and Native Americans respectively. The necessity of extinguishing Indian land titles moved into the necessity of quelling the "treacherous" acts of Indians seeking to stop the advance of Anglo Americans into the Inland Northwest. Both authors described the events in similar ways and included the same actors in their versions of the narrative. The narrative, therefore, differed not in the type of actor but in the emphasis. Meany focused on Governor Stevens and wove his version of the treaty council and wars around the activities and efforts of Stevens. Brosnan, on the other hand, chose not to focus on one central character. Familiar names emerged in both narratives. For example, Colonel George Wright and Steptoe were prominent in both narratives, as were the regular soldiers and volunteers who remained nameless. While Native Americans were present, Meany and Brosnan generally use the generic "Indians" to refer to the opponents of the United States military. Leaders' names like Kamiakin, Owhi, Peo Peo Mox Mox and others are mentioned, but always in the context of organizing resistance to the treaties or the military. C.J. Brosnan's narrative more virulently represented Indians in a generic fashion. In his version, Colonel Wright did not execute Qualchin or Owhi, but executed "murderers" and forced "savages" to restore government supplies stolen from Colonel Steptoe. Brosnan also incorrectly identified the horse herd slaughtered by Wright's men as a Spokane herd instead of belonging to the Palouse. The slaughter of the herd was also justified as a necessary means "to prevent further depravations on the part of the Spokanes."[87]

Brosnan ended his narrative of the Yakama War with a section describing Colonel Wright as "a successful Indian-Fighter."[88] Wright's success resided in his ability to inflict severe casualties without losing a man, confiscating Indian property like horses and cattle, and executing eleven "murderers" involved in the killing of white men on the Columbia Plateau. According to Brosnan, Wright completely cowed Native Americans and finally allowed the government to open up Inland Northwest for settlement. Meany also shared themes with Brosnan. For Meany, "the surprise of Colonel Wright's campaign, and the resulting confirmation of the Indian treaties removed a great obstacle from the path of the American home-seeker."[89] Both authors intimated that military action was required to make "lawless bands of roving Indians" live up to their end of the bargain as negotiated in 1855, omitting the fact that the treaties were not ratified by the United States until 1859.

In the end, Meany best summed up the impact of the treaty and war for his readers. According to Meany, the treaty and war allowed American settlers on the Columbia Plateau to build homes that "were in every way counterparts of those built more than two centuries before by the Pilgrim Fathers on the Atlantic coast and of those built by all the families of pioneers in their wonderful march across a continent from sea to sea." Meany connected the settlers involved in the settlement of the Inland Northwest to the progressive march of Anglo-American civilization across North America. Not only were they connected to a national progressive historical narrative, settlers in the Pacific Northwest also had their own examples of home building and settlement. Meany recounted his narrative by citing examples of trading posts and their role in settlement, the establishment of Astoria, British Fort Vancouver, and the stations and homes built by American missionaries in the interior. The constant theme of progress and the triumph of Anglo-American civilization re-emerged at the end of this section. Meany reminded his readers that these previous examples prepared the way "for the planting of American homes that would endure and gather others about them. By thus persisting, they would in time be looked upon as the first American homes in the commonwealth." The treaties and war that followed were merely preludes to the great pioneer saga of building homes, towns and eventually cities in a region previously inhabited by people whom Brosnan characterized as "lawless bands of roving Indians." The narrative of both authors tied the identity of people, particularly settlers, who were always faceless and nameless, into the national identity and gave Anglo Americans in the Pacific Northwest a story of their own that highlighted the bravery and initiative of their elders.

The negotiations and struggles over the Treaty of 1855 and its implications mirrored the struggle between Coyote and Monster. Initially, Coyote attempted to blend into the landscape while negotiating with Monster. Plateau communities also attempted to maintain a distance from Anglo Americans during the period before the treaty. Even with the arrival of missionaries, fur traders, and settlers, Nez Perce and other Plateau communities sought to maintain a low profile while also protecting their land and way of life. This lasted as long as Coyote could remain hidden from Monster. As more and more settlers arrived in the Pacific Northwest, it became harder and harder to remain hidden and talk to Monster from a distance. As Columbia Plateau communities entered into negotiations with Governor Stevens and General Palmer in 1855, they recognized the desire of the United States government, and Anglo Americans in general, to swallow their land and change their ways of life. Just as many Plateau communities resisted the treaty and eventually took up arms to fight for their land, Coyote also attempted to inhale Monster. In the end, both failed and Monster inhaled "like a mighty wind" and changed life for Coyote, the Nez Perce and all Plateau communities.

Chapter Five
Monster Inhaled the People

> Now Monster inhaled like a mighty wind. He carried Coyote along just like that, but as Coyote went he left along the way great camas roots and great service berries, saying, "Here the people will find them and will be glad, for only a short time away is the coming of the human race." There he almost got caught on one of the ropes but he quickly cut it with his knife. Thus he dashed right into the monster's mouth.
>
> From there he walked down along down the throat of the monster. Along the way he saw bones scattered about and thought to himself, "It is to be seen that many people have been dying."[1]

Monster inhaled and swallowed Coyote. As the nineteenth century progressed, Nez Perce and other Plateau Indian communities came under greater pressure from Anglo Americans interested in obtaining their land and confining them to the reservations set up through the treaty of 1855. Just like Monster, Anglo Americans wished to "consume" the Nez Perce, not only physically, but also in a larger manner. The swallowing of the Nez Perce was an act designed to make them "disappear" from the Columbia Plateau. Anglo Americans on the Columbia Plateau wanted to relegate Indians to reservations, destroy their culture and recreate Indians in their own image. If Indians failed to accept these conditions, like the non-treaty Nez Perce, then Anglo Americans used military force to destroy their resistance.

In the face of this swallowing and consuming by Anglo Americans, Native Americans faced enormous problems when they attempted to retain and communicate their historical and cultural knowledge to their own people and to Anglo Americans. Anglo Americans failed to understand native viewpoints and worldviews and therefore researched and recorded history from their own perspectives while ignoring Nez Perce memory and historical knowledge. Until recently, depictions of "Joseph's War" in 1877 and the struggle of the non-treaty Nez Perce against the United States Army and government dominated Nez Perce and Plateau histories created by Anglo Americans. Yellow Wolf, in the eloquent conclusion of his life story, poignantly described the dilemma of Nez Perce people when they attempted to articulate their own knowledge in the public memory of the United States. He stated:

> This is all for me to tell of the war, and of our after hardships. The story will be for people who come after us. For them to see, to know what was done here. Reasons for the war, never before told. Nobody to help us tell our side-the whites told only one side. Told it to please themselves. Told much that is not true. Only his own best deeds, only the worst deeds of the Indians, has the white man told.[2]

In essence, the fascination with the pursuit and defeat of the non-treaty Nez Perce isolated and condensed their history into an extremely short period of time and, just as Yellow Wolf asserted, silenced Nez Perce perspectives and memory. The writings of Anglo-American historians like Edmond Meany and C.J. Brosnan clearly illustrated how Nez Perce and Plateau Indian history, culture, and religion were condensed into tropes of savagery, barbarism and inferiority.

The common assumption made by historians like Meany and Brosnan, and Anglo Americans in general, was that the military defeat and exile of non-treaty Nez Perce, and the confinement of Christian Nez Perce to the reservation, demonstrated the power of Anglo-American culture and started both Indian groups on the road to assimilation into the dominant culture of the United States. However, telling something to "please themselves" did not make the story/myth of cultural dominance and assimilation true. It merely expressed the goals and desires of various groups that wished first to obtain Nez Perce land and then to see Plateau people become, in essence, white people who shared the values and culture of the larger Anglo-American community.

Until the publication of *Yellow Wolf: His Own Story*, Anglo Americans relied on texts created by non-native historians and non-historians to understand the events that occurred between 1863 and 1877, but they researched and used few Nez Perce voices. In general, these narratives shared a certain trajectory with similar cues to make the story understandable and accessible to the Anglo-American general public. The following chapter attempts to deconstruct the narrative structures created to make these events part of the regional and national story. For Anglo Americans and their historians, the treaty of 1863 and the Nez Perce War of 1877 represented the last attempts to block the "powerful" forces of progressive Anglo-American civilization by a handful of native peoples whose fate was preordained by the inexorable forces of evolution and history.

For many Anglo-American academics and authors in the early twentieth century, the narration of these events marked the climax of the story and completed the "inevitable" disappearance of Native Americans from the Great Columbia Plain. Nez Perce and Plateau peoples vanished from the pages of these narratives after the Nez Perce War of 1877. Anglo Americans believed that the defeat of the non-treaty Nez Perce completed the narration of "civilization versus savagery" and that the narrative no longer required the presence of Native Americans. The focus of the later narratives shifted to the establishment of Anglo-American political, social and economic institutions on the Columbia Plateau. Meany began his discussion of these institutions even earlier, since his regional history focused on Washington State and only mentioned the Nez Perce War in passing. For Meany, the triumph of civilization occurred earlier when the United States Army defeated Indian forces in the Yakama War. People in Idaho, like historian C.J. Brosnan, the author of *The Illustrated History of North Idaho*, and missionary Sue McBeth, viewed things a bit differently from Meany and believed that their triumph only came when the United States defeated non-treaty people within the boundaries of Washington or Idaho territories.

The triumph for Anglo Americans only came when "Monster" swallowed all the people, including Coyote. Pressure on Nez Perce and other Plateau people's land base and confinement of non-treaty people to reservations were Monster's attempt to complete the swallowing and make native peoples "disappear." This was part of the grand scheme of "Manifest Destiny" so often referred to by Anglo Americans during the nineteenth and early twentieth centuries. It was not good enough for Monster to take Nez Perce land; he also needed to consume all things Nez Perce, including land, culture, history, oral tradition, and political structure. How did this begin? When Monster inhaled, Coyote was consumed and entered the mouth of Monster. Just as in the Monster and Coyote story, the Nez Perce secured themselves within the confines of their new reservation, bound themselves with "ropes" of oral traditions, songs, ceremonies and beliefs, and awaited the inhalation of Monster, an inhalation that began shortly after the Walla Walla Council of 1855.

"NOW MONSTER INHALED."[3]

The end of the so-called Yakama War and the confinement of many Columbia Plateau Indian communities to reservations paved the way for white settlement of areas previously occupied by Native Americans. The cycle of treaty-making, war, relegation to reservations, and subsequent acquisition of land is one of the most enduring patterns of Indian-White relations in the United States. The experience of Columbia Plateau peoples failed to differ substantially from this national pattern. Plateau peoples like the Yakamas, Cayuse, Walla Wallas, and others lived through this pattern in all its brutality and violence. While some Nez Perce scouted for the United States Army, the Yakama War affected them much less since the Walla Walla Treaty of 1855 promised to uphold reservation boundaries that encompassed most of the Nez Perce homeland. As Josephy pointed out, "the Nez Perces lived on their large reservation in splendid isolation."[4]

But the isolation of Nez Perce communities on the reservation lasted only a brief time. With the conclusion of the "so-called" Yakama War in 1858, white settlers, miners, adventurers and others flooded into the Columbia Plateau region. Anglo Americans occupied the land of Yakamas, Cayuse, Umatillas and others and rather quickly began to eye the land set aside for the Nez Perce. As white settler numbers increased, they pressured state, territorial and the United States governments to renegotiate the treaty of 1855 and decrease the size of the Nez Perce reservation. Renegotiation of treaties also fell within the national pattern of Indian policy. As settlers and other white immigrants clamored for more land and encroached on land guaranteed to Indians in treaties, the United States government found it easier to renegotiate treaties instead of enforcing the ones already legally concluded with Native American groups. The desire for land and the disregard for native people's claims fostered an attitude that made it easy for government officials and the military to acquiesce to the demands of whites hungry for the lands of the Nez Perce, especially after the discovery of gold and the development of Lewiston, Idaho.[5]

The quest for valuable minerals played an important role in the settlement of many areas by Anglo Americans. As noted, miners often paved the way for settlers in many areas of the western United States. The Gold Rush of 1849 in California was only one example of the enormous impact Anglo-American greed and the desire to exploit mineral resources exercised on native populations and their land base. The search for gold eventually came to the Columbia Plateau and many prospectors, fortune hunters and miners eagerly eyed the Bitterroot Mountains as a possible location for rich veins of gold and silver. Historians like Alvin Josephy and Clifford Trafzer placed the first tentative explorations for gold in the early 1850s. Both historians noted that Ellias D. Pierce possibly discovered gold sources in Nez Perce country as early as 1852. Undoubtedly, fear of Nez Perce reprisals for trespassing kept Pierce and others out of Nez Perce Country for a short while.

In particular, the deaths of miners before and during the Yakama War discouraged Anglo Americans from venturing into Nez Perce territory since even whites regarded the Nez Perce as skilled warriors who zealously guarded their ancestral homes.[6]

Nevertheless, by the end of the Yakama War in 1858, increasing numbers of settlers and miners moved into areas directly outside of the Nez Perce Reservation. While white settlements and incursions generally remained outside of the reservation, a major problem existed for the Nez Perce since the treaty of 1855 languished in the Senate without ratification due to the Yakama War and lobbying by those opposed to the treaty. The lack of treaty ratification and the legal settlement of the reservation boundaries caused internal friction between the pro-white Nez Perce group led by Lawyer and anti-white groups led principally by Eagle From the Light, Old Chief Joseph, and others. The uncertainty of their legal status and the failure of the United States government to fulfill its promises as outlined in the treaty of 1855 caused great concern within both groups and provided impetus for anti-white groups in their dispute with Lawyer's faction. The treaty was finally ratified in March 1859 and signed by President James Buchanan in the same year. Both groups, pro- and anti-white, breathed a sigh of relief when word reached them that the treaty was legally binding.[7]

However, the stable legal position enjoyed by the Nez Perce failed to exist for any length of time. In 1858, before the ratification of the treaty, Ellias Pierce and his partner discovered gold on the Clearwater River, and news of the discovery spread when they returned to Walla Walla to organize an expedition to exploit the find. Nez Perce Agent A.J. Cain tried to keep the expedition out of the reservation, but despite his attempts, Pierce and the expedition struck gold in August of 1860 on a tributary of the Clearwater River. Agent Cain and the military stood very little chance of thwarting the avalanche of whites racing to take advantage of the discovery. The presence of miners on the reservation raised a difficult legal question for Anglo-American authorities. The treaty of 1855 specifically outlawed the presence of whites on the reservation without the permission of the tribe. Miners violated the treaty provisions when they trespassed on the reservation, but officials of the United States government refused to execute the provisions of its own treaty and to remove the miners by force if necessary. Unfortunately, the use of military force against Anglo-American miners was not very palatable to government officials since miners were citizens of the United States, voted and exercised their political rights while the Nez Perce were not citizens, had no legal status, could not vote and exercised little or no political clout.[8]

In April 1861, Oregon Superintendent of Indian Affairs Edward R. Geary and Nez Perce Indian Agent A.J. Cain negotiated with Lawyer and other "Upper" Nez Perce leaders to acquire the right of whites to explore and mine for gold along the Clearwater River and across the Bitterroot Mountains.[9] The agreement allowed both whites and Indians to search and mine for gold. According to Allen Slickpoo, Sr., Lawyer and fifty-one other leaders signed the agreement that essentially recognized the illegal presence of whites on the Nez Perce Reservation. However, under Nez Perce law, Lawyer and the other fifty-one leaders could not speak for all Nez Perce, only for the community or communities that recognized their leadership. By making this agreement with the United States government, Lawyer violated traditional Nez Perce law. The United States government never ratified the agreement, and Slickpoo asserted that the inaction of the government betrayed the desires and hopes of whites in the region and in the United States government that the land eventually would be ceded to them as the result of future treaty negotiation. Slickpoo noted that in October 1861, Lewiston, Idaho, developed quickly as a town despite the protests of Agent Cain and the illegal status of a town site on the reservation.[10]

Since expelling miners by force seemed impractical and undesirable to United States officials, they harkened back to prior experience and dealings with other Native American groups and proposed a solution that seemed equitable to them. The national pattern of treaty negotiation and relegation of Native Americans to a reservation often required more than one treaty negotiation along with increased pressure on Native Americans to give up significant portions of their reservation land to placate white settlers. This renegotiation pattern was a theme that occurred repeatedly as Anglo Americans moved west, forming an important part of Indian policy in the United States.[11] For example, this pattern existed with the Lakota and their reservation which once included the Black Hills. When miners in the 1870s trespassed on Lakota territory, they demanded protection and renegotiation of treaties to satisfy their desire to exploit the rich gold fields of the Black Hills. General Armstrong Custer even led several thousand troops into the Blacks Hills in 1874 to confirm the gold discoveries and to protect miners, all this in direct violation of the Fort Laramie Treaty of 1868 signed by the Lakota and the United States government.[12]

As mining towns sprang up on the Nez Perce reservation, white miners and settlers pressured the United States government for a renegotiation of reservation boundaries. The first step in this process required the designation of the region as the Idaho Territory by the United States government, encompassing present-day Idaho, Montana and parts of Wyoming.

Miners, settlers, and other whites now had government institutions and greater political influence available to them through their territorial government. After territorial designation, Congress voted to appropriate funds for the renegotiation of reservation boundaries with the Nez Perce. There is a paradox evident in the justifications given for renegotiation. Trafzer and Scheuerman asserted that Oregon Superintendent of Indians Calvin Hale, while negotiating with the Nez Perce in 1863, "assured the Indians that the government wished to reduce the size of the reservation for the good of the Indians, reasoning that a smaller reservation would make it easier for the army to protect them."[13] Superintendent Hale's assurances vividly illuminate the paradox. In Anglo-American eyes, the treaty required renegotiation because the federal government and military were unable to protect the Nez Perce from white intrusions on the reservation. Therefore, the United States needed to establish a smaller reservation in order to "protect" Indians. The Nez Perce must have puzzled over the unwillingness of American military and government officials to fulfill their treaty obligations while the United States government requested additional land in the name of "protecting" the people when the government could not protect them in the first place. No wonder the terms of the 1863 treaty seemed unreasonable, arbitrary and unenforceable to those native groups opposed to signing it. Nez Perce experience with the United States government failed to elicit trust or understanding.[14]

Two months after the establishment of Idaho Territory, Oregon Superintendent of Indian Affairs Calvin Hale and two commissioners arrived in Lapwai to renegotiate the 1855 treaty and decrease the land base of the Nez Perce. Before treaty deliberations started, the problems of translation and communication once again reared their ugly heads. Superintendent Hale recruited Henry Spalding, the former missionary to the Nez Perce at Lapwai, and Robert Newell, a former mountain man, as interpreters. Most of the Indians present before the start of treaty negotiations belonged to Lawyer's people, and the selection of these particular translators troubled Lawyer and others. Lawyer and other leaders like Spotted Eagle, requested that Superintendent Hale select Perrin Whitman as interpreter. The issue of translation arose from Nez Perce experience at the Walla Walla Council and their belief that mistranslations and falsehoods kept them from understanding the details and implications of the treaty.[15]

On May 25, 1863, the Lapwai council commenced inauspiciously with Superintendent Hale informing the Indians that they must agree to a smaller reservation. Since many notable leaders like Old Joseph, Eagle From the Light, White Bird and others still had not arrived, the Indians already in attendance refused to accept Hale's demand to surrender land.[16] Even Lawyer, the long-time friend of the whites, reminded Hale of previous treaty obligations under the 1855 treaty and reiterated Nez Perce refusal to sell their land. After a recess of six days, the council resumed on June 3, 1863. By this time, Perrin Whitman, the agreed-upon interpreter, and large numbers of anti-treaty Nez Perce groups arrived at Lapwai for the Council.[17]

The representatives of the United States government quickly and forcefully laid out the government's position. After Agent Howe's speech, the treaty and anti-treaty groups met to discuss the government's position and responded with a proposal that stunned and perplexed the government officials present. Alvin Josephy noted that both the treaty and non-treaty Nez Perce groups agreed to sell only the land on which whites had already discovered gold and the town site of Lewiston, Idaho. While Lawyer essentially proposed this solution earlier to the commissioners, the combined proposal of all Nez Perces present at the council unnerved government officials since their objective was not to negotiate the sale of these lands but to permanently renegotiate and decrease the total land holdings of the Nez Perce. The commissioners rejected the proposal and refused to negotiate on these points. Josephy noted that an impasse had been reached in the negotiations and that the commissioners resorted to private meetings with individual leaders to persuade them to accept the terms of the new treaty. The subversive tactics of the commissioners harkened back to the tried and true methods of "divide and conquer." By separating and applying pressure, the commissioners hoped to gain a positive outcome to their treaty proposals. According to a letter Superintendent Hale wrote about the proceedings, he concluded that the commissioners eventually persuaded all the groups, both treaty and anti-treaty, to accept the provisions of the new treaty.[18]

While Hale asserted the consent of all factions, the signing of the treaty contradicted his assertions that the entire Nez Perce nation agreed to and signed the document. In private, anti-treaty leaders, under pressure from the commissioners and interpreters, may have agreed to consider the treaty proposals or even agreed to some of the government's proposals, but no leader of an anti-treaty faction signed the treaty and notable leaders like Old Joseph, White Bird, and Toohoolhoolzote never acquiesced to government demands. As Josephy noted, "Hale secured the signature or the agreement of every headman whose lands the treaty would not affect but did not secure the signatures of Joseph, White Bird, or any leader, save Timothy and Jason, who lived outside the borders of the new reservation."[19] All fifty-two signatures on the treaty were those of Lawyer and his faction. With Lawyer's help, Hale and the other commissioners rounded up fifty-one men to give the treaty the appearance of assent by the "entire" Nez Perce nation, but only one leader agreed to the "Thief" treaty.[20] As with many treaties concluded by the United States government, the process of ratification took a great deal of time, especially since the federal government was concerned with the more pressing issues of the Civil War. Congress eventually ratified the 1863 Thief Treaty in 1867 and then ratified a supplemental treaty, signed by Lawyer and Timothy, to move non-treaty groups to the confines of the 1863 reservation. These treaties would be some of the last signed in the Pacific Northwest. The nation's Indian policy changed once again when Congress passed a law in 1871 "declaring that the United States no longer recognized Indian tribes as sovereign." From 1871 forward, the United States government exclusively dealt with Indian issues through executive orders of presidents.[21]

"WE HAD A GOOD COUNTRY UNTIL THE WHITE PEOPLE CAME AND CROWDED US."[22]

While white populations remained fairly small on the Columbian Plateau, conflicts and demands for the removal of anti-treaty Nez Perce, Palouse, and other Plateau groups remained minimal. However, as more farmers, miners, businessmen, and other whites arrived on lands previously occupied solely by Nez Perce and other Columbia Plateau Indian people, disputes surrounding property rights, alleged crimes and other conflicts increased. Trafzer and Scheuerman noted that between 1863 and 1876, growing white population in areas previously occupied by Palouse and Nez Perce people resulted in calls by Anglo Americans for the confinement of Indians onto reservations.[23] Native resistance against demands for confinement to reservations coalesced around a loose confederation of anti-treaty communities devoted to the teachings of the Washani religion as expressed by holy men like Smohalla, Toohoolhoolzote, and Husishusis Kute. Followers of the Washani faith objected to leaving or selling the land, because they believed in the "sacredness of the earth" and the intimate connection between their land, identity and existence as Indian people of the Columbia Plateau.[24]

In 1873, conflicts between non-treaty Nez Perce groups and white settlers came to a head in areas occupied by non-treaty communities, especially in northeast Oregon. Old Joseph and his people refused to sign the treaty of 1863 and continued to maintain their ancestral homes in the Wallowa area. After Old Joseph's death in 1871, Young Joseph continued his father's policy of refusing to move or to give the government or white settlers any land. As settlers moved into the Wallowa area of northeast Oregon, conflicts arose and the United States government intervened to avoid a full-scale battle between settlers and Indians. President Ulysses S. Grant signed an executive order setting up a reservation for the non-treaty communities in the Wallowa area, but somehow the treaty outlined boundaries that gave Nez Perce land to white settlers and gave white settler land to the Nez Perce. Despite the boundaries mistake, most government officials, whether at the local, state or federal level, viewed the executive order reservation as a temporary remedy to allow time for the government to extinguish Nez Perce claims in the Wallowa Valley.[25]

Anglo-American settlers in the Wallowa Valley resented the executive order and believed that Young Joseph and his people plotted to kill them or planned to use the Indian Department to remove them from their lands. Josephy noted, "Fear of the Indians gave way to a hatred of them, as well as of 'the Indian-coddling government,'" and described the furious activity of whites in the Wallowa area to undermine the executive order and somehow rid themselves of Indian claims to the land. Settlers in the area, availing themselves of the political institutions, persuaded the governor of Oregon and Oregon's Congressional delegation to lodge protests with the Secretary of Interior and the Indian Department. These protests resulted in a reexamination of the problems in the Wallowa area by a three-man commission.[26]

Throughout 1873, Joseph and his people continued to live in the Wallowa area, but white hostility and anger heightened as popular sentiment pictured the non-treaty Nez Perce as troublemakers and possible threats. By May 1874, the United States government tacitly informed an Oregon senator that it had no intention of enforcing the boundaries of the new reservation and that "the whole valley is now open for settlement by the whole people."[27] Essentially the federal government negated the executive order without officially rescinding the order and allowed settlers to remain and settle new lands within reservation boundaries. In 1875, President Grant formally rescinded the executive order and once again officially opened the Wallowa region to white settlement.

After rescinding the executive order, the government's position focused on the removal of non-treaty communities from the Wallowa region of northeast Oregon. The removal policy placed these communities in a difficult position. Some Nez Perce leaders like Eagle from the Light and White Bird argued for open conflict, while Joseph and his brother, Ollokot, argued that war was impossible and counseled the others to attempt to live peacefully with whites.[28] The issue for all these Indian communities rested not only on their legitimate legal claims to the Wallowa region, but also on their religious beliefs about the land and their place within it. Joseph, White Bird,

Eagle From the Light, Toohoolhoolzute, and others consistently argued that their land was not for sale or exchange and that leaving their homes meant giving up a part of themselves and breaking one of their most important religious precepts. To the Nez Perce, their law required them to live in the lands of their forefathers and mothers, the lands given them by Coyote, the creative force, from the rich blood of Monster. For non-treaty Nez Perce communities, their discussions with the government and their position rested deep within the earth of the Wallowa and the surrounding region. In contrast, white settlers were concerned with their own claims to the land, the improvements built on them and their profitability in a local and national market economy. From the outset, these differing perspectives about the land exacerbated misunderstandings and misperceptions about the Nez Perce and their motivations. From the Walla Walla Council of 1855 onward, Anglo Americans failed to comprehend the central and sacred position of the land for the Nez Perce and their Plateau neighbors. Indeed, most scholars have missed this central point, sometimes denigrating native views of the land by calling them inconsequential.[29]

As tensions increased in the Wallowa and other regions, the United States government restricted native groups within the bounds of the 1863 treaty reservation. While many people and agencies actively played roles in this government policy, the United States Army and the Indian Department exercised the most visible and local presence. In September 1874, the new military commander of the Department of Vancouver, General Oliver Otis Howard, assumed command. Howard would play a central role in the "drama" and "tragedy" of the Nez Perce and, from the beginning of his tenure, he worked to confine all non-treaty groups to reservations, regardless of tribal affiliation. General Howard met Joseph in the spring of 1875 for a brief time and believed, despite the brevity of their meeting, that a spark of friendship and understanding existed between them. Initially, General Howard sympathized with the Nez Perce, and in a report on the conflicting claims of whites and Nez Perce in the Wallowa area, he stated that the 1863 treaty held no legal claim on the non-treaty Nez Perce.[30]

Despite his sympathy for the Nez Perce, General Howard, from the beginning of his tenure as commander of the Vancouver Department, attempted to fulfill the government's policy of confining all Columbia Plateau non-treaty Indian communities to reservations and opening their land to white settlement. Ostensibly, these policies originated from a concern for the safety of both white settlers and Indians, but in reality they were driven by deeper impulses emanating from the experience of previous encounters with other native peoples and a national belief in Manifest Destiny. The government of the

United States, with its various state and territorial governments, supported Manifest Destiny as a national policy that viewed Indians as obstacles to the ultimate destiny of the United States and white Americans to transform the land for the benefit of mankind. As Howard and other government officials worked to confine all Nez Perce to the reservation, their methods harkened back to previous Indian-White interactions in the nineteenth century and even earlier. As white population spread, the United States government negotiated and renegotiated treaties with Native American groups and forced them to relinquish land under the auspices of protecting them from white influence. This line of reasoning can be traced back to the Walla Walla Council in 1855 when Stevens and Palmer warned the Nez Perce that whites were like grains of sand and would be everywhere. As land opened for white settlement, as in the aftermath of the 1863 Thief Treaty, contact between non-treaty groups and Anglo Americans increased and white settlers demanded that the government confine all Indians to the reservation. The government's objectives, and by extension General Howard's orders, reinforced and responded to the desires or fears of Anglo Americans. It is important to reiterate that only Anglo Americans had political clout in this situation. The Nez Perce were non-citizens without economic or political power in the United States, following in the footsteps of many other native peoples in the history of Indian-White relations. Anglo Americans feared Native Americans because they represented the "savage" character or wildness of the area and also threatened the "settled" or "civilized" ways of life associated with white settlement. In white thinking, taming the wilderness of the Pacific Northwest required taming the "wildness" of Indians, in this case the Nez Perce. Anglo Americans also were deeply concerned about the title and legitimacy of their land claims. As Meany asserted, Anglo Americans needed to clarify and lay legal claim to the land they inhabited but could only do so if Indian claims had been extinguished. The pursuit of property as protected in the Constitution of the United States animated the "liberal" imaginations of Anglo Americans and required the stamp of legal legitimacy to move them from pursuit of property to the pursuit of happiness. A settler's happiness only emerged when threats to their land disappeared into the category of past ownership without claims or liens.[31]

The decision by the United States government in 1871 not to recognize the sovereignty of Native American nations surely affected how General Howard and John B. Monteith, the Nez Perce Indian Agent, dealt with the non-treaty Nez Perce. For government officials, the time for treaty deliberations was over, and any Indians not on a reservation found themselves faced with an ultimatum to conform to the government's demands or face confinement by military force if the government deemed it necessary. On the Nez Perce side, leaders like Joseph, who took his father's place as chief after his death in August, 1871, White Bird, Toohoolhoolzote, and others adamantly defended their beliefs in not removing to the reservation and maintaining control over their homeland. At the root of their defense lay the Washani religion and Nez Perce persistence in pointing out the incongruities of white statements and promises. Nez Perce devotion to holding onto their land annoyed and angered settlers, government officials and military officers like Agent John B. Monteith and General Howard.[32]

In each of the three councils that preceded the Nez Perce War of 1877, non-treaty Nez Perce met with government officials and attempted to negotiate terms favorable to their position. In particular, Joseph was most unusual in these meetings because of his patience and belief that words, reason, and arguments would win the day for the Nez Perce and that whites would come to understand the folly of the 1863 Thief Treaty. Joseph looked to the Christian values and democratic words of white America and believed that justice would be done for the Nez Perce. After all, this was the American way they had learned about. From 1875 onward, the non-treaty Nez Perce fumed over the rescinding of the executive order reservation in the Wallowa. As more and more white settlers moved into areas previously protected for the Nez Perce under the 1855 treaty, conflict and violence erupted. For example, in March 1875, a white settler named Larry Ott murdered Tipyahlanah Siskan (Eagle Robe), a Salmon River Nez Perce headman, over a fence Ott erected around Eagle Robe's garden. Also, in June 1876, two whites murdered an Indian in the Wallowa country, further stoking the resentment and frustration of non-treaty Nez Perce in the area. As a consequence, Agent Monteith hastily asked Joseph to meet at Lapwai, Idaho, to discuss the situation. After the meeting, Monteith believed the situation warranted more military presence and requested troops in the Wallowa.[33]

The United States Army and the non-treaty Nez Perce both wished to avoid conflict and, in November 1876, Joseph accepted the call for a council with five government commissioners, including General Howard, at Fort Lapwai, Idaho, to discuss the situation and removal of non-treaty Nez Perce to the reservation. At this meeting, however, Joseph refused the commissioner's demands to move to the Nez Perce reservation in Idaho and based his arguments on his religion. The meeting ended in a stalemate and the commissioners blamed the spiritual leaders, the *tooats*, for the stubborn refusal of Joseph and other non-treaty people to give up their lands. Trafzer and Scheuerman observed that both General Howard and Agent Monteith loathed Nez Perce religious leaders like Toohoolhoolzote (Nez Perce) and

Husishusis Kute (Palouse), blaming them consistently for the failure of the United States to achieve its ends. In the minds of Anglo-American officials and military men, the pejorative label of "Dreamers" described the unwillingness of non-treaty peoples to accept Christianity and assimilate into Anglo-American society.[34]

Unwilling to acquiesce to Joseph and determined to remove non-treaty people, General Howard requested another meeting on the Umatilla Reservation near present-day Pendleton, Oregon. Joseph refused and sent his brother, Ollokot, in his place. This meeting, in early 1877, once again ended inconclusively, but Agent Monteith around the same time gave all non-treaty Nez Perce a deadline of April 1, a bad time to move onto the reservation with all their goods and livestock because of the spring run-off. In April 1877, General Howard requested another meeting with Joseph and other non-treaty leaders. Joseph declined to go but sent Ollokot (Figure 5) to Walla Walla to convey Nez Perce dissatisfaction with the government's position, ask for an extension of the deadline to remove to the reservation, and request another meeting with all non-treaty Nez Perce. At the same time, the Nez Perce knew Howard had ordered troops to the Wallowa in preparation for war. Howard's military preparations frustrated Joseph.[35]

The second Lapwai Council started on May 3, 1877 and would be the last council before the Nez Perce War. From the beginning, the council was fraught with conflicts and threats. The Indians present warned Perrin Whitman, interpreter for the council, to interpret correctly. All of them remembered the problems that arose from incorrect interpretations at earlier treaty and council meetings like the 1855 Walla Walla Council and the Thief Treaty Council of 1863. The non-treaty communities selected Toohoolhoolzote as their first speaker and Husishusis Kute as the second speaker. Both men were *tooats* and represented the religious and secular concerns of non-treaty people.[36] While the two *tooats* were to represent the people, Ollokot, Joseph's brother, was the first to argue with General Howard. On May 7, 1877, Ollokot's frustration boiled over and targeted the treatment of non-treaty people by the government and white settlers. He fumed that "they treat me as a dog."[37] Toohoolhoolzote, the leading Nez Perce *tooat*, joined the argument and challenged the government's conception of law and its inability to uphold its part of the bargains made with the Nez Perce. Toohoolhoolzote consistently pointed out that none of the non-treaty Nez Perce signed the 1863 treaty and therefore had not relinquished their land. Toohoolhoolzote's position resided deep within Washani religious doctrine about the land, a doctrine that forbade the sale or relinquishing of land to white settlers or the government.[38]

Figure 5 Ollokot, Brother of Chief Joseph, circa 1877. Photographer – E.W. Moore. Courtesy of Manuscripts, Special Collections, University Archives, University of Washington Libraries, NA 878.

Toohoolhoolzote's position angered and frustrated General Howard, a devout Christian. His constant refrain of the "chieftainship" of the earth and the importance of the land to Nez Perce identity fell on General Howard's deaf ears. As related earlier, Howard loathed the *tooats* and believed that they were at the root of non-treaty resistance to removal. Howard finally refused to listen to Toohoolhoolzote and wanted to return to what he believed to be the business of the council, the removal of non-treaty communities to the Nez Perce reservation. This refusal to hear the core arguments of the Nez Perce position disturbed and angered the Indians present. Yellow Wolf stated that Howard's failure to follow the etiquette for councils, his insistent demands to remove to the reservation, and his rudeness essentially equaled "showing the rifle" or threatening war to the Nez Perce.[39]

At its root, the argument between Howard and Toohoolhoolzote illustrated the chasm of misunderstanding between non-treaty communities and Anglo Americans. General Howard had no intention of conforming to Indian etiquette at the council or listening to lengthy Nez Perce oratory. The government, as represented by Howard and Monteith, focused on one thing only, the removal of non-treaty communities to reservations and opening land to white settlement. This was the Manifest Destiny of the nation and in the best interests of the United States and its market economy. The Nez Perce, Palouse, and other non-treaty groups came to the council with the hope of achieving an agreement that would allow them to retain their traditional lands and way of life. Howard's impatience and rudeness confirmed the Nez Perce's worst fears that the government would ignore them and simply and forcefully move them onto the reservation.[40]

General Howard's hatred of Toohoolhoolzote heightened misunderstandings and erupted in a tirade that eventually ended with Howard ordering the imprisonment of the Nez Perce *tooat*. Toohoolhoolzote's refusal to acquiesce to Howard's demands and his open defiance of the government's order to remove to the reservation also prompted leaders like Looking Glass and White Bird to reaffirm their refusal to comply with the government order. Howard again threatened them with promises of military force to remove them to the reservation and even threatened the arrest of Toohoolhoolzote. Howard announced he might even send the recalcitrant Nez Perce to the Indian Territory. When Toohoolhoolzote refused to acquiesce, Howard arrested and imprisoned him at Fort Lapwai.[41]

The arrest of Toohoolhoolzote created great tension at the council. Yellow Wolf also believed that the arrest hurt all of the Indians present since threatening force at a peace council was inappropriate and "not suited for

Indians."[42] Howard broke Indian law by his hasty and forceful action. After the arrest, Howard demanded to know if the other leaders present would remove peacefully to the reservation or whether he would have to use force. According to Trafzer and Scheuerman, all the leaders present, except Toohoolhoolzote, wanted to avoid war and consented to move to the reservation.[43] Having achieved his goal, Howard and Nez Perce and Palouse leaders toured the Nez Perce Reservation to find suitable locations for non-treaty communities. The presence of non-treaty groups disturbed the treaty groups who already lived on the reservation. Robert Ruby and John Brown noted that animosities ran high among the two groups and treaty Nez Perce feared that the non-treaty groups outgunned them and left them vulnerable to violence.[44]

After their return, Howard released Toohoolhoolzote on promises of good behavior and gave all non-treaty Nez Perce thirty days and two groups of Palouse from the Snake River thirty-five days to move to the reservation with all their stock and household goods. The council ended on May 14, 1877, and the Nez Perce and Palouse traveled home to prepare for the move. While non-treaty leaders agreed to Howard's demands in order to avoid war, many people, including numerous young men, resented the move and reluctantly complied with the government's order. Yellow Wolf (Figure 6) noted, "Some young men talked secret among themselves. To one another they said, 'General Howard has shown us the rifle.' We answer, 'Yes. We will stir up a fight for him. We will start his war.'"[45] The resentment and anger must have been quite evident as non-treaty people attempted to meet the deadline. As Yellow Wolf stated, no leader desired war, and they followed the government's demands in order to avoid conflict and death.

The move created hardship and loss of property for many Nez Perce, as well as the grief of moving away from land that held their homes for many years and the graves of their people. Rounding up stock also took time because moving large numbers of horses and cattle in such a short time proved very difficult. Crossing streams in May and June was arduous for the Nez Perce since these months traditionally saw increased run-off from melting snow pack and most the rivers and streams rose to their highest levels. Nez Perce people left behind some stock that they failed to locate and lost significant numbers of cattle and horses as they forded swollen streams to reach the reservation. Most of the non-treaty bands headed for the Camas Prairie in west central Idaho, about six miles west of present-day Grangeville, Idaho. Close to the Camas Prairie was a small lake, later labeled Tolo Lake by Anglo Americans. In this location, non-treaty people gathered to dig camas root and council together before moving onto the Nez Perce Reservation.

Figure 6 Yellow Wolf, 1909. Photographer – L.V. McWhorter. Courtesy of Manuscripts, Archives, and Special Collections, Washington State University Libraries, Lucullus Virgil McWhorter Collection, 70-0276.

Unknown to all involved, the resentment and anger of the Nez Perce at their poor treatment would lead a group of young men to seek revenge for wrongs committed by whites in the Salmon River area. These hostile actions led to the eruption of the Nez Perce War and the flight of non-treaty communities to avoid capture by the United States military.[46]

THE NEZ PERCE WAR OF 1877[47]

While General Howard met with Palouse, Cayuse, Walla Wallas and other non-treaty communities, the Nez Perce and some Palouse communities met at the Camas Prairie. As Howard conferred with leaders like Thomash of the Lower Palouses, Young Chief of the Cayuses, and Smohalla of the Wanapums, the Nez Perce attempted to enjoy a brief period of rest and freedom before moving onto the reservation.[48] Over their heads hung the depressing reality of land loss and resentment born of broken promises and ill treatment. Wahlitits, a young man at the Camas Prairie, rode around the encampment in a rage, trampling some of the roots laid out to dry by families. One of the women who had gathered the roots openly and loudly scolded Wahlitits and told him that if he was such a great warrior then why had he not avenged the death of his father, Eagle Robe. Larry Ott, a white settler along the Salmon River, had murdered Eagle Robe the previous year. On June 13, 1877, Wahlitits took the scolding to heart, gathered two of his friends and set out to avenge his father's murder. The raiding party attacked white settlers along the Salmon River, killing three white men and wounding one. News of the raid brought other Indians into the fray while sparking fear and hysteria among settlers along the Salmon River and in surrounding areas.[49]

The raids along the Salmon River were not a concerted effort by non-treaty Nez Perce and Palouse to oust white settlers. Wahlitits and his friends acted independently out of anger and pent up frustration over their treatment by white settlers and the government and the desire to avenge Wahlitits' father, Eagle Robe. These individual acts of revenge did not express the policy or desires of most non-treaty leaders or people. As Brown and Ruby noted, Joseph and Ollokot were away butchering beef when the raids occurred and they did not authorize the raiding. While unauthorized, these acts of revenge appealed to many non-treaty communities because they expressed the pent up anger many of them felt as a result of government threats and demands to move to the reservation.[50]

As news of the raids spread throughout white settlements, non-treaty communities camped at the Camas Prairie realized that the raids meant war with the United States government. Trafzer and Scheuerman observed that the people present at Camas Prairie met in council to decide a course of action and concluded that they must move south to White Bird Canyon, a place more defensible if the army attacked them.[51] Joseph (Figure 7) and Ollokot led the people to the canyon and prepared themselves for the army's arrival. On June 17, 1877, a detachment of soldiers led by Captain David Perry, the same officer who had arrested Toohoolhoolzote at the Lapwai Council, attacked the non-treaty camps at White Bird Canyon. The soldiers suffered severe casualties and quickly retreated. Yellow Wolf commented that during the Battle of White Bird Canyon, Nez Perce warriors fought in small groups or by themselves as they had done traditionally against their enemies. This style of fighting was not as "organized" or hierarchical as the tactics employed by the United States Army, but the tactics proved highly effective in a conflict based on movement and quick deployment. Yellow Wolf also disputed the reported number of warriors gathered at Camas Prairie and the number of warriors who actually participated in the war.[52] As he noted at the end of *Yellow Wolf: His Own Story*, Anglo Americans told the story of the war to please themselves. Small numbers of warriors defeating larger forces of the United States Army failed to fit into the narrative structure of the war as imagined and reported by Anglo Americans. Small numbers of warriors defeating larger United States forces also highlighted the military capabilities of the Nez Perce and other non-treaty communities.[53]

After the Battle of White Bird Canyon, confusion reigned in the Salmon River area as non-treaty Nez Perce and Palouse, who had not prepared for war, sought to protect their communities and move to safety while white settlers, fearful of Indian attack, fortified towns and mobilized to defend against Indian attack.[54] On June 27th, General Howard assumed overall command in the field and mobilized his forces to follow the Nez Perce. As he trailed the non-treaty communities, he commanded Captain Stephen Whipple to find Chief Looking Glass and his people. Looking Glass was not present at Camas Prairie or White Bird Canyon, but due to rumors and reports by treaty Nez Perce, General Howard falsely believed that Looking Glass posed a threat to his columns and worried that Looking Glass had provided recruits to the other non-treaty bands, none of which was true. While counted as a member of the non-treaty faction, Looking Glass had not participated in any of the actions before July 1 and had urged his people to maintain peace with white settlers and the government. Captain Whipple and his men, who included volunteers involved in the White Bird Battle, found the peaceful camp of Looking Glass on July 1. Without provocation, Whipple and his men fired on the camp, scattering Looking Glass's people

Figure 7 Chief Joseph. Courtesy of Manuscripts, Archives, and Special Collections, Washington State University Libraries, Lucullus Virgil McWhorter Collection, 70-0149.

and destroying their village. This action firmly placed Looking Glass and his people on the side of non-treaty people. Josephy observed that this "was a senseless and inexcusable attack," and that Whipple never addressed Looking Glass or gave his people, among them the young warrior, Peo Peo Thalekt (Figure 8), a chance to negotiate with him or his men.[55]

From July 5 to 13, 1877, several engagements ensued in the Salmon River Valley before the non-treaty bands retreated to the Weippe Prairie, reaching the head of the Lolo Trail on July 14, 1877.[56] At the Weippe Prairie, the non-treaty communities rested and convened to decide on their course of action. During the council, Looking Glass argued persuasively for a retreat over the Bitterroot Mountains along the Lolo Trail. According to Trafzer, Looking Glass reasoned that if they left the area they would leave their troubles behind and that their friends, the Crows, would welcome them. Most of the other leaders agreed with Looking Glass, and Joseph, deferring to him because of his war experience, allowed Looking Glass to lead the non-treaty communities over the Bitterroot Mountains. As the Nez Perce negotiated the difficult terrain of the Bitterroot Mountains, General Howard and his troops attempted pursuit but could not catch them.[57]

Arriving on the other side of the Bitterroot Mountains unmolested, the non-treaty bands met a small force of army volunteers at "Fort Fizzle," near present-day Missoula, Montana, who decided not to fight the Indians but allowed them to continue on their way. Believing they had escaped the United States Army, the non-treaty bands traveled south and east along well-known trails and hoped to hunt buffalo on the plains of Montana and Wyoming, places familiar to them from past hunting trips. They traveled to the valley of the Big Hole River and stopped there in early August to recuperate, hunt for food, fish and tend their wounded. Confident in their having escaped from the United States Army, some people celebrated at Big Hole, and Looking Glass posted no sentries to guard the camp against attack. However, in a dream, Wootolen saw soldiers attacking the camp, and he warned Looking Glass and others of the impending danger. Unfortunately, Looking Glass disregarded the warning.[58]

Early in the morning on August 9, 1877, troops under the command of Colonel John Gibbon surprised the Nez Perce at Big Hole (Figure 9). The first Indian to die was Hahtalekin, a non-treaty Palouse chief, shot as he checked on his horses but not before he warned the camp and fought the soldiers.[59] Colonel Gibbon's troops had crept close to the Nez Perce camp, and once the battle began, they moved quickly into the encampment and fired indiscriminately at Nez Perce people. Trafzer noted that Gibbon informed his men that he wanted no prisoners, encouraging them to shoot everyone

Figure 8 Peo Peo Thalekt wearing historical headdress, Colville Reservation, Washington, 1905. Photographer, Edward H. Latham. Courtesy of Manuscripts, Special Collections, University Archives, University of Washington Libraries, NA 949.

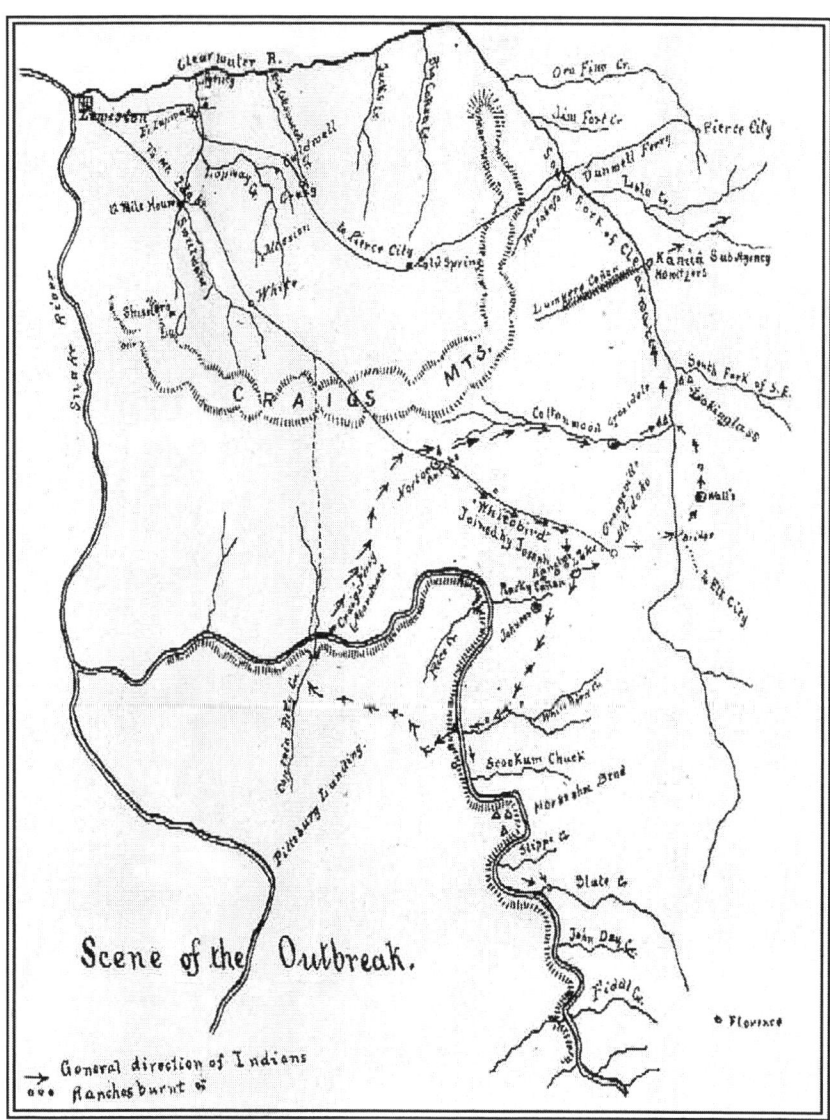

Figure 9 Map of the Nez Perce War, Scene of the Outbreak. Department of Columbia, Maps of the Nez Perce Campaign. In U.S. House, 45th Congress, Second Session, Report of the Secretary of War, 1877. (H.Ex.Doc. 1, Pt. 2) Washington, Government Printing Office (Serial Set 1794). Courtesy of the United States Government Printing Office.

in sight.⁶⁰ As the soldiers advanced, women, children, and old people rushed from the tipis in all directions. Nez Perce warriors fought back, often in hand to hand combat, while their families fled. Initially, the soldiers captured the camp, but Nez Perce warriors regrouped and drove the soldiers out of the camp. As the warriors pinned down Gibbon's troops, Nez Perce women, children and old people returned, took down the camp and moved out of harm's way. According to Ruby and Brown, the Nez Perce death toll was eighty-seven killed with thirty-seven warriors among the dead. This meant that the majority of Nez Perce dead were women and children. Among the dead warriors were Hahtalekin, his son, Pahka Pahtahank, Wahlitits, Rainbow and others. Both Joseph and Ollokot lost wives and many people lost their lodges and other property in the battle.⁶¹

As the warriors continued to pin down Gibbon's troops, Nez Perce women, children and elders escaped from the Big Hole basin on the night of August 10th. According to Trafzer, Looking Glass lost much of his power after the disaster at Big Hole. He noted that Lean Elk, a Nez Perce chief, assumed leadership and led the non-treaty bands away from the Big Hole basin, traveling south and east toward the Yellowstone country in northwestern Wyoming. As the Nez Perce rode toward the Yellowstone, additional army troops entered the pursuit of the non-treaty people. During the Big Hole Battle, General Howard continued his pursuit and eventually caught up with the Nez Perce at Camas Meadows in southwestern Montana, but was unable to overtake or defeat the Nez Perce. However, when the Nez Perce reached Crow country, the Crows rebuffed them because they did not want to anger the United States government and cause trouble for themselves.⁶²

At this point, with no support from other Indian communities and running out of options, the non-treaty bands decided to attempt an escape to Canada. The people met in council and by consensus agreed to go to Grandmother Country. Lean Elk led, but Looking Glass gave him so much trouble that he turned over leadership to Looking Glass. The year before, the Lakota had risen against the United States, defeating and wiping out Colonel Custer's command. After further confrontations with the United States Army, Sitting Bull escaped to Canada. Nez Perce leaders also hoped to reach the Lakota with Sitting Bull to escape the United States Army. As they moved north, Howard continued his pursuit and telegraphed Colonel Nelson Miles, the commander of the Tongue River Cantonment, of Nez Perce intentions to reach the Canadian border. Colonel Miles commanded 400 men and a large contingent of Cheyenne and Sioux scouts. As the Nez Perce moved toward the Canadian border, Looking Glass regained his leadership position. Knowing they had scouts behind them and that Howard trailed far behind the retreating Nez Perce, Looking Glass encouraged the people to slow down and rest before their final push to the Canadian border. The Nez Perce did not know that Miles would soon cut off their route to Canada. Suffering from wounds, illness, exhaustion, and hunger, they heeded Looking Glass's admonitions and moved slowly toward Canada.[63]

By September 29, 1877, the non-treaty Nez Perce bands decided to camp at Snake Creek, a tributary of the Milk River in northern Montana. Snake Creek was located between the Bearpaw Mountains and the Little Rocky Mountains. The Nez Perce camped only forty miles from the border and needed only one long day of travel to reach Canada and Sitting Bull's camp. As the Nez Perce rested for two days before the final leg of the journey, Colonel Miles' command closed in and Cheyenne and Sioux scouts discovered the Nez Perce camp. On September 30, 1877, Miles' force attacked the camp and caught the Nez Perce by surprise. Much of the fighting was close quarter combat with some women and children beating back soldiers with digging sticks and knives. Miles lost fifty-three killed and forty wounded, while the Nez Perce lost twenty-two killed on the first day of fighting. Among the Nez Perce killed on September 30 were Toohoolhoolzote, the leading *tooat* of the Nez Perce, and Ollokot, Joseph's brother.[64]

On October 1, 1877, Miles offered a truce and called for Joseph to come forward and discuss the situation. Nez Perce leaders conferred, some believing that Howard would hang them if they chose to parley, so they decided to send an interpreter, Tom Hill, to talk to Miles and to receive assurances that Joseph and those with him would not be harmed. Miles replied that Joseph would be safe and that they should meet halfway between the trenches of the United States Army and the Nez Perce position. At the meeting, Miles demanded that the Indians surrender unconditionally and give up their weapons. As the talks ended, Miles treacherously captured Joseph and confined him to the Army's camp. Yellow Wolf watched this from a distance and angrily remembered, "I saw Chief Joseph taken to the soldier camp a prisoner. The white flag was pulled down! The white flag was a lie!" In retaliation, the Nez Perce captured and held Lieutenant Lovell H. Jerome as prisoner until Miles and his soldiers released Joseph.[65]

On October 4, 1877, General Howard arrived on the scene, but, according to Trafzer, Howard did not engage in direct negotiations or command, allowing Colonel Miles to continue dealing with the Nez Perce. The next day, two treaty Nez Perce scouts, Meopkowit (Old George) and Jokais (Captain John), who had accompanied General Howard on the pursuit, rode into the Nez Perce camp and explained to the people present that Howard and

Miles wanted no more fighting.[66] Yellow Wolf reported that, through the Nez Perce scouts, both officers said, "We will have no more fighting." According to Trafzer and Scheuerman, this news allowed the Indians "an honorable way to end hostilities without surrendering." Trafzer and Scheuerman also asserted that many Nez Perce believed that they were agreeing to a conditional surrender that included a return to the Nez Perce Reservation and no punishment for warriors who fought in the war. In particular, the Nez Perce worried that they would be hanged as were Palouses who had fought Wright in 1858.[67]

In the evening of October 5, Joseph prepared to surrender to the United States Army (Figure 10). Joseph, along with other leaders, met General Howard and Colonel Miles between the two camps and offered his rifle as a symbol of surrender. Trafzer and Scheuerman noted that Joseph was sick and tired of fighting and wanted to surrender in order to avoid more death and misery. There is also some controversy about the famous "I will fight no more forever" speech attributed to Chief Joseph. Yellow Wolf, who witnessed the surrender, mentioned that the "Indians lifted their hands towards the sky, where the sun was then standing. This said: 'No more battles! No more war.'" According to Yellow Wolf, this was all he heard and saw of the surrender, and he does not mention the now famous speech by Chief Joseph.[68] Some Nez Perce and Palouse people refused to surrender and attempted to join Sitting Bull in Canada. Among them were White Bird and his band, Yellow Wolf, and others from Joseph's band. Some people reached Sitting Bull, but Looking Glass, who had led the Nez Perce through much of their flight, ironically, was shot by Nez Perce warriors, when he was mistaken for a Cheyenne scout working for Miles.[69]

Over four hundred Nez Perce and Palouse people surrendered on October 5, 1877 and the Army quickly sent them to Fort Keogh in present-day Wyoming. After a short stay at Fort Keogh, General William Tecumseh Sherman, commander of the United States Army, ordered the transfer of Nez Perce prisoners to Fort Leavenworth, Kansas, and then on to the Quapaw Agency in the northeastern corner of the Indian Territory (present-day Oklahoma). These movements and transfers directly violated the surrender terms negotiated by Nez Perce with Colonel Miles and General Howard at the Bearpaw Mountain battlefield. Joseph and the other Nez Perce believed that the Army would send them back to their homeland as soon as possible and did not anticipate the treatment they received at the hands of the United States Army. In particular, the Nez Perce suffered through much mistreatment and neglect at Fort Leavenworth and the Quapaw Agency, with many dying of exposure, starvation and malaria. After nearly a year and one-half

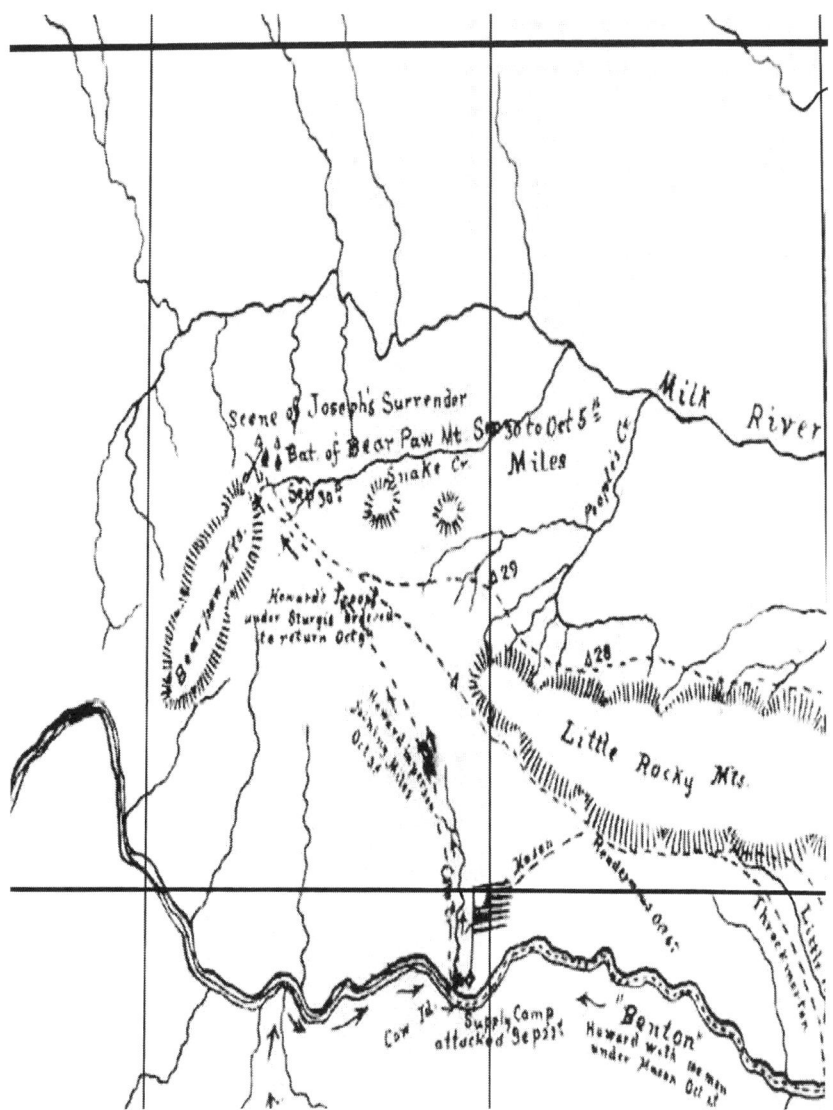

Figure 10 Bear Paw Battlefield. Department of Columbia, Maps of the Nez Perce Campaign. In U.S. House, 45th Congress, Second Session, Report of the Secretary of War, 1877. (H.Ex.Doc. 1, Pt. 2) Washington, Government Printing Office (Serial Set 1794). Courtesy of the United States Government Printing Office.

at Fort Leavenworth and the Quapaw Agency, the Bureau of Indian Affairs transferred the Nez Perce to the newly created Ponca Agency and settled them on a piece of land that Joseph and Husishusis Kute chose for their people. During this whole ordeal, many people, mainly women and children, were sick or dying. By the time of their return to Idaho in 1885, nearly half of the original four hundred had perished from various ailments ranging from malaria to malnutrition.[70] The conflict with Monster and the destructive inhalation of the Nez Perce led many Indian people to the same fate that Coyote observed in his own conflict with Monster. As Coyote traveled down the throat of Monster he thought, "Many people have been dying."[71] Non-treaty Nez Perce and Palouse people suffered the same fate as the *tewats* or the animal people, in their conflict with Monster, but just like in the Monster and Coyote narrative, people survived and remained alive and active in the belly of Monster.

MONSTER INHALED AND THE PEOPLE DISAPPEARED?

The defeat of the non-treaty Nez Perce communities and their imprisonment in *Eekish Pah* (the Hot Place) offered vast amounts of material for Anglo Americans in their quest to reorganize the historical landscape of the Pacific Northwest. At the outset of the war, Anglo Americans in the region feared for their lives, fortified their towns and organized militia forces to protect themselves from "savages." The Anglo-American hysteria that accompanied the outbreak of hostilities eventually faded away and new feelings, sometimes mixed with old fears and animosities, emerged in the wake of the non-treaty Nez Perce surrender. Though it took a while, many people in the Pacific Northwest would come to regard Chief Joseph, but only Chief Joseph, incorrectly as the "Red Napoleon," the greatest Indian general of all time. For many people living on the Columbia Plateau during the war and for those who settled in the region in the aftermath of "Joseph's War," the retreat of the non-treaty communities and Chief Joseph's surrender served as historical anchors for the new Anglo-American population of the Northwest, particularly those in the eastern portions of the Columbia Plateau and northeast Oregon. The war helped "secure" land for whites held previously by the Nez Perce and other Plateau tribes while eliminating the Indian "threat" to white settlement. Not only did the war settle the land question, but it also provided the necessary actors and events for the creation of a romantic epic with Joseph as the tragic noble savage, settlers as the victims of Indian "depredations," and the United States Army as the protector and savior of white "civilization" in the Pacific Northwest.

In the late nineteenth and early twentieth centuries, most, if not all, narration of these events, starting with the 1863 treaty through the surrender at Bearpaw, fell to Anglo Americans. Whether written by professional historians or by those writers interested in more popular versions, the narrative employed certain key elements that made the story more accessible to the Anglo-American public. Noble savages, heroic military men, frightened settlers, and focus on one "leader" of the Nez Perce were some of these common threads that made the story understandable and linked the experiences of the Nez Perce to other native peoples. For example, the United States Army fought many engagements against non-treaty people, and the stories created by Anglo Americans about these campaigns often focused on male Indian leaders with strong personalities like Sitting Bull, Crazy Horse, Cochise, Geronimo, Tecumseh, Pontiac and many others.[72] In essence, each of those Indian leaders was involved in conflicts that were portrayed in the same way as Joseph's conflict, creating a narrative that Anglo Americans wove about themselves for themselves. This story focused on the divine mission, Manifest Destiny, of Anglo Americans and the superiority of their culture *vis-à-vis* their Native American opponents. The story's appeal, as told by most Anglo Americans, lay in its romantic overtones and the tragic nature of the story. Each of the "Indian war stories" related native peoples resisting the "inevitable" onslaught of settlers and civilization, Indians filling the role of the noble but tragic "villain," and the United States Army and settlers taking on the mantle of heroes defending Anglo-American people, values and property. The story of native peoples was distilled into an account about one leader selected by Anglo Americans to serve as the tragic figure of the noble savage attempting to hold on to "primitive" ways of life and native land. For the Nez Perce, their story was condensed into a narrative about Chief Joseph and "his" tribe outwitting and outfighting the military, only to lose in the end, but capping the conflict with a monumental speech that whites could remember and recite. For many writers, the hostilities of 1877 became "Joseph's War" and Chief Joseph became the tragic romantic symbol of American history.

To discover the details of the story and how it was constructed by Anglo Americans, it is necessary to analyze a number of narratives created by different members of the Anglo-American community. Most of the narratives used in this analysis are from non-historians, like Presbyterian missionary to the Nez Perce Kate McBeth and the writers of *An Illustrated History of North Idaho*; but one particularly regional historian, C.J. Brosnan, crafted a narrative about the war which echoed many of the themes found in earlier non-professional writings. While investigating how these various Anglo-American authors wrote Nez Perce history, it is also important to answer the question of why they wrote the narrative as they did. What function(s) did these narratives serve in the Columbia Plateau, the Pacific Northwest, and America? For example, Chief Joseph and his story turn up in nearly every United States history textbook, particularly those composed for children. Stories as powerful as the ones told about Joseph and the non-treaty Nez Perce were not solely used to inform the public, but, most important, the narratives helped in the formation of a regional identity and national historical myth, a myth based on Nez Perce history but serving another master, Monster.

HOW DID MONSTER SWALLOW COYOTE?

The roots of the struggle between non-treaty Nez Perce communities and the United States government rest in the familiar story of intrusion and white pressure on reservations supposedly protected by the government and guaranteed in perpetuity by treaty. Allen Slickpoo, Sr., noted that the "Nez Perce War of 1877 resulted from many years of frustration, mistreatment, and broken promises."[73] The frustration, mistreatment and broken promises referred to by Slickpoo resonated in many other regions of the United States. Native peoples all over North America often experienced similar feelings in their dealings with the United States government and white settlers. Native Americans not only dealt with the realities of white pressure on their land and conflicting government policies, but they also confronted a myth created by Anglo Americans based on their previous experience with Native Americans. The first part of this myth was that of the "savage" versus "civilization," a comparison that relegated Native Americans to the realm of darkness, evil and ignorance while elevating Anglo Americans to the status of progressive "civilizers" and "God's servants" who knew how to tame the land and make it beneficial to mankind. The second part of the myth revolved around the circular argument mentioned above in the discussion of the Thief Treaty of 1863. This part of the myth reasoned that treaty making was an integral role of civilized man and the United States government, but rational people understood that such treaties were only temporary and required renegotiation when white pressure on "unused" Indian land reached a level that threatened armed conflict. Reservations were to be a purgatory for Indians, a temporary space where civilized man could corral and train up savages to be civilized. At that point reservations would no longer be needed and the land could be divided, through the allotment process, into individual parcels owned by Indian citizens.[74]

Echoes of the myth appeared in many Anglo-American written sources relating to the Nez Perce during the 1860s and 1870s. In this first part of the analysis of Anglo-American narratives about the Nez Perce, it is crucial to understand how Anglo Americans viewed the intrusion of whites onto the Nez Perce Reservation in the early 1860s, the treaty negotiations held in 1863, and the events leading up to the Nez Perce War of 1877. From articles in *Frank Leslie's Illustrated Newspaper* in 1877 to R. Ross Arnold's *Indian Wars of Idaho (1932)*, the narrative remained fairly consistent and formed the basis for stories about the war in 1877. Assumptions made by various Anglo-American authors about the 1863 treaty, the status of the Wallowa region, and the immediate causes of the war tell a great deal about how these stories provided a secure sense of possessing land previously owned by the Nez Perce and a feeling that the war against the non-treaty Nez Perce was justified.[75]

As the Nez Perce War of 1877 raged, *Frank Leslie's Illustrated Newspaper* provided reports and commentary on the conflict, seeking to provide reasons for the newest Indian "outbreak." Printed in New York, *Frank Leslie's Illustrated Newspaper* was distributed around the nation. The first article on the Nez Perce War, printed on July 28, 1877, sought to explain in cursory form the reasons for the war and it focused primarily on the treaty-making policies of the United States government (Figure 11). The initial foray into explaining the war completely failed to explain the exact course of events leading to the war. Leslie's writer compressed the treaty negotiations at Walla Walla in 1855 with the Thief Treaty of 1863 and confused Old Joseph for Young Joseph. Joseph, in this context, was characterized as a defiant Indian who refused the "white man's charity" and civilization. The writer suggested that Joseph taunted Lawyer, the Christian leader of the treaty Nez Perce faction and "friend" of the white man. According to the article, government policy and ineptitude were the main causes of the war, leaving the reader with the distinct feeling that the war could have been avoided if the government had acted decisively to move the non-treaty Nez Perce onto the reservation.[76]

While the mistakes of the earlier article could be attributed to a lack of information and informants, the September 1, 1877 issue contained an article specifically written to explain "the cause of trouble in Idaho." The tone of this article was much different from the July 28th piece. While still accusing the government of dishonesty and unfair treatment of the Nez Perce, this author clearly researched the situation and presented a much clearer explanation of the war. After decrying the government's dishonesty, the author laid out as the base for his argument a simple sentence that explained the

Figure 11 Frank Leslie's Illustrated Newspaper, Engravings of Eagle of the Light, Chief Joseph, and the Dreamer. October 27, 1877. Courtesy of Frank Leslie's Illustrated Newspaper.

government's Indian policy. According to the writer, "Since the earliest period of colonization in America it has been the unbroken rule to regard the Indians as the rightful owners of the territory they occupied and to make treaties with their separate tribes and nations as with so many independent political communities."[77] While recognizing Indian ownership of the land, the author implicitly stated the overriding principle of Indian policy in the United States, which relied on treaty making to abolish Indian title to the land. The purpose of this policy was to extinguish Indian title to the land, confine native peoples to reservations (the marginal land that was left), and open newly acquired territory to white settlement. For the writer, the root of the problem in Idaho lay in the inability of the government to live up to the bargain it made with the Nez Perce, which was to protect a portion of land the government guaranteed to them.

The article continued with a narrative cadence familiar from other works. As white settlers "located themselves on the Nez Perce's domain," the author asserted that a treaty was necessary and mentioned some of the difficulties of negotiating a treaty with the Nez Perce. For Anglo Americans, the decentralized nature of Plateau Indian political life meant that many different groups claimed ownership to tracts of land, with no single leader or group controlling the whole area. The article's author also noted that even when the government recognized one leader, like Lawyer, other Nez Perce groups often refused to recognize that leader or his right to speak on behalf of the entire tribe.[78]

The remainder of the article focused on the government's inability to find a solution to the Nez Perce treaty crises. The author pointed out that the government took too long to ratify the agreements and failed to pay annuities or protect reservation land. The discovery of gold in the early 1860s exacerbated the situation as whites moved onto the reservation and even built a town. According to the article, the government proposed new treaty negotiations and neglected to include the Wallowa area in the new reservation. While describing the distinction between treaty and non-treaty Nez Perce communities, the author noted that the new treaty was only made with "the more tractable portion of the tribe" and that the non-treaty communities mainly led by Joseph refused to acknowledge the validity of the 1863 treaty.[79]

The narrative framework of these articles concerning the Nez Perce War remained similar for many Anglo-American sources. Articles in *Frank Leslie's Illustrated Newspaper* offered evident tensions. While recognizing Nez Perce claims to the land, the articles assumed that some accommodation needed to be made for white settlement within the area. The war was a result of government incompetence, dishonesty and settler intrusions on Nez Perce land, but the articles clearly communicated the author's belief that decisive action by government officials could have prevented the war. The root of trouble in Idaho rested firmly on the inability of the government to clear up title of the land, allowing whites to encroach on Indian land, and then attempting to clear up the problem as tensions and conflict emerged. The authors of these narratives had no interest in recognizing Indian title to the land or their spiritual connections to the earth. This was outside of their own belief system and contrary to Anglo-American interests. For these authors, Indian religion was not an issue because such beliefs were not part of the national consciousness. Edmond Meany's *History of the State of Washington* also echoed the theme of Indian land title as he discussed the desire of settlers to have clear ownership of the land. A paradox was evident in these writings. How could a government official recognize Indians as the rightful owners of land while at the same time attempting to extinguish this title and confine them to a reservation? What maintained the balance in this paradox was the Anglo-American conquerors' belief in their own cultural superiority and the assumption that it was their destiny, assigned by God, to lay claim to all land from the Atlantic to the Pacific Ocean. It was easy for them to recognize Indian land rights when they also believed that Indians would eventually disappear because "superior" Anglo-American culture supplanted the "inferior" cultures of Native Americans. While the newspaper recognized the wrongs and injustices faced by the non-treaty Nez Perce, the "real" wrong or problem presented was that the United States government allowed the situation to degenerate into bloodshed. This story was "being told in letters of blood by the daily newspapers," as the result of government inaction and ineptitude.[80]

The writers of *Frank Leslie's Illustrated Newspaper* fashioned explanations for the Nez Perce War that continued into the twentieth century. These newspaper articles were themselves echoes of previous decades' encounters or conflicts with Native Americans, and expressed the development of narrative cues and devices familiar to many Anglo Americans. As time wore on, references to the Nez Perce War and its causes followed similar formats, but the story often emerged in a much more condensed form. For example, General Howard wrote about Chief Joseph in 1908 and, just as did Frank Leslie's writers, condensed nearly seventeen years of history into two paragraphs. Howard mentioned the treaty of 1855 and the large tract of land, the size of New York, secured by the Nez Perce, but then noted "white people began to see that this was a good place to live in, and they asked Uncle Sam to give them some of it." As narrated by Howard, "Most of the Indians agreed to sell part of their "big" reservation and live on a part called the Lapwai lands, or reservation." After the treaty was "arranged," the government of the United States discovered that "several bands of Nez Perces lived outside of this smaller reservation." This is an amazing statement since the non-treaty people present at the 1863 treaty negotiations clearly stated their grievances and resistance to the 1863 treaty, which was in violation of the 1855 treaty, and left no doubt in most minds that they would not agree to sell their land to the government. Howard's experience with the Nez Perce during the 1870s certainly argued against the assumption that all Nez Perce agreed to the provisions of the 1863 treaty, but his simplification could also be based on the magazine's need to make the narrative understandable to a wider audience of Anglo Americans.[81]

The need to reach a wider audience may have held great appeal to Howard, since during the war he took quite a beating in the national press. After the brief introduction of the Nez Perce situation, Howard moved into a detailed discussion of the Lapwai Council of April 1877. Most of the narrative focused on his "reasoned" approach to the hostility he met at the council. It is quite obvious from this discussion that Howard had received his orders and was not at the council to negotiate, but to dictate terms. He arrived in Lapwai to inform non-treaty people that they were to move onto the reservation. They had no other choice. In a twist of the narrative, Howard insinuated that Indian resistance arose from the hatred of Indians like Toohoolhoolzote and Husis Husis Kute who argued against Christian values, not from his "showing the rifle" as Yellow Wolf had contended. In the end, Howard absolved himself and all Anglo Americans of guilt in their dealings with the non-treaty Nez Perce while he extolled the military virtues of Joseph. Howard did this by focusing on Toohoolhoolzote's anger and arguments and by showing how Joseph and the non-treaty communities broke their agreement to settle on the reservation. He focused on the Nez Perce "hostiles" who went "on the war-path."[82]

One of the most telling parts of Howard's narrative described the survey of lands set aside on the Nez Perce Reservation for non-treaty people. During the ride, Joseph asked Howard what the Nez Perce could expect from the United States if the non-treaty people removed to the reservation: "what will you give us – schools, teachers, houses, churches and gardens?" To this Howard replied, "yes." Then Joseph reiterated that non-treaty people did not want these things, in essence restating that they did not want any part of Anglo-American culture, values or institutions. Joseph based his refusal on his religion and maintained that his people still wanted to live as they had previously. After Joseph's reply, General Howard simply stated,

"Yours is a strange answer." This simple statement spoke volumes about the huge cultural gulf between non-treaty people and the Anglo Americans. Howard could not have possibly understood why non-treaty Nez Perce people refused what he believed to be a crucial element of civilized living with churches, formal education, and permanent home sites. As Bruce J. Dinges stated in the introduction to *Famous Indian Chiefs I Have Known*, Howard, as well as his contemporaries, could not conceive of "anything in Native American culture worth saving." While they may have recognized the basic humanity of the Nez Perce and even agreed that they held title to the land they occupied, throughout the late nineteenth and early twentieth centuries Anglo Americans firmly believed that Indian cultures would disappear, assimilating into Anglo-American society.[83]

While *Frank Leslie's Illustrated Newspaper* and Howard's *Famous Indian Chiefs I Have Known* addressed a broader, national audience, the next two works focused specifically on events and people in northern Idaho. *An Illustrated History of North Idaho* and Kate McBeth's *The Nez Perces Since Lewis and Clark* framed their narratives differently, but shared many of the same cues as those mentioned in Leslie and Howard accounts. Of all the narratives, *An Illustrated History of North Idaho* (1903) offered the most extensive and the most vehemently anti-Indian perspective. The authors of this volume began the story of the war with an introduction explaining the necessity and inevitability of conflict with Native Americans. They stressed that the certain destruction of Indians at the hands of the "Anglo-Saxon" race was inevitable. Telling and retelling the myth of Anglo-American cultural superiority helped readers of the time understand why the war started and why it ended the way it did. For example, the authors stated:

> When the indomitable Anglo-Saxon race began following the course of destiny westward, the doom of the thriftless aboriginal peoples was sealed. The time had arrived in the progress of the world when the dusky, nomadic savage had become a cumberer of the soil.[84]

For these authors, the Nez Perce and all Native Americans "must lay aside at once his ancestral habits and adopt those of another and superior race or he must perish and perish miserably." The roots of the conflict lay in the meta-narrative of "savagery" versus "civilization." The particulars of the story were not as important as the result, which was, according to these authors, the supposed victory of the "Anglo-Saxon" race.[85]

The authors of *An Illustrated History of North Idaho* continued their analysis of the war by offering similar condemnations of the federal government. According to them, the war resulted from the "incapacity of our government officials to understand Indian character and deal with it in a sensible business like manner."[86] Following the narrative cues of *Frank Leslie's Illustrated Newspaper*, the *Illustrated History of North Idaho* authors explained the problems generated by the government during the treaty making councils and subsequent intrusions by white settlers on Nez Perce land. Recognizing the justice of non-treaty Indian claims to their land, these authors asserted that it was inconceivable for the federal government to require settlers to "relinquish their prospects of future gain, pull up stakes and set out again in search of the natural means of winning a livelihood, all for the sake of a few shiftless, nomadic Indians." It seems that Indians, Anglo-American settlers, and the United States government were unable to resist or change the "inevitable" course of history and the "victory" of the "superior Anglo-Saxon" race. The failure of the government lay in its inability to understand the course of history and to develop a strategy to gain Indian land and assimilate Indian cultures without armed conflict.[87]

In contrast to *An Illustrated History of North Idaho*'s detailed and exhaustive discussion of events related to the causes of the war, Kate McBeth's *The Nez Perces Since Lewis and Clark* took a different approach. McBeth noted that the Nez Perce Treaty of 1855 "gave" the Nez Perce "a great domain," but soon afterward white settlers, especially miners, moved onto land previously held by the Nez Perce. The necessity of a new treaty was self-evident to Kate McBeth as she confidently stated, "A new treaty must be made." Unlike other narratives discussed so far, McBeth only mentioned that Joseph did not sign the treaty of 1863 and made no comment on Indian claims of land ownership. While this may seem outside the narrative loop shared by the other works, McBeth probably failed to mention the government because she was more interested in narrating the differences between the non-treaty and treaty bands of the Nez Perce.[88]

The remarkable stability of Anglo-American narrative frameworks continued into the 1920s and 1930s. By 1926, historian C.J. Brosnan crafted a regional history focusing on the state of Idaho. As a professor at the University of Idaho located in Moscow, Idaho, Brosnan lived just north of the Nez Perce Reservation and many of the sites of the Nez Perce War. While Brosnan lacked the rabidly racial comments of *An Illustrated History of North Idaho* authors, he continued in the same narrative vein as his predecessors and outlined the treaty making process, the incursion of white settlers and the problem of the Wallowa. Brosnan did not directly blame the government for the war, but, by focusing on the treaty councils, he laid the groundwork for the reader to conclude that the actions of the United States government contributed greatly to the cause of the war. For Brosnan, the immediate cause of the war rested in the government's decision to force non-treaty Nez Perce onto the Nez Perce Reservation near Lapwai.[89]

In 1932, R. Ross Arnold also narrated the events leading up to the war in his book, *Indian Wars of Idaho*. Arnold was not a professional historian, and his text is replete with narrative flourishes and flowery language. His narrative turned first to the reasons for the war. Arnold followed the Anglo-American narrative framework, tracing the intrusion of whites into Nez Perce territory after 1860 and discussing non-treaty resistance to the 1863 treaty. From this starting point, Arnold continued with a discussion of the attempt in 1877 to remove the non-treaty bands to the Nez Perce Reservation. Arnold recognized the justice of non-treaty arguments, but he offered a new twist to the narrative framework by arguing that General Howard could do nothing but obey the orders of the United States government. However, this was merely a twist on the narrative cue of inevitable conflict and defeat of Native Americans offered by previous authors.[90]

From the brief discussion of Anglo-American texts from 1877 to 1932, three common themes emerged to dominate the narration of the events leading up to the 1877 war. One of the most important themes focused on the inability of the United States government to resolve the difficulties of non-treaty bands in the Pacific Northwest. Government ineptitude and inaction were a safe way to assign blame while still adhering to a belief in the moral rectitude of Anglo-American actions in the Pacific Northwest. Recognizing the legitimate claims of the non-treaty Nez Perce was the second theme and it reinforced the "moral" strength of the Anglo-American narrative. The card that trumped the recognition of Nez Perce ownership of the land was Manifest Destiny. Only the inevitable Anglo-American "conquest" of North America provided sufficient justification for neglecting the legitimate claims of Native Americans. The third theme of white infringement on Nez Perce land was also rooted in the belief of Manifest Destiny. While they recognized it as wrong, many of the authors described the trespasses with an air of inevitability. These three themes all share one thing in common: they all reduce the causes of strife (and deaths) between Anglo Americans and Nez Perce to forces that defy the ability of individuals or groups to interfere or change the course of these events. Under these terms, Indians were doomed to lose, while Anglo Americans had to win. The government, an institution constructed not of individuals but of faceless bureaucrats, created the circumstances leading to war, death and removal.

As the narrative shifted from the events and causes leading to the war to a narrative of the war itself, the structure of Anglo-American narratives aligned to a greater degree. The "facts" of the war, as told by Anglo Americans, remained consistent because they used similar sources. Most of the authors relied on the testimony of United States military personnel, on government documents, and on the statements of "pioneer" settlers to create their narratives while completely silencing Nez Perce sources except for Chief Joseph.[91] This penchant for using Anglo-American sources began with *Frank Leslie's Illustrated Newspaper*, one of the first narratives created in 1877 and continued in R. Ross Arnold's *Indian Wars of Idaho*. Such exclusive use of Anglo-American sources evoked fatalism in all of the narratives produced about the Nez Perce, particularly in *An Illustrated History of North Idaho*. This fatalism stemmed from beliefs in the "inevitable" demise of Indians and the triumph of Anglo Americans. Non-natives could sympathize with those who were "doomed" since their fate was already sealed. Anglo Americans recognized the injustices committed by the government and white settlers, but, in the end, this sympathy did not matter because the "inexorable forces" of history and progress had already determined the fate of the Nez Perce. Indian peoples were the doomed "savages" who were wronged by the United States government but still fought a hopeless struggle against superior, enlightened forces of "civilization." This is the classic example of a tragedy meant to explain the progressive process of history and the inevitable triumph of civilized Anglo Americans over their primitive foes.[92]

Some Anglo-American narratives mentioned that the Nez Perce trained for war and had already decided to fight before the Salmon River raids, but this was not the case. Whether Anglo-American authors believed that the Nez Perce wanted war from the beginning or if they narrated that events overtook most of non-treaty communities, the next step in the story was shared by nearly all of the narratives. One of the most common themes recurrent in Anglo-American imagination about Native Americans was the image of the bloodthirsty "savage." Narratives about the Nez Perce War also fell into this theme and described the "depredations" committed by Indians along the Salmon River, while silencing the deeds of Larry Ott and other ruthless white people. In particular, *An Illustrated History of North Idaho* spent a great deal of space describing the various "outrages" of Nez Perce at the beginning of the war. For Anglo Americans, this phase of the war was self-evident. Without depredations, the war would have been more ambiguous and less "moral" in the eyes of Anglo Americans. For the authors of *An Illustrated History of North Idaho*, it was extremely important to support claims of depredations in order to justify Anglo-American reactions. For example, the authors noted that stories "concerning the outrages during the earliest days of the Nez Perces Indian war have been verified by exhaustive investigation into all printed accounts that could be secured, and by interviews with very many of those living in the storm center at the time."[93] The previous statement clearly noted that Nez Perce accounts of the early days of the war were not gathered, studied or even required for a complete and exhaustive account of the "depredations." Later narratives produced by Kate McBeth, C.J. Brosnan and R. Ross Arnold failed to even mention specific accusations of depredations, but they noted that "some Indians from the non-treaty band began a horrible series of murders and outrages on men, women, and children in the lower Salmon River country."[94] R. Ross Arnold asserted that these acts remained in the memories of whites in the Salmon River area and that even in 1932 "people of this section of Idaho have never forgiven Joseph and his band." These two sources show that by the 1920s and 1930s, and perhaps earlier, Anglo Americans needed no accurate details to understand the code words of "outrages" and "depredations" when used in the context of conflict with Native Americans.[95]

Another important theme of Anglo-American narratives of the war revolved around the number of warriors associated with the non-treaty bands participating in the war. While *Frank Leslie's Illustrated Newspaper* does not mention the number of Nez Perce warriors, Colonel Miles, in a letter to the Assistant Adjutant General, Division of the Pacific in 1885, estimated the number of warriors at 400 strong out of 1,000 members of the non-treaty bands. This number was adjusted down to around 300 in *An Illustrated History of North Idaho*, Brosnan's *History of the State of Idaho*, and Arnold's *Indian Wars of Idaho*. All of the above numbers contrasted with those given by Nez Perce warrior and participant Yellow Wolf who estimated that the Nez Perce people perhaps mustered 120 men of fighting age at the beginning of the war, of which only less than fifty actually participated in the fighting. The number of warriors was important to the narrative since a small group of men holding off larger numbers of United States Army personnel did not paint a favorable picture of Anglo-American military prowess. Also humiliating was the notion that men, women, children and old people outsmarted and outran the United States Army for over a thousand miles. Not only were the numbers skewed in favor of larger force of Nez Perce warriors, but the narrative also required the creation of a "general," a "Red Napoleon" in Joseph. Chief Joseph's role helped place the narrative into the heroic struggle of a brilliant Indian general against the United States Army, one that out-maneuvered and out-fought a professional army.[96]

While the number of warriors was hard to determine, the narratives clearly identified the reason for Nez Perce successes during the war, in the person of Chief Joseph. The best example of this trend existed in the narrative produced by C.J. Brosnan who outlined the causes for the war and discussed briefly the Battles of Whitebird Canyon and Clearwater. Brosnan's bold section titles signaled the topic for the reader, and after the discussion of the battles, he switched emphasis and narrated "Joseph's Retreat over the Lo Lo Trail," "Joseph's Long Flight from the Lo Lo Valley to Bear Paw Mountains," "Chief Joseph's Surrender," "Joseph's Speech at the Surrender," "Chief Joseph's Genius" and "the Last Days of Chief Joseph."[97] In essence, the narrative became a story about Chief Joseph, condensing the actions of many non-treaty Nez Perce people into the figure of one man. This tendency was evident in the other narratives as well. For example, the authors of *An Illustrated History of North Idaho* mentioned the fame of Joseph at the end of the chapter on the war, but the authors preferred to narrate the story using the phrase "wily savages" instead of using Joseph's name for every Indian action. Kate McBeth referred to the war as "Joseph's War," and General Howard condensed the whole story into a short chapter about Chief Joseph. Howard also summed up the sentiment for Joseph in the final paragraph of his essay on the Chief. He noted that "Twenty-seven years later I met Chief Joseph, the greatest Indian warrior I ever fought with, at the Carlisle Indian School, and there he made a speech: 'For a long time,' he said, 'I did want to kill General Howard, but now I am glad to meet him and we are friends!'" For Howard, Joseph filled the twin roles of his greatest Indian adversary and of his friend, a suitable ending of the narrative for Anglo Americans and an appropriate mention of the Joseph myth, a myth discussed later in this work.[98]

The last major common theme of Anglo-American narratives about the war focused on the tragic surrender scene and the noble speech attributed to Joseph. Most narratives described in detail the last battle at the Bearpaw Mountains and stressed the role of Colonel Miles during the last days of the pursuit. *Frank Leslie's Illustrated Newspaper* offered a detailed description of the battle and surrender, providing a lithograph of scenes from the Bearpaw Battlefield and Joseph's surrender (Figure 12).[99] From 1877 onward, Anglo-American narratives and visual imagery memorialized Joseph, with the motion of him handing his rifle to Colonel Miles and addressing his speech to Howard and Miles. C.J. Brosnan memorialized the surrender imagery and accompanying speech in his characterization of the speech as "a masterpiece of pathetic and picturesque oratory." Brosnan then quoted the entire speech, but he did not mention that this was a translation or that no

Figure 12 Frank Leslie's Illustrated Newspaper, November 3, 1877. Illustrations of various scenes from the Nez Perce War of 1877. Courtesy of Frank Leslie's Illustrated Newspaper.

one except the translator truly understood Joseph's words. The surrender speech itself is today a much-debated part of the Nez Perce War. As Trafzer and Scheuerman noted there is no documentary evidence for the speech. However, this lack of evidence for the speech has not stopped Anglo Americans from repeating the speech at every opportunity.[100]

All of the Anglo-American sources presented in this chapter used events from 1860 onward as the foreground for the war. According to these narratives, the conflict between the non-treaty Nez Perce and the United States was "inevitable." The climax of the narrative was the war. Everything pointed to it and all actions somehow contributed to the outbreak of hostilities. In essence then, whether an author sympathized with the non-treaty Nez Perce or not, the narrative still followed the same framework of moving toward the inevitable conflict between Native American and Anglo-American: good versus evil, progressive versus savage and civilized versus barbarian. In this traditional way of telling a story in American history, just as audiences of oral narratives awaited certain cues in stories, so too did Anglo Americans respond to anticipated cues in the narrative like heroes, villains, and noble savages that focused on the presumed nature of Native Americans and the "progressive" and inevitable forces of "civilization" and history. The narrative of the Nez Perce War was intelligible because it fit into a narrative framework that required conflict between two diverse cultures that inevitably opposed each other. The narratives not only discussed the familiar territory of Indian/White conflict, but they also described how the war secured Idaho and the Pacific Northwest for the United States, fulfilling the Manifest Destiny of the United States. As the authors concluded the discussion of the Nez Perce War, the narratives switched from Indian wars to the creation and establishment of Anglo-American institutions and economic life in the Pacific Northwest, the most significant aspect of American history for the dominant society.[101]

For both treaty and non-treaty Nez Perce, non-native writers made the war and its conclusion a vehicle for the total "silencing" of Native American history. The "real" history belonged to Anglo-American historians and their narratives. White historians needed Indian actors in the stories, but once Native Americans served their purpose either as examples of "savagery" or of nobility, like Joseph, their part in the story ended. For Edmond Meany, a regional historian interested in Washington State history, Indians departed the narrative at an earlier date, around 1858-59, once the so-called Yakama War ended. For him, Native Americans had been subdued and placed on the reservation, ready for the inexorable forces of civilization and assimilation to enfold them into Anglo-American society and culture. C.J. Brosnan's narrative, a history focusing on the state of Idaho, kept Indian participants around longer, but only because Idaho's Indian wars started later than those in Washington state. Both men silenced Indian history after whites defeated and corralled the Indians.[102]

The silencing of Native Americans not only came in the form of cutting them out of narratives, but also from Anglo-American conscious efforts to not include their voices as part of the historical record. As Michel Rolph-Trouillot pointed out in his book, *Silencing the Past*, silences can occur in historical production in moments of fact creation or the making of sources and in the moment of fact assembly, or the making of archives. *An Illustrated History of North Idaho* quite plainly stated that the Nez Perce were not consulted in the moments of fact creation or fact assembly. White writers privileged printed sources from the United States government, newspapers, and letters from participants and the oral testimony of white inhabitants of the region at the moment of fact creation, fact assembly and dissemination like university teaching and publishing.[103] While non-native writers did not consult Nez Perce people or use their voices in their narratives, Yellow Wolf, Frank Oliver, Allen Slickpoo, Sr., Wotolen and other Nez Perce recognized the important role Indians had played in the creation of narratives about the Pacific Northwest. Nez Perce people clearly understood their role in the saga of the Pacific Northwest. They recognized that Anglo Americans had used Nez Perce people as instruments to create white identity and give Anglo Americans in the region a story to tell about how they came to live and occupy the land. They had told these stories to please themselves at the expense of historical accuracy, objectivity and sound scholarship

Monster had swallowed Coyote and all the people. For Monster, their silencing was complete. They now resided inside of Monster and he would digest them. Monster, in this case Anglo Americans and their systems, physically "swallowed" the Nez Perce and silenced them. In the moments of fact creation, fact assembly, the creation of narratives about themselves and their role in Pacific Northwest history, Anglo Americans imparted significance to their own actions and to the parts they played in the creation of an Anglo-American Pacific Northwest. For Anglo Americans, the silencing of the Nez Perce was complete because they were no longer needed for the progression of the narrative nor were their voices needed to confirm or deny narrative versions created by Anglo Americans. In the late nineteenth and early twentieth centuries, these narratives took on a finality that Anglo Americans hoped would end in the demise of Indian cultures and the assimilation of Native Americans into Anglo-American culture. The only problem was that Coyote was not through, not yet. Coyote, the creator of order and chaos, still lived within Nez Perce communities, indeed, in the world. He would not be denied. Coyote did not enter the maw of Monster unprepared, and he was not willing to accept his silencing or that of the people. As in the ancient story, Coyote would cause calamity for Monster, eventually succeeding in freeing himself and the people from the bowels of the beast. Coyote's creative power and that of his people would not end in a linear conclusion, but continued the circle that had always characterized the Numipu.

Chapter Six
The Consuming Silence: The Nez Perce in the Stomach of Monster

> Presently Coyote arrived at the heart and he cut off slabs of fat and threw them to the people. "Imagine you being hungry under such conditions – grease you mouths with this." And now Coyote started a fire with his flint, and shortly smoke drifted up through the monster's nose, ears, eyes, and anus. Now the monster said, "Oh you Coyote, that's why I was afraid of you. Oh you Coyote, let me cast you out."
>
> There was his fire still burning near the heart and now the monster began to writhe in pain and Coyote began cutting away on the heart, whereupon very shortly he broke the stone knife. Immediately he took another and in a short time this one also broke and Coyote said to all the people, "Gather up all the bones and carry them to the eyes, ears, mouth, and anus; pile them up and when he falls dead kick all the bones outside." Then again with another knife he began cutting away at the heart. The third knife broke and the fourth, leaving only one more. He told the people, "All right, get yourselves ready because as soon as he falls dead each one will go out of the opening most convenient. Take the old women and old men close to the openings so that they may get out easily." Now the heart hung by only a very small piece of muscle and Coyote was cutting away on it with his last stone knife. The monster's heart was still barely hanging when his last knife broke, whereupon Coyote threw himself on the heart and hung on just barely tearing it loose with his hands. In his death convulsions the monster opened all the openings of his body and now the people kicked the bones outside and went on out. Coyote, too, went on out.[1]

As Anglo Americans told and retold the story of how they "conquered" the Pacific Northwest, treaty and non-treaty Nez Perce people confronted the systematic silencing of their part in the story of Manifest Destiny and the creation of an Anglo-American state in North America. Through the confinement of treaty Nez Perce to the reservation and the pursuit, capture and exile of non-treaty people, Anglo Americans wrested control of the physical environment of the Pacific Northwest as well as control over the creation of the story about the history of the region. This silence, the muting of Nez Perce voices, resulted from a nearly total absence of Numipu voices. As the ancient story of Coyote and Monster related, Coyote and the people lived within the bowels of Monster, and the world did not hear their voices or see their actions. It is important to note that this silencing began earlier for some portions of the Nez Perce tribe. For example, once the United States government successfully confined the treaty Nez Perce on their reservation, few of the narratives described earlier in this work mentioned their involvement in the Nez Perce War. Whether acting as scouts for the United States Army or safely isolated on the reservation, the treaty Nez Perce were no longer needed in the structure of many Anglo-American narratives. Treaty Nez Perce failed to appear in these narratives because those Nez Perce people, in many Anglo-American eyes, had started their journey on the path of assimilation into white culture. The apparent success of attempts to convert the treaty Nez Perce to Christianity and to make them into farmers and contributing members of American society led them out of Anglo-American historical frameworks and into the "oblivion" that most whites believed was the destiny of Native Americans in the United States. In essence, Monster had digested these people and incorporated them into his body.

After the capture of most non-treaty people in 1877, the bulk of those people sent into exile in Oklahoma also disappeared since Anglo Americans condensed Nez Perce voices into a single voice and visage, that of Chief Joseph, their Red Napoleon, and their tragic hero of the Nez Perce War and future friend. The death of a large number of people in Eekish Pah, the hot place, aided in the silencing of most non-treaty Nez Perce. Whether dying in Eekish Pah or moving toward "civilization" on the reservation, Anglo Americans saw the situation of the Nez Perce as the fulfillment of Manifest Destiny and confirmation of their own cultural and racial superiority. The ultimate indication of Anglo-American superiority lay in vanquishing a foe as virtuous, honorable, and intelligent as Chief Joseph. The creation of the Joseph myth distilled the experience of non-treaty people into the life of one man who served as a mirror for Anglo Americans, a mirror that reflected the glory and superiority of Anglo America culture over the savage and that reinforced beliefs that the United States rested under divine sanction and blessing.

As Anglo Americans fashioned Chief Joseph into the representative of the noble savage, treaty and non-treaty Nez Perce, including Chief Joseph, attempted to find their own path in the new world of Monster. While it may have been comforting for Anglo Americans to believe that Nez Perce people were on the road to assimilation or were militarily defeated, the narrative silencing of the Nez Perce merely masked the often complex and contradictory relationships between the Nez Perce people, the United States government and Anglo Americans near the reservation. Treaty and non-treaty people sought to exercise power over their own circumstances and create their own community structures while dealing with institutions like the Bureau of Indian Affairs, missionary and church organizations, and local government authorities. Just as Coyote remained active in the belly of Monster, so too did treaty and non-treaty Nez Perce remain active and vocal as they attempted to find their own way in the face of Anglo-American assertions that their culture was moribund and doomed to disappear.

EEKISH PAH – THE HOT PLACE

After the surrender of the non-treaty Nez Perce, the United States Army considered them prisoners of war and transported them to Fort Leavenworth late in 1877. About four hundred non-treaty people remained at Fort Leavenworth until July 1878, when they were transferred to the Quapaw Agency in the Indian Territory. During their stay at Fort Leavenworth, nearly every person in the group of prisoners became sick with malaria and other maladies and twenty-one of them died. Sickness and death followed the Nez Perce to the Quapaw Agency where a further forty-seven people died in the first two months. The non-treaty Nez Perce and Palouse remained at the Quapaw Agency for a year until the Office of Indian Affairs transferred them to the Ponca Agency in hope of permanently settling the group on land near the agency. However, permanent settlement in the Indian Territory was the furthest thing from the minds of Chief Joseph, Chief Yellow Bull, Husis Husis Kute and most of the non-treaty Nez Perce. Joseph continued to hope that he and all the non-treaty people would be sent back to Idaho and perhaps even to the Wallowa, as promised by Colonel Miles and General Howard at the Bear Paw surrender.[2]

During their stay at the Ponca Agency, Chiefs Joseph and Yellow Bull traveled to Washington, D.C., in January 1879, to persuade the United States government to allow the return of non-treaty Nez Perce and Palouse to the Pacific Northwest. While they visited many politicians and dignitaries, the government remained adamant in its denial of their request. Fearing the reaction of the white population in the Pacific Northwest, particularly in the Wallowa region of Oregon and Idaho, and focusing on the specter of another Indian war, the government believed that the Indian Territory was the best place for non-treaty people. The fear of war voiced by politicians in Washington, D.C., seemed a bit overblown since the majority of survivors of the Nez Perce War were women and children. Undaunted by the refusal of the United States government, Joseph returned to Washington, D.C., in March 1879 to once again seek the repatriation of non-treaty people to the Pacific Northwest. Just as on his first trip, Anglo Americans received Joseph with great fanfare, allowed him to speak with politicians, and even granted him an interview with the *North American Review*. Despite his attempts to appeal to Anglo-American culture through language and imagery, Joseph failed to persuade the government to allow the return of non-treaty people. The reception of Joseph and the rebuff of his requests illustrate the emergence of the Joseph myth and the silencing of non-treaty people. As early as 1879, the American public could receive Joseph because of his status as a tragic hero, the defeated but glorious foe. In essence, while celebrating Joseph, Anglo Americans celebrated themselves, their achievements, and divine destiny. At the same time, Anglo Americans could decline Joseph's repeated requests to return to the Pacific Northwest since the fate of those confined to reservations, whether in Idaho or the Indian Territory, was already decided. This fate was the future of all Native Americans, except those like Chief Joseph who were raised into the pantheon of "great" chiefs, to be assimilated into American culture or to disappear, mainly through death.[3]

During their stay at the Ponca Agency, many Nez Perce attempted to make the best of the situation. A few Nez Perce from Idaho traveled to the Indian Territory to assist the exiles. Educated in white Christian schools, Archie Lawyer, Mark Williams and James Reuben taught and preached to a portion of the exiles under the leadership of Chief Yellow Bull. This group moved away from the main encampment and attempted to farm, and to raise stock to make a living while in exile. Unfortunately for the Nez Perce, the government again failed to provide the needed monetary and material support to make farming, raising stock or even planting gardens successful. Allen Slickpoo, Sr. noted that at the best of times farming was a precarious activity in much of the western United States, and the lack of help from the government made a difficult situation even worse. Not only suffering from a lack of materials and funds, the Nez Perce were also affected by their old nemesis in the form of white encroachment on their assigned portion of the Ponca Agency. In particular, white ranchers allowed their stock to stray into Indian Territory and these animals destroyed crops, fences and other improvements made by the Nez Perce. The property issue was never really resolved. The Nez Perce leased some land to white ranchers and received compensation, but encroachments continued throughout their stay at the Ponca Agency.

While attempting to make a living in Eekish Pah, some members of the exiled community took advantage of the religious and educational instruction of James Reuben and Archie Lawyer, Christian Nez Perce from Idaho. These men voluntarily came to the Ponca Agency to help the exiles. They established a school and began Christian religious instruction. According to Allen Slickpoo, Sr., Archie Lawyer conducted services close to the camp of Husis Husis Kute, a Palouse *tooat*, replicating Presbyterian services that Lawyer knew from life on the Nez Perce Reservation in Idaho. By 1882, James Reuben instructed many children of the exiles in a new frame schoolhouse. Some of the students from this school attended boarding schools in the Indian Territory. J. Stanley Clark, in his 1945 article on the exiles, identified the group attending school as those who had managed to escape the influence of "medicine men" like Husis Husis Kute, and noted that white visitors and government officials viewed this group with approval in their moves toward "civilization." Clark fell into the same narrative structure of earlier authors by frequently mentioning the progress of those who removed themselves from the influence of "medicine men" and often tied unfortunate circumstances or the suffering experienced by the "non-progressive" group of exiles to their continued devotion to *tooats* and the Washani religion. For example, Clark noted, "Chief Joseph unfortunately remained under the control of the medicine men and spent much of this time railing against his fate while clinging still to the faint hope of returning to Oregon or Idaho." Once again, Clark lamented the fact that progress was hindered by the Indians' refusal to give up the "old" ways and "cling" stubbornly to their religious faith.[4]

While the exiles attempted to survive in Eekish Pah and to make a life far away from their homes, James Reuben, members of the Indian Rights Association, some members of Congress, and other reformers agitated for the return of the Nez Perce exiles to the Pacific Northwest. In particular, Reuben hoped to bring a group of orphans and widows back to Idaho, but for several years the government rebuffed his requests. The position changed in 1883, and the government gave James Reuben permission to return thirty-three women and children to the Nez Perce Reservation in Idaho. However, due to government negligence, this group of women and children had to raise their own money for their return to Idaho. Shortly after the return of this group, the publicity surrounding the condition of the non-treaty Nez Perce influenced Congress in 1884 to pass a law allowing the Secretary of Interior to decide the fate of the exiles.[5]

The increased publicity and the enactment of the law empowering the Secretary of Interior to decide the fate of the exiles did not mean immediate repatriation to Idaho. In the Department of the Interior and the Office of Indian Affairs, government officials still worried about the reaction of whites in Idaho, Washington, and Oregon if they decided to return the exiles. Some of the exiles, particularly Joseph, were under indictment in Idaho and the government feared that conflict might arise from Joseph's return to Idaho. Indian Commissioner Atkins sent Dr. W.H. Faulkner to arrange the transfer of the exiles and eventually Secretary of the Interior Lamar, despite his fears of outbreaks of violence, approved the relocation plans developed by Faulkner. To avoid the problems of returning Joseph and those under indictment to Idaho, Faulkner negotiated a compromise that divided the group, some under Husis Husis Kute returning to Lapwai, Idaho and the remainder under the leadership of Joseph and Yellow Bull traveling to Colville, Washington. The United States government did not tell the people about this division until they arrived at Walula Junction on the Columbia River.[6]

As the group waited to embark on the trip, Joseph, Yellow Bull, Yellow Bear and Husis Husis Kute surrendered the deed to 90,000 acres of land in Indian Territory to the government. In exchange they were to receive financial support to help them become reestablished on the Nez Perce and Colville Reservations. The United States passed an act on March 3, 1885 that included $18,000 of reimbursement for the exiled Nez Perce. The train trip from the Indian Territory to the Northwest took seven days, and the Nez Perce exiles arrived in Wallula, Washington, in May 1885. At this point, the government agents divided the Nez Perce people into two groups. Agent Monteith took charge of 118 people led by Husis Husis Kute returning to Lapwai, Idaho, and the remaining 150 people, including Joseph and most of his family, continued on to the Colville Reservation. Allen Slickpoo, Sr. noted that the exiles returning to Lapwai, Idaho were greeted with joy and most were integrated fairly quickly back into various Nez Perce communities on the reservation. Joseph and the other exiles were not so fortunate; they faced hostility from some of the mostly Salish-speaking Native American communities on the Colville Reservation.[7]

The concerns of government officials about the reaction of local whites were genuine and justified. Some Anglo Americans, particularly in local papers, vehemently opposed the arrival of the exiles in Lapwai, Idaho. For example, one editor asserted, "We need their room more than their company." Allen Slickpoo, Sr., maintained that this sentiment was not shared by everyone and mentioned that the *Portland Oregonian* accused local citizens in northern Idaho of being more concerned with acquiring Indian lands than with the return of the exiles. Fortunately for the exiles and all

Nez Perce on the reservation, the anger and frustration vented in local newspapers remained on the printed page and, generally speaking, resistance to the return of the exiles "was allowed to die a quiet death," eventually it became a non-issue.[8]

The return of the exiles to the Nez Perce and Colville Reservations ended the immediate suffering of the non-treaty people sent to the Indian Territory, but their return also marked their official disappearance from Anglo-American narratives and the national consciousness. The United States government now confined all Nez Perce people to reservations in the Pacific Northwest and entered a period of silencing that extended well into the twentieth century. Once these people returned to the Pacific Northwest, Anglo Americans expected that the process of assimilation would slowly but surely move the Nez Perce from the category of semi-savagery to civilized participants in American society. The major exception to this process was Chief Joseph. Anglo Americans froze Joseph in time, perpetually holding up his rifle during his eloquent speech or after the surrender, nobly speaking to whites about the beauty of the Wallowa and his desire to return to his homeland. Joseph became the symbol of the Nez Perce, both locally and nationally. In fact, Joseph would become a "meta-symbol" in the Anglo-American narrative, the ultimate personification of the noble savage and honorable enemy. In Joseph, Anglo Americans saw the "glory" and "victory" of white culture and Manifest Destiny, since even a great Indian leader like Joseph could not withstand the forces of "civilization" and Christianity. Savagery had lost, given way to the superior race, just as the noble Joseph, the worthy foe, had lost and been confined to silence.

THE MYTH AND CULT OF JOSEPH

While many non-treaty Nez Perce honored Chief Joseph and recognized his leadership and rhetorical skills, Anglo Americans would take veneration of Joseph to a new level after the 1877 Nez Perce War. Throughout the late nineteenth and early twentieth centuries, Joseph's words, actions and image appeared in letters, books and newspapers throughout the Pacific Northwest and the rest of the United States. Joseph became the fare of American history textbooks. This fascination and obsession with Chief Joseph elevated him to levels that unfortunately made Joseph almost inaccessible as a human being. He became a legend who personified Native American honor and the Indian's "tragic" and "misguided" struggle against the United States. The creation of the Joseph myth led this researcher to two very important questions. Why was Chief Joseph the only visible Nez Perce after the Nez Perce War of

1877 and throughout the twentieth century? And more importantly, what did Joseph represent for Anglo Americans during the late nineteenth and early twentieth centuries?

The placement of Nez Perce exiles on the Nez Perce or Colville Reservations depended largely on their religious beliefs. The United States government sent Nez Perce people who had accepted Christianity to the Nez Perce Reservation at Lapwai, Idaho, while those, like Joseph, who continued to follow the Washani religion, were sent to the Colville Reservation. As noted by J. Stanley Clark, Joseph continued to remain devoutly attached to Washani belief and practice while in the Indian Territory, and the move to the Colville Reservation did not change Joseph's or the other 149 exiles minds about their religion. This group fought white cultural incursions and refused to take up farming or any activity that entailed disturbing the soil since Washani belief taught that this was a sin.

Joseph's devotion to the Washani religion elicited curiosity and loathing depending on the background and interests of Anglo Americans. For example, Colville Indian Agent Major Albert M. Anderson detested Joseph and any Indian who followed the "old" ways. For Anderson, Joseph was a hindrance to the objectives of assimilating and civilizing the Indians on the Colville Reservation. Other Anglo Americans, like Edmond Meany, shared Anderson's view of Indian religion, but he personally liked Joseph, invited him to Seattle to speak, and participated in the memorial and statue dedication after Joseph's death in 1904. For Anglo Americans, Joseph's devotion to the Washani religion created a dual image of him that played both to those who detested Indian culture and its "backwardness" and to those who continued to create images of the noble savage. This was a love/hate relationship expressing ambivalence evident in many of the narratives created by Anglo Americans about the Nez Perce and other Native Americans. In the case of Joseph, Anglo Americans easily loved the chief who outran and outfought the United States Army while hating his stubbornness when rejecting white culture, Christianity or farming.[9]

This Anglo-American ambivalence with Joseph expanded beyond his religious beliefs. Mick Gidley maintained that Joseph always evoked a number of different responses from Anglo Americans.

> When war came he was immediately credited both with starting it (and was called a murderer) and with holding out for peace (and was considered weak). During the course of the war he was admired for skillful strategy and damned for the Nez Perce victories. In defeat he was reverenced for his eloquence but treated by the governing representatives of the people with respect and contempt in varying portions.[10]

These dualities expressed the nature of Anglo-American views of Indians in general. Anglo Americans could admire Joseph's military prowess, his desire for peace and his eloquent rhetoric, but they found it difficult to admire the part of Joseph that reminded them of his status as a former enemy of the United States government. This duality also extended to the very core of Joseph's identity as an Indian. Americans elevated Joseph to the status of noble savage, but at the same time whites grew increasingly frustrated with Joseph as he remained Nez Perce and refused to accept the "benefits of civilization." Joseph, as well as other Nez Perce who rejected Christianity and white culture, caused minor problems for Anglo Americans in their recitation of the eventual assimilation of Native Americans into American society. Office of Indian Affairs officials often referred to Indians like Joseph as the "non-progressive," "blanket," "long hairs" and "dreamer" elements and compared their status with those Indians on the reservation labeled as "progressive" or "advanced." These "dreamers" refused to comply with the Anglo-American belief in the progressive development of culture, and government officials hoped that these groups would disappear as "progressive" Indian elements became more "civilized" and dominated the politics and culture of the reservation. White government officials could not understand why people like Joseph preferred to live in their tipis on the Colville Reservation instead of living in the perfectly good houses built for them by the Indian agent.

Into the midst of this dualistic atmosphere, Edmond Meany came to the Colville Reservation in 1901 to interview Chief Joseph for a thesis he was preparing for his degree from the University of Wisconsin. Frederick Jackson Turner supervised Meany's biography of Chief Joseph, a work that clearly fit into the regional focus of historical research that Turner desired to encourage students to pursue. Even though he completed his degree, Meany never finished the biography of Joseph for publication. Mick Gidley noted that perhaps Meany failed to complete the biography because Joseph's myth had already grown to such an extent that any work he produced could not do justice to the complex nature of Joseph's life and mythical image. Meany instead seemed to be satisfied to participate in two important parts of Chief Joseph's life. In 1903, Meany arranged for Chief Joseph and Red Thunder to visit Seattle. The visit was punctuated by two speeches given by Joseph, one in a Seattle theater and the other before the weekly assembly of students at the University of Washington. During both speeches, Joseph continued to appeal for his return to the Wallowa region and emphasized his desire to live at peace with white people. The speeches failed to mention the Nez Perce War and were very short, but each of the speeches was greeted with much applause and great enthusiasm; Mick Gidley noted that Joseph evoked a mixed response in Seattle. Meany, in longer speeches given shortly after Joseph completed his brief talks, explained the significance of Joseph's life and his role in Pacific Northwest history. While in Seattle, Chief Joseph and Red Thunder allowed Edward S. Curtis to photograph them in his studio. In one of the photographs, Meany stands between Joseph and Red Thunder and looks quite pleased to be included in one of the portraits (Figure 13).[11]

Meany also participated in the ceremonies surrounding the death of Chief Joseph in 1905. On September 21, 1904, Chief Joseph died while sitting in front of his tipis on the Colville Reservation. Colville Agency Doctor Edward H. Latham (photographer of Figure 14) believed that Joseph died of a broken heart, perpetuating the myth of the doomed, noble savage. Members of his family and community temporarily buried Joseph in the Agency cemetery. After Joseph's death, a debate occurred over his final resting place. Friends and family struggled with whether to rebury him on the Colville Reservation, close to friends and family, or rebury his remains in the Wallowa, his birthplace and home. After a council of Joseph's relatives and friends on October 29, 1904, Henry Steele, a friend of Meany who worked on the Colville Reservation as a subagent serving Chief Joseph's band, wired Meany to inform him of the relatives' decision to inter Joseph's remains permanently on the Colville Reservation. Along with this information, Steele also passed on a query from the Indians at the council about who would cover the cost of a monument if one were to be erected.[12]

The question of erecting a monument and covering its cost directly affected Meany. His active membership in the Washington State Historical Society and their monument creation activities throughout Washington State made Meany the logical choice for organizing Chief Joseph's memorial. By the time he received Steele's telegram, Meany had already corresponded with Chief Joseph's widow in Kamiah, Idaho and assured her that the State Historical Society would take care of the details regarding a monument. During the early months of 1905, Meany ordered the monument, raised money and kept interested whites apprised of the project's progress. Once the reburial ceremony was set, Meany forwarded the inscription for the monument to the New England Granite and Marble Company.[13] On June 20, 1905, a large group of Nez Perce people and Anglo Americans met to rebury Chief Joseph. The event started with a procession of Nez Perce people circling Joseph's body and mourning his death. By noon Nez Perce people completed the reburial and the participants returned at 2:00 p.m. to unveil the monument. At the unveiling, Chief Yellow Bull spoke first (Figure 15), followed by Chief Albert, the newly elected successor to Chief Joseph, and Edmond

The Consuming Silence 155

Figure 13 Nez Perces Chief Joseph and Red Thunder pose with Edmond S. Meany, Seattle, Washington, circa 1903. Photographer – Edward S. Curtis. Courtesy of Manuscripts, Special Collections, University Archives, University of Washington Libraries, NA 610.

Figure 14 Chief Joseph posed on horseback. The caption reads, "Joseph, the famous Chief of the Nez Perces, one of the greatest Indians that ever lived. Before the Chief would pose for this picture and the next he exacted $10 from the artist." Photographer – Edward H. Latham. Courtesy of Manuscripts, Special Collections, University Archives, University of Washington Libraries, NA 1285.

Figure 15 Chief Yellow Bull delivering a speech at the Chief Joseph monument ceremony, Colville Indian Reservation, Washington, 1905. Photographer – Edward S. Curtis. Courtesy of Manuscripts, Special Collections, University Archives, University of Washington Libraries, NA 617.

Meany concluded the speeches with a review of Chief Joseph's life. The following day, the relatives of Joseph held a "give away" to distribute Joseph's possessions, and Joseph's family gave Meany one of Joseph's buffalo robes as a token of appreciation.[14]

Meany's active participation in Joseph's life and death revealed the underlying tension in Anglo-American portrayals of Native Americans. On the one hand, Meany could befriend Joseph, write his biography, and arrange for a monument to be erected over his grave, but in the midst of these acts, Meany also adhered to the dominant ideas about Native Americans popular during his life. While admiring Joseph, Meany also noted that Columbia Plateau native communities obstructed progress and civilization, and he believed and wrote that their title to land must be extinguished so that settlers, the carriers of civilization, could have clear title to their land. For Meany, Joseph was the perfect example of the noble savage, the tragic Indian hero who valiantly led his people in war, but ultimately faced defeat by the forces of civilization.

The images, words and ultimately the body of Chief Joseph existed on many symbolic levels and could be manipulated to meet the various needs of diverse parts of the Anglo-American community. For example, Kate McBeth, one of the Presbyterian missionaries to the Nez Perce, called Joseph "a scoundrel" in her book, but in the next sentence she redeemed his image by pointing out his staunch support of temperance and his personal abstinence from alcohol. Joseph could be both scoundrel and temperance advocate because the myth created by Anglo Americans was malleable enough to allow construction of numerous images of Chief Joseph. This malleability extended to his participation in the Nez Perce War. Joseph was considered not only the tragic Indian hero of the war, but he also filled the role of villain, ready to be hated by local residents for "reported" depredations and on a national level for his unrelenting opposition to the United States government and its policies.[15]

Dual visions of Joseph continued to emerge from Anglo Americans well into the twentieth century. One of the most interesting illustrations of the complexity of Chief Joseph's myth revolved around the debates between Lucullus V. McWhorter and Colonel J.W. Redington, a former Indian scout, over the erection of a monument to Chief Joseph. McWhorter and Redington corresponded frequently, and Redington provided material for McWhorter's research into the Nez Perce War. In a 1929 editorial, Redington decried the effort to erect a monument to Chief Joseph and based much of his opposition on his belief that "a monument to Joseph would mean that all the white men who lost their lives in defense of civilization during the Nez

Perce War died in vain and did not know what they were dying for." For Redington, the monument was "a mockery of history," and any monument would glorify "murderous marauders." Redington continued with a detailed list of various "murders" committed by Joseph and his followers during the war. Those murdered white people, Redington contended, " have no monuments and our generous government allowed their murderers to go free." The very thought of a monument to Joseph assaulted the personal experiences of Colonel Redington, experiences that he said included many murders and "the barbarous cruelties of the noble red man, whose nobility was the bunk to all who had seen him as is."[16]

While Redington railed against any monument project, others in the Pacific Northwest region defended the project. In an *Idaho Statesman* article of 1930, L.V. McWhorter carefully used testimony from United States Army personnel and some civilians to counter Redington's assertions that Joseph incited murders and atrocities during the Nez Perce War. Based on his research for *Yellow Wolf: His Own Story* and *Hear Me My Chiefs*, McWhorter persuasively argued for a much different picture of Chief Joseph, praising him "for meeting the exigencies of the war with humane principles far above the traditions of their race." McWhorter noted that the killings of the first few days of the war were more the result of whiskey, but he asserted that none of the killings "can be charged to Chief Joseph or other of the head men." Despite the disagreement over Joseph's monument, the men remained friends and continued to correspond.[17]

Other Anglo Americans supported L.V. McWhorter in his defense of Chief Joseph. McWhorter clipped an editorial from the *Yakima Republic* newspaper supporting the monument. In the editorial, Joseph's image remained intact as the author noted that "When hopelessly beaten he submitted gracefully, making an eloquent speech to his own people and Col. Nelson A. Miles to whom he surrendered." The author of the editorial almost seemed resigned to the fact that "Congress will probably erect a monument to the memory of the Napoleon of Indians, as Chief Joseph has been designated. He was an outstanding character as well as a great general."[18] As if to reinforce the *Yakima Republic* editorial, McWhorter also saved a very interesting short article that mentioned the designation of Chief Joseph as one of five great Idahoans named by Idaho Secretary of State Fred E. Lukens. That article maintained Joseph's image as the "greatest soldier, diplomat and statesman of the American Indian races," and referred to him as the "Napoleon of the Northwest."[19]

In the end, Joseph's myth served Anglo Americans, not the Nez Perce. His image could be held up to Anglo Americans as a noble leader who was devoted to his people, and as a brilliant warrior-general. At the same time Anglo Americans rested in the fact that Chief Joseph and other Indian leaders like Geronimo, Crazy Horse, and Sitting Bull were vanquished foes, demonstrating in their defeat the prowess of the forces of civilization and progress over savagery. Joseph could be both loved and hated by Anglo Americans, a multi-purpose icon capable of entertaining and teaching the American populace depending on the needs of the time. Kate McBeth's "temperance Joseph," Edmond Meany's "tragic Joseph," and C.J. Brosnan's "military genius Joseph" illustrated the multiple meanings and multiple persons created to fit the needs of various Anglo-American communities and narratives. Many of these narratives included a photograph of Chief Joseph, particularly regional histories like *An Illustrated History of North Idaho*, C.J. Brosnan's *History of the State of Idaho*, and A. Arnold's *Indians Wars of Idaho*.[20] Situated in the front of the works, Joseph stared out on the readers and reminded them of the great struggle in Idaho and the Pacific Northwest between the forces of "civilization" and the forces of "savagery" and the ultimate triumph of Anglo-American culture. Omitting Joseph's image from the narration of the events of the Nez Perce War was impossible in the structure of these narratives. To eliminate Joseph would be to strike out the very heart of the heroic tragedy woven around the remnants of Native Americans. Without Joseph and the Nez Perce, the narratives made little sense. In order to progress, struggle was necessary and an opponent, Chief Joseph, needed to be plucked out and placed on display for those who had fought to isolate Native Americans on reservations and to destroy their culture and history.

IN THE BELLY OF MONSTER: LIFE ON THE NEZ PERCE RESERVATION

While the exiles remained in the Indian Territory and Anglo Americans praised Joseph for his courage and daring, the treaty Nez Perce continued to live on the Nez Perce Reservation in Idaho (Figure 16). Just as the *tewats*, the animal people, stayed alive in the belly of Monster, the treaty Nez Perce and the returned exiles lived within the confines of a reservation that functioned physically and psychologically very much as the stomach of Monster. Anglo Americans envisioned reservations as places to isolate Native Americans and then consume them, either through death or their assimilation into Anglo-American society. The ultimate goal of silencing Nez Perce voices continued, whether reservation or non-reservation, Christian or Washani, died or assimilated. Coyote saw many bones of people as he traveled

The Consuming Silence 161

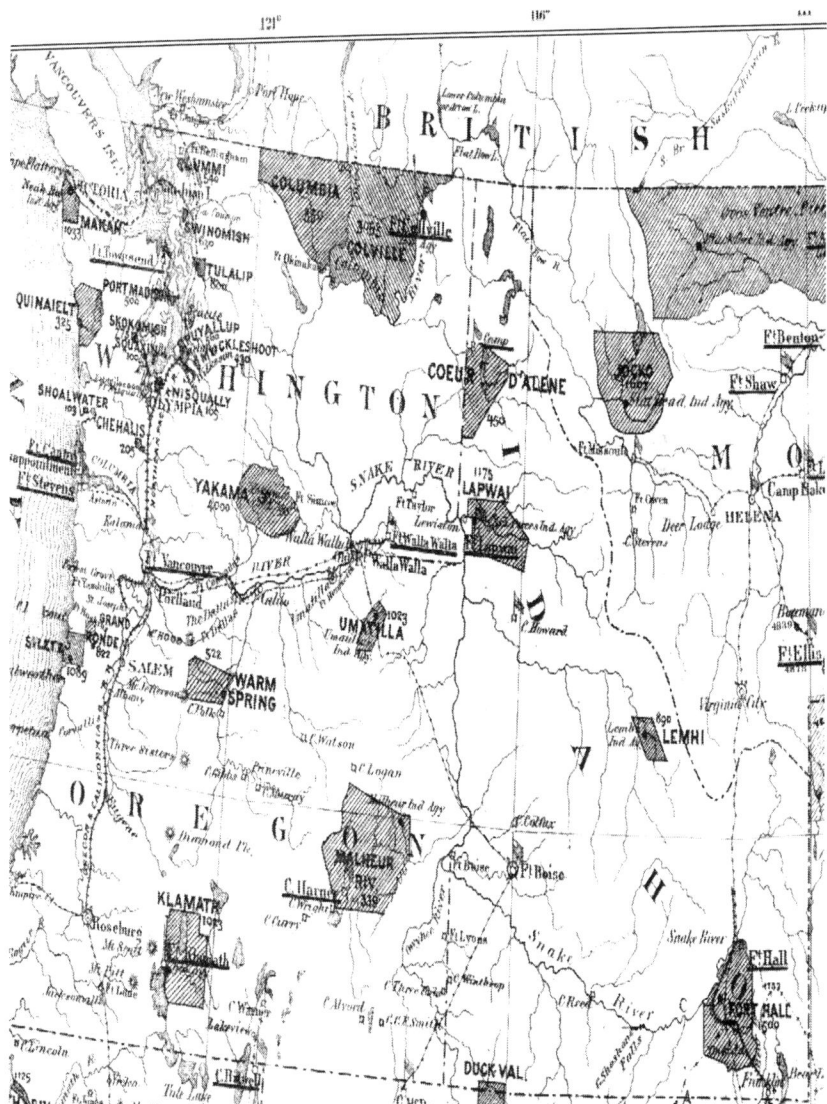

Figure 16 Map of Pacific Northwest Indian Reservations, 1879. In U.S. House, 46th Congress, Second Session. Annual Report of the Secretary of the Interior 1879 (H.Ex. Doc. 1, Pt. 5, Vol. 1) Washington, Government Printing Office, 1880 (Serial Set 1910). Courtesy of the United States Government Printing Office.

through Monster and noted their passing from the living. He also met the survivors and scolded them for acquiescing to Monster's actions while also pointing out how the people could survive in the belly of Monster until Coyote set them free.

Anglo Americans silenced treaty Nez Perce on the reservation at an earlier date than they silenced the exiles in Indian Territory. Once on the reservation, Anglo Americans believed that treaty Nez Perce people came under the influence of "civilization," either through missionaries or government officials from the Office of Indian Affairs. As Indians traveled down the road to civilization, most Anglo-American narratives failed to mention Nez Perce people who chose to adopt some or all of Anglo-American culture. The treaty Nez Perce only re-emerged in narratives when Anglo Americans needed them as examples of the benefits of civilization or if the treaty Nez Perce helped the United States in the war against the non-treaty communities. During the Nez Perce War of 1877, around fifty-one treaty Nez Perce men served as scouts for General Howard and the United States Army. James Reuben, a Nez Perce preacher who went to the Indian Territory to teach and preach, was one of these scouts, and his own people among the non-treaty bands wounded him in a small engagement during the war. Two other scouts emerged in some of the narratives about the war, Meopkwit (Old George) and Jokais (Captain John). Both men participated in the fighting at the Bear Paw Battlefield and helped arrange the final surrender of the remaining non-treaty people. Anglo Americans mentioned these scouts in their narratives because they chose to support the forces of "civilization," the United States Army, and thereby demonstrated their commitment to accepting white culture and "civilization."

Despite the participation of Nez Perce scouts in the war, most treaty Nez Perce people remained in Idaho on the reservation. Their story and the story of the exiles, once they returned to Idaho, generally failed to appear in the annals of Anglo-American history. The silencing of their voices was assumed to be complete, but the belief in the silent and vanishing Indian was premature and not supported by activities and life on the reservation. Documents produced by various Indian agents and agency personnel demonstrate the determination of Anglo Americans to transform Nez Perce people into progressive, Christian citizens of the United States. While these documents often extol the virtues of assimilation, they also voice the sentiments and responses of Nez Perce people, both treaty and non-treaty, as they dealt with the pressures to surrender their culture and melt into American society. As with narratives created by Edmond Meany, C.J. Brosnan, and Kate McBeth, documents created by the Office of Indian Affairs bureaucracy followed certain patterns and frameworks. Most of the Annual Reports of the Office of Indian Affairs contained a narrative section describing the reservation and providing a brief historical overview for officials in Washington, D.C. After the overview, the Indian agent or other agency employees often delved into matters of interest or difficulty, depending on the circumstances. In the next section, these documents will be used to provide a glimpse into the life of the Nez Perce on their reservation in northern Idaho. These documents demonstrate that although Monster swallowed Coyote, the good trickster-creator remained active in the belly of Monster and caused Monster grief and pain.

The Nez Perce Reservation

As a result of the Thief Treaty of 1863, the Nez Perce possessed a much smaller land base ($1/10^{th}$ the original size) than they traditionally held during most of their history (Figure 17).[21] The Annual Reports filed by Indian agents posted to the Nez Perce Reservation frequently started with a narrative section describing the reservation. While varying a bit from year to year, the Indian Agents related geographic, population and general information about life on the reservation. For example, the 1916 Annual Report prepared by Supervisor of Indian Schools Otis B. Goodall noted that the Nez Perce population was around 1,551 and that most people earned a living through agriculture and raising stock. Principally concerned with "Industries" on the reservation, Goodall spent a great deal of time describing the state of agriculture. The 1919 Annual Report prepared by the superintendent of the agency started the narrative section with a description of the agency buildings and then moved into common themes covered by most Annual Reports. After describing the buildings, the agent outlined various problems with dancing, gambling, marriage customs, and liquor. These themes were echoed five years later in the 1924 Annual Report. The superintendent started with a brief narrative and then moved on to the problems he faced when attempting to impose white cultural practices on the reservation. In particular, the topics of dancing, gambling and liquor consumption caused the superintendent great concern.[22]

While describing problems with uncooperative Indians, Indian agents almost always made some mention of the treaty Christian Nez Perce faction. Most of the comments made by agency staff praised the Christian faction for their progress. During a visit to the Nez Perce Reservation in 1922, Hugh L. Scott, a member of the Board of Indian Commissioners, "was deeply impressed by the fine strong faces, the reverent attitude and the quality of the pastors and congregations. I saw for the first time churches built and run solely by Indians without intervention of white men." Scott

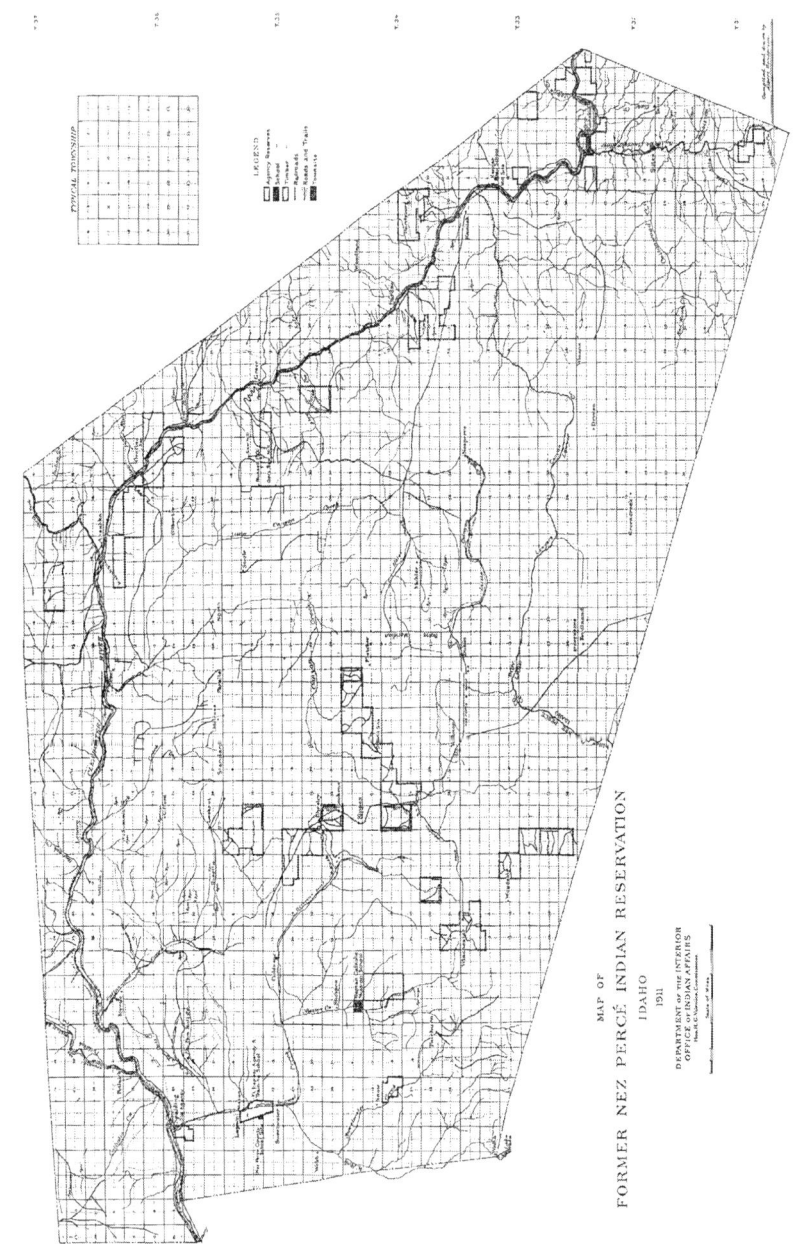

Figure 17 Map of Nez Perce Reservation, 1911. Courtesy of National Archives and Records Administration, Pacific Alaska Region, Seattle, Washington.

ended the paragraph by praising the "stable community of high class, patriotic, God-fearing Indians that would compare favorably with the best of our own farming communities in any state." The situation described by Scott took nearly fifty years to accomplish and required the active participation of missionaries, government officials, and the Christian Nez Perce themselves. Scott's observations painted an idyllic picture. How did this come about?[23]

From 1885 to 1940 on the Nez Perce Reservation, the efforts of the United States government focused on attempts to assimilate Nez Perce people into American society. These efforts came in many forms, sometimes in the guise of missionary activity, at other times in the guise of allotment. While not limited to Christianization or allotment, the assimilation policies of the Bureau of Indian Affairs and the United States government confronted Nez Perce people with the difficult choice of whether to adopt the culture of Anglo Americans or remain, more or less, Nez Perce. For Christian Nez Perce, this question seemed to be answered more easily. Missionary activity almost always included the preaching of the Gospel, and missionaries taught their converts aspects of a cultural Christianity based on Anglo-American values and practice. For example, it was not enough for a Nez Perce person to profess faith in Jesus Christ, but he or she must also give up wearing traditional clothing, attempt to farm a piece of land, learn English and cut his long hair if he were male.

The Christian conversion of treaty Nez Perce began before the Nez Perce War and was probably precipitated by the arrival of George Waters, a Yakama Methodist preacher on the Nez Perce Reservation. In 1871 and 1872, both Protestant and Catholic missionaries on the Nez Perce Reservation reported an estimated 800-900 Nez Perce converts. Deward Walker, Jr., noted that many of these conversions occurred at the village or band level with the leader of the village assuming the role of church leader or elder. According to Walker, church membership in some cases began to substitute for village or band membership. Presbyterian missionaries conducted most Protestant missionary activity on the Nez Perce Reservation. By 1875, the conversion process was fairly complete, and the missions and churches entered a period of consolidation. Deward Walker, Jr., asserted that churches solidified around village/band localities with principle Protestant churches located in the Lapwai and Kamiah areas, accommodating the large communities in those areas.[24]

In 1879, Sue McBeth, a Presbyterian missionary, arrived on the Nez Perce Reservation and took over from the part-time white preachers serving the Nez Perce churches, basing her activities in Kamiah, Idaho. McBeth started a program for the education of Nez Perce men, to prepare them for the ministry. Allen Slickpoo, Sr., observed that McBeth's charge from the Board of Missions "was to teach young men who seemed to have promise in this field *(Christian ministry)*."[25] During her tenure at Kamiah, McBeth trained twelve Nez Perce men as pastors who were then ordained by the Presbyterian Church. Many of these men returned to the Nez Perce Reservation to lead Nez Perce churches. Walker noted that by 1888 "all Nez Perce Presbyterian churches were under the control of native preachers, who essentially stepped into newly created status left vacant by departing missionaries." These preachers contended with traditional authority figures like village headmen, *tooats* and chiefs for power and control over people in an area. Generally, the Indian agent and agency employees favored Christian Nez Perce over traditionalists or as they called them "blanket Indians," providing both material and moral support for their activities.[26]

By 1878, approximately 900 Nez Perce were members of the Presbyterian Church on the Nez Perce Reservation. According to Allen Slickpoo, Sr., Christians formed a majority of enrolled members of the Nez Perce tribe in 1878. This Christian majority led to some very important social and cultural transitions on the reservation during the 1880s and 1890s. Walker noted, "Presbyterian Church organization in conjunction with the church-village complexes and native-preacher elite came to substitute for much of the older social organizations." Church-village complexes were governed by elected and ordained elders who held their position in the church for life. Children of elders inherited these positions, often creating a very powerful family-based church leadership. The church leadership governed through meetings called sessions, and Walker asserted that these governing bodies energetically pursued the policy of eliminating cultural practices associated with earlier Nez Perce life. In particular, many offenses heard by the sessions concentrated on problems with breaking the Sabbath, gambling, adultery, and, most importantly, curing the sick through shamanistic practices.[27]

Records of the Office of Indian Affairs also showed that Christian factions on the reservation often appealed to Agency officials to help in their fight against "heathen" practices. For example, in a 1891 letter from Indian Commissioner T.J. Morgan to Nez Perce Indian Agent Warren D. Robbins, Commissioner Morgan addressed the problems of "immoral practices" on the Nez Perce Reservation. While white officials at the Nez Perce Agency were deeply concerned about so-called "immoral practices," Christian Nez Perce also organized and wrote letters and petitions of protest concerning these practices. Morgan noted that:

> Edward Conner "In behalf of Committee" addressed a letter to this Office dated Fort Lapwai, Idaho, June 8, 1891, presenting the request of the Christian Nez Perce Indians that this office prohibit a continuance of the custom among the Nez Perces of having horse racing and "circling war-hoop processions" on every 4th of July.[28]

Morgan agreed with the Christian Nez Perce and recommended to Indian Agent Robbins that he regard these practices as demoralizing, leaving to the agent's discretion " the question of the advisability of taking action to prohibit or break up these practices entirely, especially the 'processions' referred to, if it can be done without bringing on serious trouble with the Indians."[29]

If Christian Nez Perce felt that agency personnel failed in their duty to prohibit or discourage "immoral practices," like dancing, gambling, horse racing and Indian custom marriage, they could organize to remove employees whom they disliked. In a letter from Acting Indian Commissioner A.C. Tonner to Superintendent, Fort Lapwai Indian School, Spalding, Idaho C.T. Stranahan, the same Nez Perce Elder, Edward J. Conner, filed a petition with the Office of Indian Affairs in Washington, D.C., recommending that the Indian Service not retain Stranahan as superintendent of the Fort Lapwai School. Tonner stated that Edward Connor and others believed that Stranahan "may have been less active in suppressing Indian customs than you should have been." Commissioner Tonner noted with concern that "the opposition to you comes from the enlightened, civilized class, and the advocacy from the non-progressive Indian." While unsuccessful in their bid to have Stranahan replaced, Christian groups on the reservation caused considerable difficulties for employees if Indians viewed them as hindrances to the civilizing mission.[30] Protestations by Christian Nez Perce continued into the 1920s and 1930s. The 1924 Annual Report of the Fort Lapwai Agency mentioned:

> The Nez Perces are not much given to Indian dances. The tribe is divided into what is known locally as the Christian Indians and the Non-Christian Indians. Probably two-thirds of the tribe are affiliated one way or another with either the Presbyterian, Methodist or Catholic churches. The majority of the church Indians are of the Presbyterian faith. These are strongly opposed to Indian dances and discourage them in every way possible.

Opposition to dancing and gambling remained strong among Christian elements and it even extended to attempts to have Idaho law changed to prohibit the "Indian stick-game."[31]

The strength of the Christian groups dwindled from its high influence during the late 1870s and the 1880s. This decline was due to many factors that included the end of proselytizing and the reliance on biological reproduction for continued membership. Allen Slickpoo, Sr., noted that church membership dwindled from the high of 900 in 1878 to around 200 in the early 1970s. While church membership remained primarily a function of children joining their parents' church, another factor worked to decrease church membership in the 1890s and early twentieth century. Walker and Slickpoo both mention that the process of allotment and dissatisfaction with its effects created great discontent among Christian and non-Christian peoples on the reservation. Walker argued that Nez Perce conversions to Christianity served more than a religious purpose. Treaty groups on the reservation also adopted Christianity for political and economic reasons. Many of these reasons were based on the fear of losing their land just as the non-treaty people had, and Walker argued that this fear, coupled with a realization of the benefits of adopting Christianity after the agency came under the control of the Presbyterian church in 1871, contributed to the large number of converts in 1871 and 1872. In the early 1890s, the allotment process began, ending in 1895 with the opening of the Nez Perce reservation to white settlement. Walker asserted that allotment changed the political and economic situation on the Nez Perce Reservation, and many Christian Nez Perce came away from the process disillusioned, convinced that adopting Christianity and white culture would not protect their land from white exploitation. Kate McBeth noted, "Many were opposed to allotment - not just to receiving their land in severalty, but to the giving up of the surplus land, and to the settlement of the whites among them, which they knew would follow the allotment."[32] Allotment would not only affect the membership of Christian factions, but it also slowly changed Nez Perce economic and social relationships throughout the time period of this work.

Allotment

Unfortunately for Christian Indians on the reservation, their mere acceptance of Christianity did not change the desire of white settlers to acquire reservation land for their own use. Slickpoo maintained that Anglo Americans during the 1880s strongly opposed the reservation system and resented that Indians retained any portion of their land, particularly lands optimal for settlement. This Anglo-American lust for Indian land conveniently coexisted with assimilationist government policies, endorsing the private ownership of land by Indians as a way to further their acculturation. Judith Ann Jones stated that many Anglo Americans believed that "white farmers would present examples of a wholesome, farming life that the Nez Perce people could emulate in order to make a comfortable living from their lands."[33] In 1887, Congress passed the Dawes Act and began the process of distributing reservation land in severalty to Native Americans. Allen Slickpoo, Sr., briefly described the workings of the Dawes Act:

> Under this act, the president could, whenever he saw fit, divide up a reservation, and give each member of the tribe on that reservation a certain number of acres depending on the status and age of the individual. For example, each head of family was to be given 160 acres, each single person over eighteen and all orphans eighty acres, and every person under eighteen and single was to be given forty acres. Each individual could choose his own tract, but he had only four years in which to do so. At the end of that time, the government would choose for him if he had not yet made his decision. Upon making a choice, the individual was to receive a patent, which stipulated in part that the land would be held in trust by the United States government for twenty-five years, after which time the allottee would receive a fee patent in exchange for the temporary trust patent.[34]

Government officials and white reformers believed that twenty-five years was enough time for the Nez Perce and other Native Americans to learn how to use their land "responsibly." The government paid for the surveying of the allotments. The United States government purchased from the Nez Perce land not allotted on the reservation and then opened those lands for white settlement.

In 1906, the United States Congress amended the Dawes Act through passage of the Burke Act which allowed the Secretary of the Interior to declare any Indian "competent" any time before the end of the twenty-five year trust period, once "an individual was capable of taking up the responsibilities of the citizenship."[35] As soon as the government declared an Indian competent, he received title to his land, whether he wanted the title or not, and was liable for all taxes and assessments on the land. Deward Walker argued that the Burke Act devastated Nez Perce land holdings as Indians were forced to sell land to pay taxes or debts. By the 1920s, the Nez Perce had lost nearly half of the land allotted to them in 1895.[36]

The process of allotment was fraught with much confusion and opposition on the Nez Perce Reservation. In 1889, Alice C. Fletcher arrived on the reservation to conduct the survey for allotment. Fletcher, a Harvard trained anthropologist, was accompanied throughout the years of her work by Jane Gay, her friend, helper and informal photographer of the allotment process. Believing deeply in the efficacy of allotment as a means to help Indians, Fletcher, employed by the Bureau of Indian Affairs, allotted the Omahas in Nebraska and then moved on to the Nez Perce Reservation. This vast and complex process took nearly four years and required the help of the Nez Perce to complete the job. During her survey, Fletcher asked the tribal council to appoint men to act as a liaison committee between the government and tribal members.[37] Slickpoo remarked that the appointment of this committee affected future political institutions and leadership on the reservation. The nine-man committee, while lasting only through the allotment process, served as "the prototype of the present executive committee in charge of tribal affairs."[38]

Even with the help of the nine-man committee, Alice Fletcher was unable to satisfy many Nez Perce people during the survey and allotment process. During Inspector William M. Junkin's visit to the Nez Perce Reservation in January 1893, he reported that:

> It appears that Miss Fletcher's allotments were very unsatisfactory; could not find an Indian who had a certificate of his allotment, majority of them do not know even the section, township or range in which their allotments are situated. Of the opinion this not the season to make an investigation or to report intelligently upon the complaints made by the Indians against Miss Fletcher's allotments; thinks she has, no doubt, done her work faithfully. Thinks a mistake was made in not giving each Indian a certificate of his allotment. This failure has been the great stumbling block in the way of success of the Commission in inducing the Indians to sell their unallotted land. They say they do not know where their land is and hence do not know how much unallotted land there will be.[39]

Junkin discovered the discontent and reluctance of the Nez Perce to "sell" their "surplus" land when he met with the Nez Perce in council on December 29, 1892. At this meeting he heard complaints from Nez Perce people concerning the allotment process and Miss Fletcher. Some complained of incorrect survey lines, while others complained about the process itself. One of the participants, Charlie Waters, complained bitterly about the whole procedure:

> I am going to make a complaint about her (Alice Fletcher) now. It will take me sometime to get through. When she first came here she told the people she was going to allot them their lands. The people told her to wait a little longer. They told her they were not ready to take their allotments, as they had no material to work them. Then she said you must take your allotments. She said I will explain everything to you. I am going to give you your allotments but the rest of the reservation will remain as it is. After you have received your allotments the Government will help you improve them. It will be twenty-five years that the Government will help you on your reservation. Addressing my people: "You all

know about this." That is the reason that my people have accepted their allotments. Because she promised them all these things. I think the Government have cheated us when they come and say we want to buy your surplus land, when we don't know our lands yet. The people are not looked after as they out to be, and therefore, we cannot sell our lands. So much of our trouble I have explained to you.[40]

It is obvious that Junkin's main concern was the reluctance of the Nez Perce to sell their unalloted land. Charlie Waters spoke forcefully about government promises and Nez Perce unwillingness to sell land that was not carefully surveyed. Waters' fear most likely arose from Nez Perce experience with the United States government and the long history of government attempts to confine Indians to an ever shrinking land base. Since 1855, the United States government first negotiated then deceived the Nez Perce into giving up land, and in 1893 it wanted to confine each Indian to 160 acres.

Despite the concerns of many Nez Perce, on May 1, 1893, the United States government and important Nez Perce leaders completed an agreement, completing the allotment process. In this agreement the Nez Perce agreed to take allotments totaling 178,812 acres, while ceding 542,074 acres to the United States government. The government set aside 34,000 acres for the agency, school, mission, cemetery and timberlands for the tribe, while paying the Nez Perce tribe $1,626,222.00 for the ceded land. While Anglo Americans viewed the Dawes Act as the best means to produce independent farmers among the Native Americans, in reality allotment created two parallel conditions that thwarted this goal. The first condition rested in the fact that very few Nez Perce became farmers as a result of allotment. Instead, many Nez Perce people preferred to lease their land to white ranchers and farmers, preferring the steady lease income to working their own land.

By 1941, a survey of employment among Nez Perce men between the ages of eighteen and sixty-five found that of the four hundred fifteen men covered by the survey only thirty-six were full or part-time farmers. Nearly as many men, thirty-one, lived off of trust income and fishing and seasonal work.[41] The other condition created by allotment was the obvious decrease in land holdings. Deward Walker, Jr. mentioned that, by 1923, Nez Perce owners had sold nearly half the original allotments. By 1933, this figure had risen considerably due to the economic conditions of the Great Depression. As lease income decreased drastically during the early 1930s, Nez Perce people were forced to sell their land to pay taxes and debts. According to a 1932 Annual Report of the Northern Idaho Agency, the Nez Perce received 55,052 acres in fee patent, but had sold 41,139 acres of allotted land. The government continued to hold nearly 80,000 acres in trust.[42]

As the Nez Perce leased their allotments or sold their fee-patented land, the reservation transformed from a fairly isolated area primarily populated by the Nez Perce to a region overwhelmingly settled by whites. Many towns sprang up and between 1890 and 1910; the white population on the reservation rose from approximately 4,000 to around 10,000. Oscar H. Lipps, Supervisor of the Fort Lapwai Indian School, observed with satisfaction that:

> Road and bridges have been built on all parts of the reservation; five railroad lines penetrate it; towns have been built; public schools and churches dot it throughout all its parts, and save for the few Indians living within its boundaries, what was once the Nez Perce Reservation presents now a spectacle no less attractive and prosperous than may be found in many of the best agricultural sections of the Northwest.[43]

Lipps' description of the reservation in 1910 was a picture of "civilization," with its towns, churches, railroads and schools. Many Anglo Americans shared Lipps' devotion to the outward signs of Anglo-American progress and hoped that the "few" Indians remaining on the reservation would be influenced by the presence of whites.

By 1960, the white population of the region reached 59,000 while Nez Perce opening of the reservation to White settlement in 1895 the Nez Perces were flooded with alien cultural influences on a scale previously unknown."[44] As Christian Nez Perce came into greater contact with Anglo Americans, they became disgusted and disillusioned with the behavior of many whites who violated the morality and ethics taught by the missionaries to the Nez Perce. Walker maintained that this disillusionment led to a decline in religious fervor by 1900 and that by 1930 only a small nucleus of Nez Perce worshippers remained in the Presbyterian churches.[45] The decrease in church attendance, leasing or selling land rather than farming it, and the extension of the trust period to 1940 conclusively demonstrated the complete failure of the Dawes Act to achieve its purpose of creating small, independent farmers out of Native Americans. By 1963, only 57,062 acres out of 175, 026 acres allotted in the original survey remained in Nez Perce hands. Through financial hardship, government taxation, and white pressure, Nez Perce people lost more of their estate. Government policies forced Nez Perce people to live among an ever-growing number of Anglo Americans. Just as Monster consumed all the people and covered the land with his enormity, Anglo Americans through government policies consumed Native American land and covered the Nez Perce estate in their enormity.[46]

"The Burdens of Civilization"

While allotment and its goal to create Indian farmers loomed as one of the largest experiments in assimilation on the Nez Perce Reservation, government officials, missionaries, and neighboring whites placed other pressures on the Nez Perce to conform to Anglo-American culture. The struggle to assimilate the Nez Perce, both Christian and non-Christian factions, played out in the fields, churches, forests and prairies of the Nez Perce Reservation. Anglo-American policies of assimilation relied on confining Native Americans to a small area where government officials and missionaries could oversee the social experiment of converting "Indians" into "white people." Despite their best efforts, agency officials often voiced disappointment and frustration with the Nez Perce, especially those who refused to give up important cultural practices like dancing, hunting, fishing, gambling and Indian custom marriage for more "civilized" activities like farming and participating in the church. Not only frustrated with these practices, agency officials also contended with those desiring to challenge the United States government over treaty rights and obligations, especially concerning the Wallowa area. Throughout the first four decades of the twentieth century, white government officials hoped that the Nez Perce would forget their former ways and adopt Anglo-American culture, but as Oscar H. Lipps, long-time employee of the Office of Indian Affairs, noted in 1926:

> The Indian has not yet reached the point where he is willing to bear many of the burdens of civilization, though he is very anxious to receive all of the benefits. He resents the restrictions which surround his land by reason of its being held in trust by the Government, when those restrictions impose any sacrifice on his part, but he is very eager to demand all the benefits, such as exemption from taxation and having the Government collect his delinquent rentals, paying all the expenses of necessary court proceedings in cases where suits must be brought, etc.[47]

At the quote revealed, the Nez Perce developed their own ways of dealing with the assimilation policies of the United States. Some individuals and communities, exercising agency regarding acculturation, chose to accept and adopt Anglo-American culture and to abandon their previous way of life, while many others selected a middle ground that attempted to balance Nez Perce and Anglo-American culture, living as they did after allotment as a minority on their own land. Some simply chose to reject Anglo-American culture and refused to cooperate with government attempts to assimilate or indoctrinate them into the dominant society. Whether Indians assimilated or not, whites often believed that the process was taking too long and grew frustrated with the pace of change, no doubt wishing that there was some way to prod the Nez Perce along more quickly. In essence, the irritation of government officials and missionaries over remaining Nez Perce cultural practices was an irritation born out of the choices of Nez Perce people regarding their own lives. Even Christian Nez Perce caused concern as they looked out for their own best interests and sometimes disregarded the goals of the government.

Regardless of the desires of agency employees, missionaries, or government officials in Washington, D.C., the Nez Perce continually charted their own course through the reefs of assimilation. From the 1870s onward, groups of Nez Perce, mainly non-Christian factions, participated in activities that incurred the wrath and disappointment of government officials and missionaries. In particular, disputes over dancing, gambling, and children's school attendance loomed large on the reservation. These disputes often involved many different factions on the reservation with Christian factions, in most cases, siding with the Indian agent in attempts to discourage these cultural practices. Kate McBeth in *The Nez Perces Since Lewis and Clark* related one of the most interesting examples of these disputes. The life and work of Kate and Sue McBeth are excellent examples of the missionary fervor and vision that drew many Christian workers to the Nez Perce and other Native American groups in the Pacific Northwest. Sue McBeth arrived in Lapwai, Idaho, in 1873 and her sister Kate joined her in 1879 under the commission of the Presbyterian Board. In 1908, Kate McBeth wrote *The Nez Perces Since Lewis and Clark* as a vehicle to preserve what she believed to be Nez Perce history with a large dose of biography and autobiography thrown in.[48]

The most illuminating chapter of McBeth's book recounted the struggles over Fourth of July celebrations on the reservation. This chapter, above all others in the book, spoke volumes about the attitudes and perceptions of Anglo Americans, especially missionary attitudes, when confronted with Nez Perce cultural practices. During the course of Kate McBeth's long missionary tenure, she experienced many frustrating instances of Nez Perce resistance to demands for abandonment of activities described as "heathenism." In particular, the weeklong Fourth of July celebration caused great tension among some of the Christian Nez Perce. Before 1897, the celebration and encampment was a communal activity held on the grounds of Fort Lapwai. McBeth described the "unfortunate" consequences of these celebrations, and she was particularly concerned about Christian Nez Perce participation and the potential for corrupting influences to gain sway over her flock. Drinking, gambling and alleged wife swapping concerned McBeth and some of the Christian Nez Perce. For

McBeth, this celebration symbolized everything that hindered the Nez Perce from entering into and gaining all of the benefits of white culture, civilization and Christian belief that she so earnestly thought would help integrate the Nez Perce into Anglo-American society.[49]

The Fourth of July encampments were visible expressions of the cultural struggles extant between Nez Perce groups. Christians often participated in or attended the activities of the "heathen" camp and continued to interact with relatives and friends who practiced the "heathenism" so abhorrent to McBeth. In 1897, the situation distressed a number of Christian Nez Perce and the missionaries so greatly that they decided to form their own camp away from the "corrupting" influences of the larger gathering and to celebrate in ways more appropriate to Christian practice and ethics. However, McBeth noted that simply separating the camps failed to stop intermingling, and she asserted that Christian Nez Perce often required "heroic measures" to deal with their disobedience. These disciplinary actions included expulsion from the church, involuntary confessional sessions, and withholding communion from unrepentant members.[50]

The chapter ended with a stirring affirmation of the triumph of Christianity and Anglo-American culture. McBeth assured her readers that the "heathen" camps lost their power to attract Christian Nez Perce, and that each year church encampments grew in number and participation. According to McBeth's version of the cultural superiority myth, the "dark side" of Nez Perce culture expressed itself in the activities of the heathen camp and was often encouraged, to the consternation of missionaries and Christians alike, by white men who hoped to make money off the remnants of Nez Perce culture. The message behind McBeth's indignation over white support for the heathen camp was that the Nez Perce failed to possess the cultural strength to continue their former "heathen" practices without the help of misguided white men. McBeth clearly believed, despite the efforts of her misguided countrymen, in the ultimate triumph of the Christian camp over the heathen camp. The chapter ended with the reassurance that, "Each year there are numbers leaving the heathen ranks to camp with the Christians." It was only a matter of time before the heathen camps would no longer hold interest, and then the "true" celebration of the Fourth of July could commence at the Christian camp.[51]

Despite McBeth's best attempts and the attempts of Nez Perce Agency officials, cultural practices like dancing, gambling and alleged "wife-swapping" continued into the twentieth century. For agency personnel, those practices directly countered their efforts to assimilate Nez Perce people and flouted their authority. In most annual reports mentioning those "offenses," the Agent often voiced his frustration over a lack of personnel to enforce stricter behavioral norms on the reservation. They also were incredulous with state officials who rebuffed their requests of assistance. For example, the Superintendent in the 1919 Annual Report observed:

> The Indians of this reservation are citizens and all minor offenses are handled by the local courts. However, we find it difficult to get the local officials to take action in many cases because the officials feel that since it is Indians there is no reason why they should spend their time and money of the county in prosecuting these cases.

He continued:

> It is difficult to outline a policy that would be successful in controlling these dances. In fact, the state officials would rather encourage the dances than discourage them for it creates amusement for a certain class of people who must be entertained.[52]

In this instance, the Nez Perce exercised influence and control over a portion of the assimilation process. Not every Nez Perce participated, but those who did disregarded the power of agency officials and even seemed to have gained the tacit support of state officials to continue traditional dances. Most likely this situation existed because the surveillance on the reservation was not very "deep" or effective by agency personnel who could not even rely on local or state officials to cooperate with them to achieve the desired goals of assimilating the Nez Perce.

The debate over dances and July Fourth celebrations continued into the 1920s. During 1924, the leaders of the Nez Perce Indian Camp Association sent a petition to the Commissioner of Indian Affairs. In the petition, members of the Association hoped to persuade the Commissioner to block a grant of land to a group desiring to "indulge in war dances and other irreligious rites or ceremonials," particularly since the land in question was close to the location of their regular summer meeting place. Accompanying the petition was a lengthy letter from Superintendent Oscar H. Lipps. The dispute centered on the use of tribal timberlands. In 1920, the Bureau of Indian Affairs set aside some of this land for a permanent camp ground for the Nez Perce Indian Camp Association to conduct religious summer camps. A year later, a group of non-Christian Nez Perce also petitioned the Indian Office for a section of the timberland two miles from the Christian campsite for camping during the summer months. The proximity of the two camps created friction between the two factions and the Christian Nez Perce complained to the Agent that the non-Christian camp drew away young people from their camp and was "a source of annoyance to them." As the spring of 1924 wore on, the conflict over the use of tribal timberland remained unresolved with the Christian faction voicing its opposition to any compromise with those who danced and held more "traditional" celebrations on the Fourth of July.[53]

The matter appeared to remain unresolved as both sides claimed the right to use tribal timberlands to camp and hold celebrations. George Peo Peo Tah Likt, a leader of a non-Christian faction, even used the memory of Chief Joseph to bolster his arguments for the same rights and privileges as the Christian Nez Perce. He stated, "I am one of the Indians who celebrates the Fourth of July by having our old dances and we like these dances because Chief Joseph had them, and we want to keep them up."[54] As Oscar Lipps attempted to mediate between the two groups, the Christian faction remained steadfast in their objections to the dancing camps and refused to meet with representatives from the non-Christian factions to work out a compromise. Lipps came to the conclusion that he could not prevent the Christian faction from using the campground, but he also realized that unless the non-Christian group broke a law, he would be unable to intervene in the situation. While opposing the dances, Lipps observed that the

> celebration proper was very impressive. A long-haired Indian read in somewhat broken English the Declaration of Independence. Patriotic talks were made and the stars and stripes were much in evidence, and altogether the day was more patriotically celebrated than is done by many white people who gather for the observance of this holiday.[55]

This dispute illustrates the complex web of power relationships surrounding the issue of assimilation. The Christians recognized the power of labeling the non-Christian Fourth of July celebrations as "evil rites" and hoped to use this label to achieve their ends. The non-Christians also possessed power in the situation and used Chief Joseph's name with assurances that they were "as much opposed to drinking, gambling and other evil practices as are the Christian Indians" to sway opinion in their favor. In the end, Lipps' options were limited, and he decided to post an Indian policeman at the campsites to ensure orderly conduct and to discourage drinking and drunkenness.[56]

While concerned about dancing and gambling, agency officials and Nez Perce people also worried about issues of school attendance. With the dissolution of the Nez Perce Reservation after the 1893 agreement with the United States government for purchase of "surplus" reservation land, many Nez Perce children began attending local schools instead of government boarding schools. While attempting to create Indian farmers through allotment, government officials also hoped that education, either at boarding schools or at local schools, would further the goal of assimilating the Nez Perce into Anglo-American culture. However, as fewer Nez Perce sent their children to government boarding schools, they gained more time with their children and were able to include them in family activities. Retaining control over their children's education meant a great deal to the Nez Perce. A 1900 petition drafted by Starr Jacob Maxwell and signed by 160 Nez Perce men and women demonstrated their keen interest in retaining their children in local schools. The petition, addressed to the Senator Fred T. Dubois, listed a number of grievances against Superintendent of the Fort Lapwai School A.T. McArthur, and requested that the Senator join the undersigned Nez Perce in requesting that the Commissioner of Indian Affairs transfer McArthur. The first complaint centered on McArthur's alleged abusive behavior toward the Indians of the agency, but the second charge alleged

> That he opposes the sending of our children to the public schools of Nez Perce County and attempts to coerce us into sending them to the Government School, threatening to withhold our rents and refusing us the privilege of leasing our lands at all, until we comply with his wishes.[57]

The petition also alleged "that he uses poor judgment in selecting and recommending guardians over Indian children."[58] These concerns voiced strong support for Nez Perce control over their children and their education. While the government's response to these allegations did not accompany the petition, it is evident that Nez Perce people demanded certain behavior from agency officials and responded through government channels when confronted with government employees whom they viewed as unfair, arbitrary, or abusive.

Agency officials often mentioned educational matters in their annual reports and in correspondence with the Office of Indian Affairs in Washington, D.C. Some of these reports mentioned the difficulty of maintaining strict attendance at public or boarding schools. Charles E. Monteith, Nez Perce Indian Agent, wrote a letter to J.D.C. Atkins, Commissioner of Indian Affairs, in 1885 describing the difficulty of persuading the Nez Perce to send their children to school, most likely, in this case, to a boarding school. Monteith, believed that "If attendance at school is to be had, it can be secured only by adopting compulsory measures," and he noted that he had "concluded to send the policemen out this week, and bring in the brightest and best of school children who returned with the Nez Perces of Joseph's band, also some of those who attended school last season."[59] Agency officials, like Monteith, often resorted to threats in order to compel school attendance by Nez Perce children, particularly those of non-Christian factions.

Twenty years later, Oscar H. Lipps faced similar problems with school attendance. In 1924, Lipps hoped "that some plan be worked out whereby the Nez Perce Indian children attending public schools be required to enter at the beginning of the year rather than travel over the country attending fairs, rodeos, and similar attractions." (Figure 18 and Figure 19) Lipps noted:

> Unlike white people, Indians as a rule take their camping outfit and spend the entire week at or near the fair grounds. The man takes his wife and children with him as a rule, and as the Nez Perce Indians are citizens and have all the privileges of any other citizen, I know of no way by which they can be forced to stay at home and put their children in school promptly at the beginning of the school year.[60]

Lipps attempted to gain the cooperation of local law enforcement officials, but he related that "they say they have no authority to go outside of their jurisdiction and round up these people and force them to put their children in school."[61]

In 1925, Lipps continued to voice his frustration with Nez Perce attendance at school and observed:

> From time immemorial these Indians have been accustomed to making an annual exodus to the mountains about the time the public schools opened in the fall. Whole families go on these trips, taking their children with them – they go far back in the Bitter Root Mountains, one hundred miles from the agency, and remain there all the way from three weeks to two months, camping, fishing and hunting. Last fall one family, the father and mother of which are both Carlisle graduates, took their children out of school and went back into the mountains and were gone for several weeks. This family has been regarded as one of our most progressive Nez Perce families.[62]

Consternation and incredulity can be sensed in Lipps' words, especially as he related the case of the "progressive" couple who took their children into the mountains. While these children missed the first few weeks of school, Lipps maintained that most showed fairly good attendance once they returned to class.

This brief foray into problems of school attendance reveals some of the varied ways that the Nez Perce attempted to circumvent assimilation and the loss of their culture. Agency officials viewed school attendance as necessary and of utmost importance for Nez Perce children. Nez Perce parents may have shared a desire for their children to attend school, but they managed to negotiate this on their own terms. Family hunting trips, rodeos, and visits to

Figure 18 Caption reads, "Parade Day, Toppenish Roundup," Toppenish, Washington. Courtesy of Manuscripts, Archives, and Special Collections, Washington State University Libraries, H.E. Mares Collection, PC 93, Box 1, Folder 44.

The Consuming Silence 181

Figure 19 Caption reads, "Drunken Indian ride Toppenish round-up," Toppenish, Washington. Courtesy of Manuscripts, Archives, and Special Collections, Washington State University Libraries, H.E. Mares Collections, PC 93, Box 1, Folder 31.

relatives often took precedence over school attendance. While serving valuable social functions, these trips also allowed Nez Perce people to evade the supervision they experienced on the reservation, allowing them greater control over their own lives and over the lives of their children. Once again, the Nez Perce used the land to their advantage and staked out areas in their lives that they refused to allow others to dictate for them.

"Their Story"

Despite the best efforts of the Christian and non-Christian Nez Perce to secure a measure of autonomy in their lives, they still faced, even when they succeeded, the same Anglo-American narratives about their land and history. Anglo Americans measured the "progress" of all Nez Perce by the degree of their acceptance of Anglo-American culture. For example, in the 1922 inspection of the Nez Perce Reservation by Hugh L. Scott, member of the Board of Indian Commissioners, Scott related the story of one Nez Perce that "fit" the progressive label. He wrote:

> I was driven to Kamiah, seventy miles, by Jesse Paul, a full blood Nez Perce, in his own high powered touring car. I was quartermaster of the wagon train that took the Nez Perce prisoners of war from the mouth of the Yellowstone in 1877 to put them on the train to Fort Leavenworth, Kansas. Jesse Paul was a boy on those wagons; he is now one of the most respected citizens of this part of the country. He has a comfortable home with electric lights and other modern conveniences, owns a two hundred acre farm which he cultivates himself, together with leased land. He has mortgages on the farms of his white neighbors and can borrow money to any reasonable amount in any bank in this section, solely on his known character.
>
> This is the most remarkable case of Indian progress in the same generation of which I have knowledge and shows what the Indian is capable. Paul was educated at Carlisle, which has turned out many men and women of high character in various walks of life in spite of its unsuitable location for western Indians.[63]

For Paul and all other Nez Perce, the narrative was still the same. According to this story, Indians could not resist the strength of Anglo-American culture and must drop their "savage," "uncivilized" culture for superior Anglo-American ways. Scott told Jesse Paul's story to illustrate what Indians were capable of and in what cultural direction they should be taking.

While narratives of cultural dominance and superiority persisted, Nez Perce people also faced continued recitation of Anglo-American historical narratives as they attempted to deal with the United States government, particularly over matters of land and treaty rights. Four years after Hugh Scott's visit to the Nez Perce, another member of the Board of Indian Commissioners, Flora Warren Seymour, visited the reservation. Her report lauded the Nez Perce and stated that "If all the Indian tribes who have received lands in severalty reached the state of progress attained by the Nez Perces the general allotment policy of the Government might well be deemed a satisfaction of the needs of the Indian."[64] After praising the Nez Perce, Seymour moved into a brief description of the physical aspects of the reservation and then told "Their Story," the story of the Nez Perce. Seymour narrated many of the mileposts that Anglo Americans knew as familiar territory. She mentioned Lewis and Clark, the Nez Perce delegation to St. Louis, the arrival of the Spalding missionary party, the Whitman Massacre, the Nez Perce "troubles" of 1877-78, and last, but not least, the allotment process. This narrative cadence was the one shared by most, if not all, agency officials well into the twentieth century.[65]

The narrative recited by Flora Seymour helped officials to "understand" the Nez Perce people and their contemporary situation. Seymour even mentioned, "The story of the development of the Nez Perces in the main tells of cooperation on the part of the Government authorities, the missionaries, and the Indians themselves."[66] In essence, according to Seymour, the story was about cooperating to bring about the appropriate result for the Nez Perce, their entrance into "civilized" Anglo-American culture.

Seymour's short version of Nez Perce history also served as a vehicle to render powerless Indian land or treaty claims. At the end of her report, Seymour noted that on the morning of her arrival the Nez Perce held a meeting with their lawyer, F.M. Goodwin, former Assistant Secretary of the Interior, to discuss various claims against the government. Seymour explicitly observed that the meeting focused on educating those present in finding evidence to back up Nez Perce claims and that this was merely the first step in a long process. At any step in the process, Nez Perce claims could be found unsubstantiated by the Department of Interior, Congress or the Court of Claims. Most of the claims dealt with hunting and fishing rights, compensation for gold taken from the reservation in the 1860s, and occupancy rights for Joseph's band in the Wallowa Valley. However, each of these claims would have to stand up to competing claims and narratives attested to by Anglo Americans and reinforced by people like Flora Seymour.[67]

Even though Coyote would eventually free the people from the bowels of Monster, a long period of time passed in which Monster controlled the people and attempted to consume them. Once Monster swallowed all the people, including Coyote, Monster believed he had completed his task and could rest. This was false thinking on Monster's part. While in Monster's stomach, Coyote and the people caused him discomfort and pain because they did not accept their situation. Coyote remained alive and harassed Monster on the Nez Perce Reservation through the many interstices of local action and memory. Nez Perce people, following the example of Coyote, found their own ways out of Monster, even the Christian Nez Perce eventually gained control over their churches and decided what directions to take their faith. The simple act of going to the mountains for two weeks to a month or visiting relatives on other reservations irritated Monster and eventually wore him down. By 1940, while still laboring under the Anglo-American narrative, Coyote and the people found voice in a narrative from one of their own, Yellow Wolf, a Nez Perce warrior and chief, a member of Chief Joseph's own family.

Epilogue

Then he told the people, "Gather up all the bones and arrange them well." They did this, whereupon Coyote added, "Now we are going to carve the monster."

Coyote then smeared blood on his hands, sprinkled this blood on the bones, and suddenly there came to life again all those who had died inside the monster. They carved the great monster and now Coyote began dealing out portions of the body to various parts of the country all over the land; toward the sunrise, toward the sunset, toward the warmth, toward the cold, and by that act destining and forenaming the various peoples; Coeur d'Alene, Cayuse, Pend Oreilles, Flathead, Blackfeet, Crow, Sioux, et al. He consumed the entire body of the monster in this distribution to various lands far and wide. Nothing more remained of the great monster. And now Fox came up and said to Coyote, "What is the meaning of this, Coyote? You have distributed all of the body to far away lands but have given yourself nothing for this immediate locality." – "Well," snorted Coyote, "and did you tell me that before? Why didn't you tell me that awhile ago before it was too late? I was engrossed to the exclusion of thinking. You should have told me that in the first place." And he turned to the people and said, "Bring me some water with which to wash my hands." They brought him water and he washed his hands and now with the bloody washwater he sprinkled the local regions saying, "You may be a little people but you will be powerful. Even though you will be little people because I have deprived you, nevertheless you will be very, very, manly. Only a short time away is the coming of the human race."[1]

The story of Monster and Coyote did not end with the consumption and disappearance of Coyote and the people. In the end, Coyote brought about the death of Monster, saved the people and created numerous Indian peoples from the body of Monster, including the Numipu. Through their experience inside of Monster, Coyote and the people realized that their re-creation must use the very substance of their captivity, Monster's body and blood, in order to start anew. Coyote started by bringing back those who had died by sprinkling their bones with the blood of Monster. After resurrecting the people, Coyote set out to create human beings using the carcass of Monster. Just as Coyote sought to reinvigorate or resurrect the people, Nez Perce people like Yellow Wolf sought to re-create their place in the Pacific Northwest by revising and resurrecting the Nez Perce side of the story. For the Nez Perce, Coyote constantly created and re-created as part of his role as trickster and creator, and Nez Perce people also sought to emulate Coyote in their attempts to keep their story alive in Anglo American society. The Nez Perce understood that non-native historians and settlers intended to silence Nez Perce voices and interpretations of their past, but the people persistently brought forth elements of their own stories.

The situation for the Nez Perce in the first half of the twentieth century required all Nez Perce people to re-create their lives using the body of Monster. One of the principal players in this re-creation was Yellow Wolf who possessed intimate knowledge of "Monster." He gained this experience as a Nez Perce warrior who had fought in the Nez Perce War and escaped to Canada, eventually returning to the United States and the Colville Reservation. Through his work with L.V. McWhorter, Yellow Wolf hoped to preserve his culture and his identity as a Nez Perce by telling his side of the story, a story that Anglo Americans failed to include in their histories. While attempting to preserve his culture, Yellow Wolf and all Nez Perce people struggled with the question of how to remain Nez Perce and survive in a hostile American society.[2]

Yellow Wolf answered the question of how to remain Nez Perce by continuing to live his life in a manner that honored the traditional ways of Nez Perce culture. Growing up in Wallowa Valley, Oregon, Yellow Wolf lived among Joseph's family and participated fully in the culture of his people. As a young man, he attended the councils leading to the Nez Perce War and fought bravely as his people retreated over 1,200 miles toward Chief Sitting Bull's camp in Canada. Instead of surrendering with Joseph's people, Yellow Wolf escaped to Canada, but he returned with a group of refugees in 1878. The government subsequently sent him to the Indian Territory. When the non-treaty exiles returned to the Northwest, Yellow Wolf accompanied Joseph's band, his people, to the Colville Reservation. During his exile in the Indian Territory and after his return to the Colville Reservation, Yellow Wolf maintained his identity as a Nez Perce, refusing to accept the United States government's policies of assimilation. While refusing to accept assimilation, Yellow Wolf and others still needed to make a living. Like many other Nez Perce people attempting to survive in the white man's world, Yellow Wolf and his family hunted, fished and gathered plant foods on the Colville Reservation. To supplement these activities, Yellow Wolf and other Nez Perce people traveled to Yakima Valley, Washington, to pick hops for wages.[3]

Returning from picking hops in October 1907, Yellow Wolf met Lucullus Virgil McWhorter. At this first meeting, Yellow Wolf asked McWhorter to care for one of his horses. McWhorter held onto Yellow Wolf's horse and returned it ten months later, never asking for a dime to pay for the hay or boarding. This was the Indian way of sharing friendship. This was the beginning of a unique and close friendship that lasted nearly thirty years. In 1908, McWhorter received the first part of Yellow Wolf's narrative regarding the Nez Perce War. Speaking through an interpreter, Yellow Wolf related his experiences of the war and many other facets of Nez Perce life. For the next twenty-seven years, Yellow Wolf and McWhorter worked to complete a history of the Nez Perce War from a Nez Perce participant and native perspective. Through correspondence and personal interviews, McWhorter assembled Yellow Wolf's story and finally published the volume in 1940, five years after Yellow Wolf's death.[4]

While Yellow Wolf related his story to McWhorter, he was very concerned about the next generation of Nez Perce, as well as Anglo Americans who would hear a story created by Anglo Americans, not by the Nez Perce. Refusing to be consumed by Monster or allow Anglo Americans to tell the story of his people "to please themselves," Yellow Wolf hoped, through his work with McWhorter, to provide a different perspective and offer a Nez Perce voice, a story that had the power to re-create and revise the story. Yellow Wolf hoped his story would live long after his passing, recreating through the blood and bones of so many people who had died and gone on. McWhorter noted that:

> During one of our interviews in 1931, Yellow Wolf made the following remarks, which may be taken as a just summary of his feelings about the long-suppressed truths of the Nez Perce War:
>
> "The story I gave you long ago – if people do not like it, I would tell it anyway. I am not strong, and do not expect to be better any time. I would like finishing it as truth, not as lie.
>
> "We have worked together a long time. You always helped me from first time we met. I am aging where I can not do much more.
>
> "White people, aided by Government, are smothering my Indian rights. The young generation behind me, for them I tell the story. It is for them! I want next generation of whites to know and treat the Indians as themselves.

Figure 20 Chief Joseph. National Archives and Records Administration, College Park, Still Pictures Branch.

> "We came from no country, as have the whites. We were always here. Nature placed us in this land of ours – land that has been taken from us. I am telling my story that all may know why the war we did not want. War is made to take something not your own."[5]

Through his work with McWhorter, Yellow Wolf created an enduring narrative that countered prevailing historical accounts of the Nez Perce War. Just like Coyote, Yellow Wolf dealt Monster a blow that started the process of re-creating stories about the Nez Perce and their place in Pacific Northwest history. Just as Yellow Wolf hoped, his story continues to help native and non-native people alike to retell the story of the Nez Perce people. Yellow Wolf's narrative set an example for other historians and writers creating narratives about the Nez Perce in the twentieth century. Through the inclusion of Nez Perce oral histories and a distinctive Nez Perce voice, Yellow Wolf and McWhorter broke the bonds of Monster and released others to create narratives that contested the narrative structures of earlier works. Works like Archie Phinney's *Nez Perce Texts*, Josephy's *The Nez Perce Indians and the Opening of the Pacific Northwest*, Slickpoo and Walker's *Noon Nee-Me Poo (We the Nez Perce)*, Trafzer and Scheuerman's *Renegade Tribe*, Steven Ross Evans' *Voice of the Old Wolf: Lucullus Virgil McWhorter and the Nez Perce Indians* and many other works followed in Yellow Wolf's footsteps and created narratives that valued and included Nez Perce voices. As historians and Nez Perce people challenged the earlier Anglo American narratives about the Nez Perce War, other narratives, of a more personal nature, emerged to give insight into the circumstances of Nez Perce people in the second half of the twentieth century. For example, Horace Axtell, Nez Perce elder and teacher, wrote a book detailing his life and the life of his people on the Nez Perce Reservation during the twentieth century. Told from a personal perspective, Axtell related the story of his life as an act of re-creation, finding his way out of Monster and into new life by returning to the roots of his Nez Perce identity.[6]

The question of how to remain Nez Perce in the face of Anglo American narratives bent on silencing Nez Perce history still exists today. This question is not for Anglo Americans to decide. Rather Nez Perce people must decide this for themselves, every day. Throughout most of their contact with Anglo Americans, the native peoples of the Columbia Plateau faced a Monster that decided who was Nez Perce, Cayuse, Palouse, or Umatilla. Monster tried to determine how these people fit into narratives created by Anglo Americans. Many Nez Perce people, both Christian and non-Christian, resisted this effort and exercised autonomy on a local level. They wished to avoid the control of whites, whether physical or cultural, and re-create for themselves a story, a place, that expressed their identity as Nez Perce people. This exercise of intellectual sovereignty, the re-telling of the story, is Coyote freeing the people from Monster and re-creating the people, not through Anglo Americans narratives or desires to assimilate Indian people, but through Nez Perce definitions and actions.

Notes

NOTES TO CHAPTER ONE

1. Michel-Rolph Trouillot, *Silencing the Past: Power and the Production of History* (Boston: Beacon Press, 1995), 22.
2. William G. Robbins, "In Pursuit of Historical Explanation: Capitalism as a Conceptual Tool for Knowing the American West," *Western Historical Quarterly* 30, (Autumn 1999): 282. Modern Capitalism, in this context, was best described by Raymond Williams. In *Keywords: A Vocabulary of Culture and Society*, Williams noted that in most languages, capitalism has been increasingly used to indicate a particular and historical economic system rather than any economic system as such. In this sense, modern capitalism, as used in this work, referred to the specific context of the United States and the changes in "capitalism" that occurred in the late nineteenth and early twentieth century. As William Robbins noted, capitalism "also represents a body of ideas and values that are lived at great depth and that permeate our culture."
3. William G. Robbins, "In Pursuit of Historical Explanation: Capitalism as a Conceptual Tool for Knowing the American West," *Western Historical Quarterly* 30, (Autumn 1999): 282.
4. T.J. Jackson Lear, *No Place of Grace: Antimodernism and the Transformation of American Culture*, 1880-1920 (Chicago: The University of Chicago Press, 1981): xvii and 10.
5. Robert Young, *White Mythologies: Writing History and the West* (London: Routledge, 1990): 175.
6. Ibid., 11.
7. Calvin Martin, ed., *The American Indian and the Problem of History* (Oxford: Oxford University Press, 1987): 33.
8. Robert Young, *White Mythologies: Writing History and the West*, 175.
9. Some of these sources include: *Frank Leslie's Illustrated Newspaper*, Volume 64, June 16-November 10, 1877, Western Historical Publishing Company, *An Illustrated History of North Idaho Embracing Nez Perces, Idaho, Latah, Kootenai and Shoshone Counties, State of Idaho*, Western Historical Publishing Company, (1903), Oliver O. Howard, *Famous Indian Chiefs I Have Known*, Originally Published in St. Nicholas Magazine, November 1907 through October 1908, (Reprinted by Lincoln: University of Nebraska Press, 1989), Edmond S. Meany, *History of the State of Washington* (New York: the Macmillan Company, 1910),

Kate C. McBeth, *The Nez Perces Since Lewis and Clark*, New York: Fleming H. Revell Company, (1908), Cornelius J. Brosnan, *History of the State of Idaho* (New York: Charles Scribner's Sons, 1926) and R. Ross Arnold, *Indian Wars of Idaho* (Caldwell, Idaho: The Caxton Printers, Ltd., 1932).
10. Michel-Rolph Trouillot, *Silencing the Past: Power and the Production of History*, 29.
11. Ibid., 28.
12. Ibid., 26.

NOTES TO CHAPTER TWO

1. Archie Phinney, *Nez Perce Stories*, in *Columbia University Contributions to Anthropology*, Volume 25, (New York: Columbia University Press, 1934), 26-27. Reprinted with the permission of the publisher. Archie Phinney, a Nez Perce anthropologist, collected this version of the Coyote and Monster narrative from his mother in the 1930s. The Coyote and Monster narrative serves as a lens for viewing the results of Anglo-American historical production on Nez Perce history and culture. The Nez Perce themselves would most likely not use this narrative in this manner but, for the purposes of this work, the author believes that the metaphor of Coyote struggling with the Monster over the fate of the people is appropriate when describing the relationship between the Nez Perce and Anglo Americans.
2. Allen P. Slickpoo, Sr. and Deward E. Walker, Jr., *Noon Nee-Me-Poo (We, the Nez Perces): Culture and History of the Nez Perces, Volume One*, (Lapwai, Idaho: Nez Perce Tribe of Idaho, 1973), 201-202. Just two years earlier, the U.S. Army captured the non-treaty Nez Perce in Montana. The army treated most of these people as prisoners of war and sent them to Oklahoma. Many treaty Nez Perce remained in Idaho and some even served as scouts for the U.S. army. Those who chose not to flee with the non-treaty groups remained on the new reservation generally under the influence of Christian missionaries, the army and Bureau of Indian Affairs personnel.
3. *Eekish Pah* is the Nez Perce term given to the reservation in Oklahoma used as a place of imprisonment for non-treaty Nez Perce after the 1877 war. The word means "the hot place" and also refers to the despair and death that came to many Nez Perce during their imprisonment. Eekish Pah meant separation from their lands in the Pacific Northwest and also denoted the despair of imprisonment and the longing to return to their homes in Idaho and Oregon. Joseph worked hard for a return to the Wallowa Country but failed in this. In 1885, some Nez Perce returned to Lapwai, while others were forced to move to the Colville Indian Reservation in northern Washington State.
4. A note about words that identify groups of people in this work is necessary at this point. Throughout the work, "Nez Perce" and Numipu will be used interchangeably in reference to the various communities that constitute this group of Native Americans. "Numipu" is the word used by many Nez Perce to distinguish themselves from other Native Americans and from Anglo-American communities. This work uses Archie Phinney's transliteration

for ease of spelling and pronunciation. While Europeans created the name Nez Perce, it seems fitting to use this designation in this context since this work focuses on the Anglo-American production of historical knowledge about the Nez Perce. This recognizes that "Nez Perce" is a European invention and must be used carefully to avoid replicating older visions of Native Americans. This work also uses the phrase "Anglo American" with reservation. The generalizing tendencies of such all-inclusive words like Anglo American and Nez Perce often lead readers to assume that these groups form a monolithic social group with shared values, memory and experience. This simply is not the case. While sharing some values or sense of common historical knowledge, individuals and groups within these larger communities interpreted and used history and culture in differing ways that express conflicting interests and agendas.

5. This work uses the phrase "myth of cultural superiority" to describe broad academic and popular conceptions of Anglo Americans concerning native peoples in the United States and the world. Anglo Americans in the late nineteenth and early twentieth centuries believed deeply in the struggle between "civilization" and "savagery" and the inevitable ascendancy of "civilization." Anglo Americans created these two tropes to provide justification for the belief that "primitive" cultures were farther down the evolutionary ladder. The myth supported many different responses to Native Americans from paternalism, racist ideologies, and efforts to assimilate them into Anglo-American society to fascination with Indians cultures and material objects. For a discussion of Anglo-American beliefs in cultural superiority see Reginald Horsman, *Race and Manifest Destiny: The Origins of American Racial Anglo-Saxonism*. (Cambridge: Harvard University Press, 1981).

6. Lucullus Virgil McWhorter, *Yellow Wolf: His Own Story*, (Caldwell, Idaho: The Caxton Printers, Ltd., 1940), 291. Yellow Wolf and L.V. McWhorter worked on Yellow Wolf's story for decades before its publication in 1940. Yellow Wolf was a cousin of Chief Joseph and joined the non-treaty flight during 1877. His story is a great contribution toward rectifying the lack of Nez Perce voices narrating this event and also serves as a valuable resource for historical research.

   Anglo Americans controlled the process of historical narration, thereby communicating in narrative modes unfamiliar to Native Americans, while developing histories that failed to include them or to allow agency to exist on the part of Native Americans. As Kerwin Klein asserted, the discipline of history up to the 1940s narrated the history of Native America in a manner that moved humanity from savagery to barbarism to civilization. The emplotment of Anglo-American history was generally done through two modes: nature and history, savagery and civilization. One of the spoils of civilization's conquest of savagery was to narrate the history of Native Americans.

7. See Calvin Martin, ed. *The American Indian and the Problem of History* (New York: Oxford University Press, 1987), 27-34. The series of articles in this book wrestles with the problems researchers face when attempting to

write Native American history. Another text that wrestles with this problem, but on a broader level, is Michel Rolph-Trouillot, *Silencing the Past: Power and the Production of History.* (Boston: Beacon Press, 1995).

8. Verne Ray, "Native Villages and Groupings of the Columbia Basin," *Pacific Northwest Quarterly* 27, (Number 2), 101. Verne Ray, however sensitive to reconstructing Nez Perce or other Plateau cultures, accepted the prevailing attitude of most Anglo-American academics that oral narratives and sources were at their root unreliable and therefore could not be trusted with the same degree of trustworthiness as written sources. The practice of denigrating oral sources and material continued and still continues to some extent. For example, Deward Walker continued to privilege missionary over Nez Perce sources in his discussion of Nez Perce acculturation. The problem exists in attributing characteristics, actions, beliefs, customs and other cultural attributes to Nez Perce through the observation and statements of Anglo Americans, a group who uniformly misunderstood and misinterpreted Nez Perce practices, culture, and historical knowledge. Ray's qualification of oral sources can also be applied to written and other sources created by Anglo Americans about the Nez Perce. Many of these sources show a great deal of bias and misunderstanding due to language barriers, cultural biases, and prejudices that the observers carried with them.

9. See Kerwin Klein, *Frontiers of Historical Imagination: Narrating the European Conquest of Native America, 1890-1990.* (Berkeley: University of California Press, 1997), for an in-depth discussion of how Anglo Americans used these words during the early twentieth century. Klein's work provided a national context for this work's analysis of narratives created in the Pacific Northwest about Native Americans. Kerwin Klein is Assistant Professor of History at University of California, Berkeley.

10. Douglas Cole discussed the interrelationship between collecting, commodification and the discipline of anthropology in Douglas Cole, *Captured Heritage: The Scramble for Northwest Coast Artifacts,* (Norman: University of Oklahoma Press, 1985) and *Franz Boas: The Early Years, 1858-1906,* (Seattle: University of Washington Press, 1999).

11. Verne Ray and other anthropologists testified before the Indian Claims Commission during the late 1920s. Ray, a specialist in Columbia Plateau cultures, assisted the Indian Claims Commission in its investigation and rulings centered on the disposition of reservation and traditional lands. Researchers like Verne Ray provided crucial information that influenced Indian possession of land and they occupied a crucial role in providing fundamental information for a legal decision regarding the possession of this crucial resource in a modern capitalist country like the United States. Verne Ray worked at the University of Washington in the Department of Anthropology during the 1920s and 1930s.

12. This work often refers to the Nez Perce as a single or united entity. The reality is that the Nez Perce community consisted of different groups and interests. Two broad groups emerged after the War of 1877, the Christian and non-Treaty Nez Perce. This method of grouping the Nez Perce Com-

munity still does not take into account family or geographical means of group affiliation.
13. Many different communities lived on the Columbia Plateau. Salish and Chinookan communities also resided on the Columbia Plateau, forming deep and lasting relationships with Sahaptin communities on the Plateau.
14. Jeff Zucker, Kay Hummel and Bob Hogfoss, *Oregon Indians: Culture, History and Current Affairs, An Atlas and Introduction*, (Corvallis: Western Imprints; The Press of the Oregon Historical Society, 1983), 7.
15. Ray, "Native Villages and Groupings," *Pacific Northwest Quarterly*, 103.
16. Eugene S. Hunn with James Selam and Family, *Nch'I-Wana – "The Big River": The Mid-Columbia Indians and Their Land* (Seattle: University of Washington Press, 1990), 89. Eugene S. Hunn is professor of anthropology at the University of Washington. *Nch'I-Wana – "The Big River"* focused primarily on mid-Columbia Indians who shared the Sahaptin language and cultural traits with other Plateau communities like the Nez Perce, Cayuse and Umatilla. Hunn's work was the result of over a decade of close personal work and collaboration with James Selam, a mid-Columbia Indian elder.
17. Donald W. Meinig, *The Great Columbia Plain: A Historical Geography, 1805-1910* (Seattle: University of Washington Press, 1968), 16.
18. Ibid., 16.
19. Ibid., 20.
20. Ibid., 21.
21. Slickpoo and Walker, *Noon Nee-Me-Poo*, 30.
22. Clifford E. Trafzer, ed., *Grandmother, Grandfather, and Old Wolf: Tamanwit Ku Sukat and Traditional Native American Narratives from the Columbia Plateau*, (East Lansing: Michigan State University Press, 1998), 89-96.
23. The word 'land' implies a great deal more in the context of Nez Perce culture than the common assumptions of Anglo-American culture surrounding this word. Land, for Europeans and Anglo Americans, is a commodity, tied up with ownership and possession. The protection of property is one of the fundamental purposes of the Constitution and American jurisprudence. For the Nez Perce and many other Native American cultures, the land is not a possession, but rather a relationship. The land, the ancestral home, is a crucial source of identity.
24. Kerwin Lee Klein, *Frontiers of Historical Imagination: Narrating the European Conquest of Native America, 1890-1990*, (Berkeley: University of California Press, 1997), 80. Boundaries created by differences of belief were particularly important for the non-treaty Nez Perce and their struggles with the United States government in the late nineteenth century. Government representatives failed to understand the deep connection between the land and Nez Perce identity and religious belief. For example, General Howard arrested Toohoolhoolzote, a Nez Perce *tooat* or shaman, in the midst of some of the most delicate negotiations during the Lapwai Council of May 1877, because he insisted that he must remain consistent with his religious beliefs and not sell or give away his land to the government or any white settler. The unwillingness of Anglo Americans to view Nez Perce religious

beliefs as legitimate intensified disputes and led to a great deal of anger among the Nez Perce.

25. Since land took on such significance for Anglo Americans within the context of capitalism, it was inevitable that different ideas about the land, its use and its role in forming identity would create conflict. The Nez Perce, as part of the Washani religion, valued the land for its sacredness and its importance to their cultural identity. The earth was not to be sold or transferred and was the source of power and relationship for the Nez Perce. Anglo Americans, on the other hand, saw the land as a commodity but also gave this commodity religious significance. Protestant Christianity in particular believed that God had given them dominion of the land and its creatures (Genesis). This dominion translated into working the land and making it "productive" or, in other words, profitable. These religious motivations are evident in the desire of missionaries to teach Indians in North America to farm the land and put it to "constructive" use. This struck at the heart of Nez Perce values and engendered great misunderstanding and resentment among the Nez Perce.

26. Hunn, *Nch'I-Wana – "The Big River"*, 228.

27. Ibid., 235.

28. Ibid., 230. In contrast to Hunn's subtle but deep reading of Plateau community's religious beliefs, Herbert Spinden, in his anthropological work on the Nez Perce in the early twentieth century, remarked that Nez Perce religious beliefs "were marked by simplicity, rationality, and freedom from ceremonial restraint." While this may have seemed a generous appraisal at the time, Spinden continued with the observation that the Nez Perce must have realized the "paucity" of their religious beliefs and responded eagerly to Christianity as a result. Unfortunately, Spinden misinterpreted Nez Perce and other Plateau Indian responses to Christianity and Christian missionaries. Many Nez Perce responded to Christianity within the context of their cosmological framework. They did not see Christianity as superior to their own beliefs, but believed initially that Christianity offered a route to the white man's spiritual power just as the quest and the wyakin gave Nez Perce their spiritual powers.

29. Ibid., 231.

30. Ibid., 231.

31. Ibid., 232. Since the Nez Perce believed that everything in the natural environment was animated by spirit, they recognized the importance of treating all things within their local ecosystem with respect, as if they were a person. The significant part of the relationship and the imbuement of power came as a result of believing in and acting on the moral principle described by Eugene Hunn. The spirit sickness described by Allen Slickpoo Sr. expressed the violation of the moral principle of treating all things with respect, but in particular treating the "person," whether in the shape of an animal, inanimate object, wind or other manifestation, with proper respect.

32. Gregory Evans Dowd, *A Spirited Resistance: The North American Indian Struggle for Unity, 1745-1815* (Baltimore: The Johns Hopkins University Press, 1992), 3. This concept of power is very difficult for "modern" Anglo

Americans to understand. Yellow Wolf, in a brief oral interview about his "power" or wyakin noted the same difficulty. He said, "It is hard to explain to the white man about the Indian's wy-akin." Undated oral interview with L.V. McWhorter, in the L.V. McWhorter Collection, Cage 55, Box 15, Folder 97, Washington State University, Manuscripts and Special Collections, Pullman, Washington.
33. Slickpoo and Walker, *Noon Nee-Me-Poo*, 57.
34. Ibid., 57.
35. Ibid., 30.
36. Ibid., 58. Quests were not always successful. Oliver W. Frank, Nez Perce tribal elder and activist, mentioned in a brief oral history that he "spent three days and nights up on the Rocky Ridge Mountain top, but no words appeared or were spoken. So I became a common ordinary Indian." He continued that Jackson Sundown, a famous Nez Perce rodeo champion, possessed an unknown spirit guardian during his lifetime that helped him become successful in rodeo competitions. At his death, his family found a pouch with a horsefly within and determined it to be his spirit power. Oliver W. Frank Oral Interview, interviewed by Clifford Trafzer, Los Angeles, California, July 1973.
37. Lucullus Virgil McWhorter, *Yellow Wolf: His Own Story*, (Caldwell, Idaho: The Caxton Printers, Ltd., 1940), 297.
38. Slickpoo and Walker, *Noon Nee-Me-Poo*, 58-61.
39. McWhorter, *Yellow Wolf: His Own Story*, 28-29. See also Horace Axtell and Margo Aragon, *A Little Bit of Wisdom: Conversations with a Nez Perce Elder*, (Lewiston, Idaho: Confluence Press, 1997), and Slickpoo and Walker, *Noon Nee Me Poo* for further discussions of contemporary Nez Perce religion. Nez Perce culture, including religion, changed over time and adapted creatively to the stresses and opportunities of the last 150 years. Religious practice has changed and will continue to change but still maintains its roots in the body of oral narrative and physical practices of relatives and kin. For an excellent discussion of how societies transmit memory and physical practices see Paul Connerton, *How Societies Remember*, Themes in Social Sciences Series, John Dunn, Jack Goody, Eugene A. Hammel and Geoffrey Hawthorn, eds. (New York: Cambridge University Press, 1989).
40. Slickpoo and Walker, *Noon Nee-Me-Poo*, 61.
41. Consequences could range from spirit sickness to death, depending on the circumstances. For example, Herbert Spinden related a story from Nez Perce informants about how Beaver and Muskrat killed a boy who used their names inappropriately. See Herbert Joseph Spinden, "The Nez Perce Indians," *Memoirs of the American Anthropological Association 2* (1908): 258. Herbert Joseph Spinden collected ethnographic and archaeological information on the Nez Perce from 1907 to 1908. His research was funded by the Peabody Museum of Harvard University and the American Museum of Natural History.
42. Hunn, *Nch'I-Wana – "The Big River"*, 232.

43. Herbert Joseph Spinden, "The Nez Perce Indians," *Memoirs of the American Anthropological Association* 2 (1908): 258.
44. Deward E. Walker, Jr., *Conflict and Schism in Nez Perce Acculturation: A Study of Religion and Politics*, (Pullman: Washington State University Press, Revised Edition, 1985), 30.
45. A more thorough discussion of religious change on the Columbia Plateau can be found in Chapter Three of this work.
46. Verne E. Ray, *Cultural Relations in the Plateau of Northwestern America* (Los Angeles: Southwest Museum Press, 1939), 24.
47. See Verne Ray, Herbert Spinden, and Deward Walker for discussions of the egalitarianism of the Nez Perce. Egalitarianism equals simplicity for these researchers. According to these researchers, lack of political structure and institutions ensured "freedom" and decentralization of power.
48. Spinden, "The Nez Perce Indians", 175-176.
49. Ray, "Native Villages," 113. Most importantly, Ray asserted villages did not interact with one another during peace, but only came together out of necessity in times of war or crisis. This notion of isolation seems a bit far-fetched and unrealistic. During the seasonal round, villages came together to collect and gather food, and also for social interaction. The Winter Dance or Guardian Spirit Dance in the winter involved villages from the surrounding area. This interaction was not limited to Nez Perce villages, but also included Palouse, Cayuse, Umatilla, and other communities that participated in food acquisition, celebrations, and also mutual defense against enemies. Again, it appears that the simplistic thesis prevails here. By asserting that villages were isolated, atomistic entities, it became easier to label Nez Perce society and social relations as "primitive".
50. Spinden, "The Nez Perce Indians", 242.
51. Ibid., 243.
52. Slickpoo and Walker, *Noon Nee-Me-Poo*, 52.
53. Spinden, "The Nez Perce Indians", 243.
54. Slickpoo and Walker, *Noon Nee-Me-Poo*, 46.
55. Hunn, *Nch'I-Wana – "The Big River"*, 201.
56. Ibid., 201.
57. Slickpoo and Walker, *Noon Nee-Me-Poo*, 47.
58. Ibid., 48.
59. Hunn,, *Nch'I-Wana – "The Big River"*, 205.
60. Spinden, "The Nez Perce Indians", 251 and Slickpoo and Walker, *Noon Nee-Me-Poo*, 48.
61. Hunn, *Nch'I-Wana – "The Big River"*, 206.
62. Ibid., 206-207.
63. Ibid., 208.
64. Ibid., 208.
65. Ibid., 209.
66. Ibid., 210.
67. Trafzer, *Grandmother, Grandfather, and Old Wolf*, 268-270.
68. See Herbert Spinden, "The Nez Perce Indians", 251-253 and Allen Slickpoo, Sr., and Deward E. Walker, Jr., *Noon Nee-Me-Poo*, 51-52 for a complete

discussion of burial practices. Both Eugene Hunn in *Nch' I- Wana* and Clifford E. Trafzer in *Death Stalks the Yakama* include detailed descriptions and insight into the death and burial practices of Columbia Plateau Native Americans.
69. Hunn, *Nch'I-Wana – "The Big River"*, 118.
70. Ibid., 118.
71. Slickpoo and Walker, *Noon Nee-Me-Poo*, 30 and Hunn, *Nch'I-Wana – "The Big River"*, 119. Sahaptin words and terms transliterated into English often are spelled differently in various sources. Since Sahaptin Plateau cultures used oral means of transmitting information and ideas and did not possess their own form of writing or alphabet, academics and researchers have attempted to use English characters for this language as a means to write down Nez Perce knowledge and oral narratives.
72. Hunn, *Nch'I-Wana – "The Big River"*, 119-121.
73. Slickpoo and Walker, *Noon Nee-Me-Poo*, 30.
74. Ibid, 30.
75. Slickpoo and Walker, *Noon Nee-Me-Poo*, 30 and Hunn, *Nch'I-Wana – "The Big River"*, 127.
76. Slickpoo and Walker, *Noon Nee-Me-Poo*, 35.
77. Verne E. Ray, "Native Villages and Groupings of the Columbia Basin," The *Pacific Northwest Quarterly*, Volume 27, Number 2, (1936), 13.
78. The photograph on the following page shows the Heart of the Monster located outside of Kamiah, Idaho.
79. Allen Slickpoo, Sr., "IEPBS/History of Idaho #15," interview by Idaho Educational Public Broadcasting/Idaho Public Television, 19 September 1988, 11. Slickpoo's observations of Coyote are crucial for understanding how the Nez Perce creatively and constructively adapted their cultural and historical knowledge to reflect their understanding of present circumstances.

NOTES TO CHAPTER THREE

1. Phinney, *Nez Perce Texts*, 27.
2. The use of the Coyote and Monster story as a narrative device in no way assaults or disregards the importance of this story to the Nez Perce. As Allen Slickpoo, Sr., noted, Coyote is still alive and teaching the people. Using the narrative does not detract from its centrality in Nez Perce historical knowledge and cultural practice.
3. Phinney, *Nez Perce Texts*, 27. The author hopes not to repeat earlier historical myths by encouraging a belief that even Coyote knew the consequences of confronting Monster and had simply resigned himself to his destiny. In the narrative, Coyote prepared himself to be swallowed, but it is far from certain that Monster would swallow Coyote. The important aspect of the story was that Coyote prepared for all contingencies. Within the narrative, Coyote voluntarily confronted Monster and prepared for the consequences.
4. Hunn, *Nch'I-Wana – "The Big River"*, 19.

5. Christopher L. Miller, *Prophetic Worlds: Indians and Whites on the Columbia Plateau*, (New Brunswick, New Jersey: Rutgers University Press, 1985), 23-26.
6. Eugene Hunn noted that Christopher Miller's assertions about the extent of cultural change resulting from the "Little Ice Age" were overstated and that these climatic changes did not significantly affect Plateau culture. Hunn's criticism was correct and the use of Miller's argument was used in the above text to describe how environment created conditions that challenged the strength of Plateau culture. While climatic change may not have changed Nez Perce culture, it certainly influenced how the Nez Perce practiced their seasonal round, where they spent time during various seasons of the year, and how they collected and distributed resources.
7. The reader must keep in mind that the three forces set in motion by the arrival of Europeans interacted and often created situations that affected communities far removed from areas controlled by Europeans. As Europeans forced Native Americans to move or conquered their territory, these communities moved to areas often occupied by other communities. The introduction of the horse to North America and its distribution conferred advantages to those communities that controlled this resource. It also made movement much easier as well as resistance to white incursions. Disease also impacted the depth of population movements and the survival of various communities and was directly related to contact with Europeans or Euro-Americans.
8. Hunn, *Nch'I-Wana: 'The Big River*, 20-22.
9. Ibid., 22. While James Selam is not Nez Perce, his experience and communal memory serve as good indicators of the attitudes and beliefs of other Plateau cultures. While much of the glorification of Nez Perce horsemanship originated with Anglo Americans, Nez Perce like Allen Slickpoo Sr., Horace Axtell, and Yellow Wolf reiterated the importance of the horse to Nez Perce culture.
10. Ibid., 23.
11. Francis Haines, "The Northward Spread of Horses Among the Plains Indians," *American Anthropologist* 40 (1938): 429-431. See also Hunn, *Nch'I-Wana*, 23.
12. Alvin M. Josephy, Jr., *The Nez Perce Indians and the Opening of the Northwest*, (Lincoln, Nebraska: University of Nebraska, 1965), 24-25. See also Robert Boyd, *People of the Dalles, The Indians of Wascopam Mission: A Historical Ethnography Based on the Papers of the Methodist Missionaries*, Studies in the Anthropology of North American Indians, eds. Raymond J. DeMaille and Douglas R. Parks, (Lincoln Nebraska: University of Nebraska Press, 1996), 12.
13. Hunn, *Nch'I-Wana*, 24.
14. Alvin M. Josephy, Jr., *The Nez Perce Indians*, 27-28. The introduction of the horse increased the scope and distance of intercommunity relationships experienced by the Nez Perce. Nez Perce and other Plateau cultures maintained elaborate and deep relationships with one another despite their lack of horses. For a detailed discussion of the adoption of Plains style clothing

and material culture see Erna Gunther, "The Westward Movement of Some Plains Traits," *American Anthropologist* 52, No. 2 (1950): 174-180.
15. Ibid., 25. See also Boyd, *People of the Dalles*, 63-71. Boyd asserted that Native Americans practiced trade differently along the mid-Columbia and these practices were not well understood by Anglo Americans infused with the values of capitalism.
16. Eugene S. Hunn, *Nch-I-Wana: "The Big River,"* 25.
17. This was perhaps best illustrated by the name Nez Perce, given to the Numipu by Europeans. Allen Slickpoo, Sr. contended that the practice of nose piercing was never widely practiced by the Numipu and that this designation or name was a European misnomer that lumped the Numipu into the cultures of other Native American communities. Allen Slickpoo, Sr., "IEPBS/History of Idaho #15," interview by Idaho Educational Public Broadcasting System/Idaho Public Television, 19 September 1988, 11.
18. Boyd, *People of the Dalles*, 140-141. According to Eugene Hunn, most researchers assumed that diseases arrived in the Columbia Plateau as a result of traveling up the Missouri River in 1782. It was likely, Hunn noted, that this later epidemic might have spent itself on the now immune survivors of the 1775 epidemic. Robert Boyd and Eugene Hunn both agreed that the first epidemic occurred in the late eighteenth century as a direct result of contact with Europeans along the Pacific Coast. The spread of disease from coastal groups inland to the Columbia Plateau directly contradicts the notion of Native American community isolation expounded by many Anglo-American scholars and popular opinion in the late nineteenth and early twentieth centuries.
19. Hunn, *Nch'I-Wana: "The Big River,"* 27. Robert Boyd also supported the contention that by 1829 the Native American population in the Pacific Northwest was less than half the number of seventy-five years earlier. See Boyd, *People of the Dalles*, 141.
20. Boyd, *People of the Dalles*, 143. Boyd detailed the different outbreaks of disease related to the influx of Anglo Americans into the Pacific Northwest. He also noted the direct relationship between these disease outbreaks and the Whitman Massacre. The measles outbreak of 1847 in the vicinity of the Whitman Mission directly led to the "Massacre." Native Americans, in this case the Cayuse, understood the relationship between the intrusion of Anglo Americans and the eruption of disease within their communities.
21. The Whitman "Massacre" will be discussed in more detail in a section of the next chapter. Clifford Trafzer in *Death Stalks the Yakama* (East Lansing: Michigan State University Press, 1997) discussed the physical, spiritual and psychological impacts of massive disease introduction. While mainly focusing on twentieth century Yakama death records, it is plausible to extrapolate these findings to earlier epidemics and to their impact on Native American communities. Of greatest importance was the impact on the transmission of cultural knowledge, both historical and practical. The most vulnerable members of these communities were undoubtedly children and old people. Epidemics most likely hit these groups the hardest. The death of old people

in the community meant the loss of knowledge and a lack of transmission to the younger generation.
22. Christopher Miller contended that traditional religious practices "died" in the face of these forces and that a new religious movement emerged mixing new revelation with the old. It is difficult to determine the validity of Miller's claim. This transformation occurred before the arrival of Anglo Americans on the Columbia Plateau, and as noted earlier, whites generally misunderstood and often despised the religious practices of Native Americans and therefore often misinterpreted religious practice among Plateau cultures. Anglo Americans arrived on the Columbia Plateau during a very dynamic period and with little regard for understanding Nez Perce and Plateau culture before the arrival of whites. As with most cultural transformation or change, new practices or institutions firmly sit on the base of older traditions and practices.
23. Eugene Hunn also discussed a transformation in Plateau religion around 1800. His description is more nuanced since he related and integrated the evolution of new rituals and practices into the flow of time and history. Hunn argued that this change of form was not a break with former religious practice but should be viewed as a continuum and he found its inspiration and theology within traditional religious corpus and practice of pre-1800 Plateau culture.
24. Miller's explanation of this transformation is related in pages 37 to 50. For Miller, the new practices were evidence of the development of a new system of religious thought and practice. Miller relied on psychological anthropologist Anthony F.C. Wallace for insight into religious transformation, "Once the system reaches the point where stress can no longer be relieved or tolerated, Wallace continues, the entire system has to be scrapped. While some traditional elements of the culture may remain the same, they and all of reality come to be seen in a new and revolutionary way: a way that helps diffuse stress rather than concentrate it." This view took the changes in form as evidence of a new structure for Plateau religion able to deal with and dissipate the stress related to the outside forces instigated by the presence of the Euro-Americans in North America. Miller's contentions failed to address the continuity evident in the new forms and practices. The Nez Perce and other Plateau peoples continued to sing songs, go on vision quests, fall sick from spirit sickness, pray and rely on shamans just as they had for centuries.
25. Eugene S. Hunn, *Nch'I-Wana: "The Big River,"* 241.
26. Ibid.
27. Clifford Trafzer discussed in detail Yakama views of death and disease in *Death Stalks the Yakama*. The Yakama shared Plateau cultural traits and religious practices. Not all illness was attributed to misuse or abuse of spiritual power. Accidents, age, war and infection also caused death. For Plateau cultures, sickness generally emerged from a moral infraction or the malevolence of an enemy or of a community member. As the epidemics raged, it struck at the very heart of how Plateau Indians understood disease and created great stress and moral dilemma.

28. Hunn, *Nch'I-Wana: "The Big River,"* 241.
29. Boyd, *People of the Dalles,* 174.
30. Hunn, *Nch'I-Wana: "The Big River,"* 242. While shamans' traditional methods proved powerless to deal with new diseases introduced by Euro-Americans, many people continued to go to shamans for relief and for attempts to cure the disease. Shamans continued to use their knowledge of herbs, medicinal plants, and other remedies to attempt to relieve the suffering of their people. It seems plausible to suggest that shamans often suffered a great deal as a result of their efforts since they were exposed to contagion on a continuous basis. The epidemic not only stripped communities of doctors and those able to deal with disease, but also demonstrated to Plateau communities that these epidemics resulted from very powerful forces that needed to be dealt with on some level. Trafzer and Hunn both maintain that the changes in religious practice stemmed from attempts to deal with the impact of disease and later the intrusion of Anglo Americans into their land.
31. Eugene Hunn remarked that these prophecies cannot be documented historically but had a powerful impact on the reception of white explorers and fur traders in the Pacific Northwest. David Thompson remarked in his journal that he was greeted everywhere as a god. He probably misinterpreted Plateau reactions, but, as a whole, the prophecy concerning the arrival of whites may have signaled the closeness of the end of the world. Columbia Plateau Indians did not know how soon these prophecies would come to fruition.
32. Hunn, *Nch'I-Wana: "The Big River,"* 248.
33. The Nez Perce formally met their first Anglo Americans with the arrival of Lewis and Clark, but there were other Euro-Americans who visited the Pacific Northwest. While Meany and others spend a great deal of time describing the exploits of explorers, the author consciously decided not to recount these activities since those explorers failed to physically come in contact with the Nez Perce and other Plateau communities. The subversive turn of this narrative structure attempts to undermine the emplotment of history in the Pacific Northwest as heroic and romantic by seeing explorers like Drake, Captain Cook, and Captain Robert Gray as the Nez Perce perceived them at the time, as non-participants in their history.
34. The economic motives of the purchase and the expedition are evident in the instructions Jefferson gave to Lewis in 1803, "The object of your mission is to explore the Missouri river, & such principal stream of it, as, by it's course & communication with the waters of the Pacific Ocean, may offer the most direct & practicable water communication across this continent, for the purposes of commerce." Bernard DeVoto, ed., *The Journals of Lewis and Clark,* (Boston: Houghton Mifflin Company, 1953), xlv.
35. James Rhonda, *Lewis and Clark among the Indians* (Lincoln: University of Nebraska Press, 1984), 113.
36. Rhonda, *Lewis and Clark among the Indians,* 142.
37. Carlos Schwantes, *The Pacific Northwest: An Interpretive History* (Lincoln: University of Nebraska Press, 1989), 50-51. Schwantes provided a well-writ-

ten synopsis of the expedition and its impacts on the Pacific Northwest. For a more thorough description of the meeting between the Corps of Discovery and the Nez Perce Indians see Rhonda, *Lewis and Clark among the Indians*, 162. Also see Bernard DeVoto, ed., *The Journals of Lewis and Clark*, Boston: Houghton Mifflin Company (1953).
38. Rhonda, *Lewis and Clark among the Indians*, 157-160.
39. Ibid., 168-173.
40. Schwantes, *The Pacific Northwest: An Interpretive History*, 51-52.
41. Ibid., 53.
42. Ibid., 55-56.
43. Ibid., 58-59.
44. Ibid., 59-60.
45. Ibid., 60-64.
46. Ibid., 64.
47. For a detailed discussion of the historical profession and the development of interpretive frameworks during the late nineteenth and early twentieth centuries, see Peter Novick, *That Noble Dream: The "Objectivity Question" and the American Historical Profession*, (Cambridge: Cambridge University Press, 1988).
48. While Meany worked under Turner and accepted his interpretative scheme, he also attempted to create a unique place for Pacific Northwest history. Meany contested some of the interpretative framework of his mentor in a brief article "The Towns of the Pacific Northwest were not founded on the fur trade," disputing his claims that towns and cities originated from early fur trading posts. The particulars of the dispute were not as interesting as the larger agreement between the two men. Whatever the means, whether through fur-trading posts, missionaries or settlers, the structure of the narrative remained the same, namely narrating the "evolution of civilization" in the Pacific Northwest and other regions of the United States.
49. An examination of Meany's course syllabi for his Pacific Northwest Course shows a growth in detail and material included but the overall structure is maintained throughout. The publication of his History merely solidified in print the oral and classroom framework Meany used and developed during the course of his early career. See <u>Undated Syllabus</u> Accession Number 106-70-12, Box Number 60, Folder 23. *The Pacific Northwest: A Syllabus*, Accession Number 106-70-12, Box Number 70, Folder 1, undated. *History 13: Northwestern History*, Accession Number 106-70-12, Box Number 79, Folder Number 13, undated. Edmond S. Meany Papers, University of Washington Library.
50. Monster, in this context, must be defined. The author does not contend that Meany or other individual Anglo Americans were monsters. Instead, Monster is used to represent all the efforts of Anglo Americans and their institutions to consume or destroy Native Americans and their cultures in the Pacific Northwest. "Monster" is figurative and non-literal and is not meant to describe any person in particular.
51. Even this work falls into the need for creating a starting place, and the penchant for American historians to place Native Americans into a narrative

framework leaves them waiting for the arrival of Europeans and Anglo Americans. The author chose to focus the first two chapters on Nez Perce and Columbia Plateau cultures but still follows, to some degree, the standard format used in most texts by historians of United States history. The term "civilization" was used in the above sentence to show how historical texts imagine the time before the arrival of Europeans in North America. For most of the past century, historians continued to write about and imagine North America as a pristine, natural place inhabited by those incapable of creating their own "civilization".

52. Edmond S. Meany, *History of the State of Washington* (New York: the Macmillan Company, 1910), 5.
53. Ibid., 5.
54. Klein, *Frontiers of the Historical Imagination*, 129.
55. Meany, *History of the State of Washington*, 6.
56. Klein, *Frontiers of the Historical Imagination*, 81.
57. The authors of Western Historical Publishing Company, *An Illustrated History of North Idaho Embracing Nez Perces, Idaho, Latah, Kootenai and Shoshone Counties State of Idaho* (Boise: Western Historical Publishing Company, 1903) are not mentioned by name anywhere in the text of the book. It is assumed that the book was a product of a cooperative effort of Western Historical Publishing Company employees or contract writers. The book was published to sell to pioneers and their families in the various counties mentioned in the book.
58. Western Historical Publishing Company, *An Illustrated History of North Idaho Embracing Nez Perces, Idaho, Latah, Kootenai and Shoshone Counties State of Idaho* (Boise: Western Historical Publishing Company, 1903), 44-45.
59. Undated Syllabus Accession Number 106-70-12, Box Number 60, Folder 23. The Pacific Northwest: A Syllabus, Accession Number 106-70-12, Box Number 70, Folder 1, undated. History 13: Northwestern History, Accession Number 106-70-12, Box Number 79, Folder Number 13, undated. Edmond S. Meany Papers, University of Washington Library.
60. See Meany, *Pacific Northwest Syllabi* and *History of the State of Washington* as well as *An Illustrated History of North Idaho* for further examples of these narrative structures.
61. Klein, *Frontiers of Historical Imagination*, 139.
62. Meany, *History of the State of Washington*, 57. Meany used this type of language, combining romanticism and heroism, to describe many of the "discoverers" and explorers in his text. The depth and appeal of heroic and romantic narrative structures in historical texts was illustrated by two words in the text selection. Meany used the phrase "undaunted courage" to describe Jedediah Smith and his exploits. Stephen E. Ambrose's recent book about the Lewis and Clark Expedition is also titled *Undaunted Courage* and harkens back to the same types of narrative cues and symbols created by earlier writers and historians. Popular imagination and historical consciousness continued to rely on discoverers and explorers as tropes for the heroic and romantic. Native Americans, on the other hand, often failed to

appear in these scenes of heroism except to help the heroes or as reminder of their eventual demise.
63. Klein, *Frontiers of Historical Imagination*, 141.
64. Ibid., 142.

NOTES TO CHAPTER FOUR

1. Archie Phinney, *Nez Perce Texts*, 27.
2. Meany, *History of the State of Washington*, 106.
3. Clifford E. Trafzer and Richard D. Scheuerman, *Renegade Tribe: The Palouse Indians and the Invasion of the Inland Pacific Northwest*, 21. The two boys selected by George Simpson were Nicholas Garry and J.H. Pelty. When these young men returned to the Northwest in 1829, they created a great deal of interest because they spoke English and knew about Christianity. Trafzer and Scheuerman noted that these and other contacts with Christianity elicited interest in learning about Christianity. Concerns about disease and death also may have contributed to this interest since it appeared that whites did not suffer in the same way and may have possessed some power to end the disease and misery associated with the epidemics.
4. Kate McBeth, *The Nez Perces Since Lewis and Clark*, 27-29. McBeth was a Presbyterian missionary deeply devoted to and inculcated with evangelical thought and theology. Missionaries, lay people and clergy in this tradition often narrated their actions in the context of native peoples or non-Christians preparing the way for their arrival or even, through the actions of the Holy Spirit, inviting missionaries to their homeland. These assertions by McBeth illustrated the filter of Christianity used by Anglo Americans when perceiving and explaining Nez Perce behavior, culture, society, and religion. The Nez Perce practiced the Washani religion and did not worship the sun. Contrary to McBeth's assertion, there is no evidence to support the contention that Lewis and Clark affected Nez Perce religious belief and practice.
5. Slickpoo and Walker, *Noon-Ne-Me-Poo*, 71. Slickpoo disputed the importance of the delegation to St. Louis and offered alternative ways of understanding the arrival of the delegation in St. Louis. According to Slickpoo, the four men may have been motivated by desire for trade goods, hopes of gifts and wealth and perhaps just simple curiosity about the religion of white people. It was clear that Slickpoo and other Nez Perce treat this episode with ambiguity and most certainly dispute the notion that these men represented all Nez Perce or Flathead.
6. Trafzer and Scheuerman, *Renegade Tribe*, 21-22.
7. Meany, *History of the States of Washington*, 107. The reference to the Macedonian cry was crucial to understanding how Anglo Americans understood the delegation of Nez Perce and Flatheads. While completely disregarding the desires and requests of Native Americans, Anglo-American evangelicals reverted to a previous narrative to understand the request of Nez Perce and Flatheads to find out about the Christian religion. Paul's vision remained a central text and narrative justification for preparing and sending missionaries to various regions of the world. In the nineteenth

century, some Anglo Americans interpreted the delegation's mission in light of their interpretations of the Bible and their own religious experiences. In a broader context, the Second Great Awakening occurred during the same period as the delegation and some of the religious fervor and energy generated by this movement gave impetus to mission organizations. The Macedonian cry implied that those practicing an "inferior," "lower" or less "civilized" religion understood the power of Christianity and wanted to know more. Meany's Indians thirsting for the spiritual advantages of the white mans religion fell directly into this type of thinking.
8. All of the missionaries involved in missionary activity in the Pacific Northwest did not act by themselves but worked within the existing institution of the American Board of Commissioners for Foreign Missions. The board represented a number of denominations with Methodists and Presbyterians heavily represented in the organization. Jason Lee, Samuel Parker, Marcus Whitman and Henry Spalding belonged to and were endorsed by this mission agency. The American Board also sought an international presence and sent missionaries to Hawaii and other regions of the Pacific Slope. Missionaries represented a Christian Manifest Destiny seeking to expand both Christianity and Anglo-American values and culture as they moved west.
9. Trafzer and Scheuerman, *Renegade Tribe*, 22-23.
10. Slickpoo and Walker, *Noon Nee-Me-Poo*, 72.
11. *An Illustrated History of North Idaho*, 11.
12. Slickpoo and Walker, *Noon Nee-Me-Poo*, 72.
13. Ibid., 72 and 75. Allen Slickpoo lists the laws on page 75. Most of the laws sought to protect property like homes, outbuildings, and personal property. Most of the punishments were fairly severe with hanging, whippings, and restitution as standard options. The Nez Perce most likely perceived these laws as intrusions on their own legal and political institutions and values. Henry Spalding also contributed to resentment and conflict through his volatile and harsh character. Alvin Josephy narrated a number of conflicts emanating from Spalding and souring his relationship with a number of Nez Perce. See Josephy, *The Nez Perces Indians*, 155-158.
14. Alvin M. Josephy, Jr., *The Nez Perce Indians*, 159.
15. Ibid., 197.
16. Ibid., 214.
17. The balance of power between Britain and the United States shifted as more and more American settlers journeyed to the Oregon Country. The British foresaw the impact of this migration and realized that joint occupancy was threatened and would not last. Native Americans responded with similar trepidation as they watched greater numbers of settlers. In particular, many Nez Perce and other Plateau communities heard from other Indians from the east how settlers took their land and brought diseases with them.
18. Trafzer and Scheuerman, *Renegade Tribe*, 25. The problems and conflicts between the missionaries and Native American communities on the Columbia Plateau were discussed in detail by Trafzer and Scheuerman as well as by Josephy in *The Nez Perce Indians and the Opening of the Pacific Northwest*.

19. Trafzer and Scheuerman, *Renegade Tribe*, 26-27.
20. Ibid., 24.
21. Ibid., 30.
22. Cornelius James Brosnan was born in Michigan on June 14, 1882. He received an A.B. degree from the University of Michigan in 1905 and became a teacher and superintendent of schools. In 1912, Brosnan moved to Idaho as superintendent of Nampa, Idaho schools. From 1920-19212, Brosnan was an Austin Scholar at Harvard University, receiving his M.A. in 1921. In that year, he joined the faculty of the University of Idaho. He completed doctoral work at the University of California, Berkeley in 1929 and became chair of the Department of American History, University of Idaho in 1930. Brosnan wrote a number of books on Pacific Northwest History, focusing primarily on Idaho. His most noted works were his book on Jason Lee, an Oregon missionary, which was nominated for a Pulitzer Prize in 1932 and his *History of the State of Idaho*, used for many years as a textbook in public schools throughout Idaho. Brosnan retired from the university in 1952, was promoted to emeritus status, and taught as a visiting professor at Whitworth College, Spokane, Washington. In January 1961, C.J. Brosnan died of a stroke in Sacramento, California.
23. Kate McBeth, the sister of Sue McBeth, worked with her sister as a missionary to the Nez Perce. She arrived on the reservation in 1879 while her sister Sue had been there since the resumption of the old mission site in 1873. Kate McBeth wrote her book, *The Nez Perces Since Lewis and Clark*, in 1908 and the book is still printed in limited editions to this day. The focus of the book was not about all Nez Perce, but principally the Christian segment of the community. This is understandable since McBeth's informants and knowledge about the Nez Perce came from that segment of the Nez Perce community. While presenting interesting contrasts to Edmond Meany and C.J. Brosnan, the author decided to introduce her work later in this work. The later chapters of McBeth's book provided valuable insight into the struggles between various portions of the Nez Perce community and on the use of Nez Perce history by a non-academic.
24. Meany, *History of the State of Washington*, 106.
25. C.J. Brosnan, *History of the State of Idaho*, 68.
26. Ibid., 68.
27. Meany, *History of the State of Washington*, 117.
28. The popularity and long life of the Turner thesis can be explained through its value as a narrative device for Anglo Americans, particularly in the late nineteenth and early twentieth centuries. Kerwin Klein discussed the creation and strength of this narrative device in *Frontiers of Historical Imagination*.
29. Western Historical Publishers, *An Illustrated History of North Idaho*, 17. Since the end was known, there was only one way to narrate the history of the Pacific Northwest and the contact/conflict between Anglo Americans and Native Americans. As noted earlier, to step outside of this narrative framework, particularly for non-historians, created an untenable situation for the person consuming the narrative. The identity of Anglo Americans

was supported and bolstered by narratives like the ones mentioned in the section above.
30. Meany, *History of the State of Washington*, 116.
31. Cornelius J. Brosnan, "The Legend of Marcus Whitman: A Practical Exercise in Historical Criticism." Unpublished Manuscript, date unknown, 14-15.
32. C.J. Brosnan, "The Legend of Marcus Whitman: A Practical Exercise in Historical Criticism." Unpublished Manuscript, date unknown, 7-14. Some of the earliest book forms of the legend were written by Oliver W. Nixon, *How Marcus Whitman Saved Oregon: A True Romance of Patriotic Heroism, Christian Devotion and final Martyrdom, with sketches of life on the plains and mountains in pioneer days* (Chicago: Star Publishing Company, 1895), Myron Eells, *Father Eells, or the results of fifty-five years of missionary labors in Washington and Oregon: a biography of Reverend Cushing Eells* (Boston: Congregational Sunday school and Publishing Society, 1894), and Charles Carleton Coffin, *Building the Nation: Events in the History of the United States from the Revolution to the beginning of the War between the States* (New York: Harper and Brothers, 1883).
33. See George A. Frykman, *Seattle's Historian and Promoter: The Life of Edmond Stephen Meany* (Pullman, Washington: Washington State University Press, 1998). Frykman's biography of Meany detailed the many different roles he played in the Seattle area, but principally focused on his academic career and his struggle for recognition as a regional historian. The use of history and the creation of narratives about Anglo Americans in the Pacific Northwest not only silenced or swallowed Native Americans, but also worked in a similar way on groups within the Anglo-American community. The debate over Whitman's role in the acquisition of Oregon illustrated the tension between popular stories about missionaries, explorers and others and the professional historical community that sought to standardize their narrative and agree on methods for using texts and evidence. The debate focused on the "silencing" of popular memory by the historical profession because it failed to meet the evidentiary standards of the profession. For Brosnan, the texts supporting the myth were those that revealed "an unfamiliarity with modern historical methods" and "the spirit of the advocate, and not that of the open-minded investigator." In essence, the narrative created by the historical profession worked dually to silence Native American voices and perspectives as well as more "common" Anglo-American voices. The broad swath of Anglo-American characters, the settlers, fur traders, thrifty gold seekers and others remained as faceless and anonymous as many of the Native Americans. They do not lend themselves to the same romantic devices that characters like Marcus Whitman, Lewis and Clark, and others so aptly fit.
34. Meany, *History of the State of Washington*, 122.
35. Ibid., 127.
36. C.J. Brosnan, "The Legend of Marcus Whitman: A Practical Exercise in Historical Criticism." Unpublished Manuscript, date unknown, bibliography Brosnan's description of texts devoted to the Whitman myth would have also applied to a pamphlet printed and distributed by Whitman College.

The pamphlet described in detail how Whitman saved Oregon for the United States and consistently painted Whitman as the Savior of Anglo-American civilization in the Pacific Northwest. On the front of the pamphlet, three red stars stand out on an American flag. The author(s) continually referred to the stars and asserted that the three stars represented the three states Whitman saved for the United States. They were his legacy to everyone in the country and, most importantly, to those living in the region he "saved". The author(s) tied Whitman's heroism to the heroism required to build a college in a region that still may have seemed uncivilized to many in the east. Of course, Whitman College, run by the Congregational Church at the time, was the bearer of Whitman's name and harkened back to its founding by Reverend Cushing Eells. The college used the Whitman myth as a means to tie itself to the same progressive narrative framework that narrated the arrival and flourishing of civilization on the Columbia Plateau.

37. The flexibility of the narrative structure, as first articulated by Frederick Jackson Turner, was evident in Brosnan's introductory sentence in Chapter eight of *History of the State of Idaho*. The general plan of development must follow the cadence of explorer, fur trader then missionary. In 1926, Brosnan continued to use portions of Turner's thesis but avoided placing Whitman at the center of the missionary narrative by choosing Idaho as the location for the progressive development of Anglo-American civilization. While he mentioned Whitman and the murders, he circumvented popular historical imagination and focused on Spalding and his role in Idaho. The devotion to the achievements, the "firsts" of the missionary was still present in the text but did not focus on Whitman. Whitman still maintained an important part in the story, but Brosnan's focused the narrative on the broader implications of missionary work in Idaho rather than relying on the more popular myth to explain the progression of Anglo-American civilization in the Pacific Northwest.
38. Meany clearly stated this connection on page 123 of *History of the State of Washington*. He noted, "Whitman held that white men were bringing civilization into the wilderness, and should be helped in doing so even by men sent as missionaries among the Indians."
39. Michel-Rolph Trouillot, *Silencing the Past: Power and the Production of History*, Boston: Beacon Press, (1995), 27.
40. Schwantes, *The Pacific Northwest: An Interpretive History*, 104.
41. Ibid., 104. Schwantes noted that the creation of Washington territory was unusual because of the lack of population in the new territory. Washington would not become a state until 1889, thirty-six years after designation as a territory. The lack of population hindered statehood, and both Washington and Idaho territories experienced much violence and conflict between Anglo Americans and Native Americans in the following twenty-five years.
42. Isaac I. Stevens was thirty-five years old when appointed Washington's territorial governor. He was a veteran of the Mexican American War, serving with the Corps of Engineers. He was also a graduate of West Point.
43. Trafzer and Scheuerman, *Renegade Tribe*, 31. The combination of seemingly conflicting roles is a hallmark of nineteenth century political and social

networks that connected Anglo-American elites and rewarded them with lucrative and powerful positions.
44. Ibid., 31.
45. Ibid., 39. Stevens relied on others to counsel and instruct him about various Plateau communities and to translate for him during the councils. The distance of the divide between Stevens and those with whom he was sent to negotiate is palpable in the minutes of the negotiations for the Treaty of 1855. Stevens used language and terms that often were insulting, or at least perplexing, to the Nez Perce, Yakama, Palouse, Walla Walla, Cayuse and others present at the council. Allen Slickpoo, Sr., noted that the use of "My Children" was particularly offensive. See Slickpoo and Walker, *Noon Nee-Me-Poo*, 78.
46. Kamiakin was an extremely influential leader among the Yakama and was well respected among many groups on the Plateau. He was related to Nez Perce people, Salish people, and others through a broad network of family. See Josephy, *The Nez Perce Indians*, 286-290 and Robert H. Ruby and John A. Brown, *Indians of the Pacific Northwest*, 125 for more detailed biographical data on Kamiakin.
47. The Hudson's Bay Company employed many Native Americans and those people came into contact with Nez Perce and other Plateau peoples in their fur trading and trapping roles. The Iroquois and other eastern peoples, told Plateau people about their treatment in the east and warned them about United States Indian policy.
48. Trafzer and Scheuerman, *Renegade Tribe*, 39-45.
49. Ibid., 42-45.
50. Ibid., 46-49. This council was generally called the Walla Walla Council. All Plateau communities sent representatives to talk with Governor Stevens. As Clifford Trafzer pointed out, Stevens and his party acquired a great deal of experience dealing with Indians through the Puget Sound negotiations. Nez Perce, Cayuse, Palouse, Walla Walla, Umatilla, Wanapums, Wenatchees, and Klikitats represented the bulk of Native American participants at the council.
51. Robert H. Ruby and John A. Brown, *Indians of the Pacific Northwest*, 131.
52. Slickpoo and Walker, *Noon Nee-Me-Poo*, 77. Clifford Trafzer and Richard Scheuerman also noted that language problems existed from the beginning of the proceedings. William Craig, Andrew Pambrun, Nathan Olney and John Whitford, all Anglo Americans, were appointed translators at the start of the council. They note that even with good translators the process of negotiations was distorted since neither Stevens nor Palmer could talk directly with Indian representatives and relied on the skills of others to faithfully translate meanings and nuances. See Trafzer and Scheuerman, *Renegade Tribe*, 46-59, for a detailed discussion of the Walla Walla Council. Another excellent resource on the Council is Alvin Josephy's *The Nez Perce Indians and the Opening of the Northwest*, (Lincoln: University of Nebraska Press, 1965).
53. Slickpoo and Walker, *Noon Nee-Me-Poo*, 77. Allen Slickpoo's remarks conveyed the importance of this event for the Nez Perce community and the lingering discontent with the proceedings in 1855. It is safe to say that

many Native American communities throughout the United States view treaty negotiations with the United States in similar ways. For the Nez Perce, the Walla Walla Council continues to influence their daily lives and remains present in their historical consciousness. The Nez Perce live on a daily basis with the consequences of the council and the treaty and therefore struggle to comprehend the process and its implications in a deeper and more intimate way than do Anglo Americans on the Columbia Plateau.

54. Ibid., 78.
55. Trafzer and Scheuerman, *Renegade Tribe*, 60.
56. Slickpoo and Walker, *Noon Nee-Me-Poo*, 78.
57. Schwantes, *The Pacific Northwest: An Interpretive History*, 105.
58. See Slickpoo and Walker, *Noon Nee-Me-Poo*, 87-103 for the speeches given by Stevens and Palmer. These speeches revealed the underlying motivations of the United States government in the treaty negotiations. They also illustrate the depth of devotion that Anglo Americans had for their own notions of civilization.
59. According to Clifford Trafzer, Stevens, impatient with the pace of the council, revealed his hand too early and with too much clarity. The passage clearly outlined United States Indian policy of the time. Stevens and the government wanted the Plateau peoples confined to reservations and then to undergo a transformation of culture that implied the death of their own culture and assimilation into Anglo-American society and culture.
60. See Slickpoo and Deward Walker, *Noon Ne Mee Poo*, 104 for an example of Peo Peo Mox Mox's concern. The entire text of the council and the treaty are included in the book.
61. Trafzer and Scheuerman, *Renegade Tribe*, 105-106.
62. Ibid., 55.
63. Ibid., 57-58.
64. Signing, in this instance, meant making a mark on the paper. Signing, especially in the sense of a legal document, probably was not viewed in this way by Native American participants.
65. Alvin Josephy mentioned that Kamiakin "insisted that he only made a pledge of friendship by touching a little stick as it made a mark." As noted above, the misunderstandings arising from various perspectives or interpretations surrounding actions and intent were based in the different perceptions and values held by the participants. Anglo Americans perceived and constructed the document as a legal binding text that extinguished Indian title to enormous tracts of land and opened the way for settlers to purchase the land and move into the area. For Indians, it was difficult to know exactly how they viewed the document. It was evident that "selling" the land was problematic for Plateau Indians and created tension and anxiety as Stevens and Palmer threatened them with coercion. See Josephy, *The Nez Perce Indians*, 322.
66. Josephy, *The Nez Perce Indians*, 323.
67. Slickpoo and Walker, *Noon Nee-Me-Poo*, 143. The 800 square mile Umatilla reservation was located in northeastern Oregon and included Walla Walla, Umatilla, and Cayuse people. The Nez Perce reservation included 5,000

square miles and encompassed much of traditional Nez Perce territory. A reservation was established in south central Washington for the Yakamas, Klickitats, and twelve other groups of approximately 1,200,000 acres. See Slickpoo and Walker, *Noon Nee-Me-Poo*, 142-143 for a more detailed discussion of the treaty provisions.
68. A brief discussion of the Yakama War will follow the discussion of how the treaty was interpreted by Edmond Meany, C.J. Brosnan, Kate McBeth and the authors of the Illustrated History of North Idaho.
69. Trafzer and Scheuerman, *Renegade Tribe*, 60-61.
70. Ibid., 62.
71. Ibid., 63.
72. Josephy, *The Nez Perce Indians*, 336.
73. Trafzer and Scheuerman, *Renegade Tribe*, 72.
74. Ibid., 73.
75. Meany, *History of the State of Washington*, 170.
76. Ibid., 174. The figure of 100,000 square miles included the land given up by communities on the Puget Sound, as well as the land of Plateau communities.
77. Brosnan, *History of the State of Idaho*, 134. Brosnan's paragraph briefly sketched Governor Stevens treaty exploits in 1855 and specifically mentioned the Walla Walla Council. He mentioned a few of the Nez Perce present and then moved into a discussion of the Treaty of 1863. Brosnan subordinated the Walla Walla Council and the Treaty of 1855 to his narration of Indian Wars and in particular the "Nez Perce War."
78. Meany, *History of the State of Washington*, 168.
79. Ibid., 170-171.
80. Ibid., 166. Meany contended that the United States government selected Stevens as the best person to implement its policies in the Northwest. It was only by virtue of Stevens "patience, courage, skill and industry" that this task was accomplished. For Meany, Stevens represented the struggle between civilization and savagery. This hero adeptly performed his duty and secured the land for Anglo Americans while also following the dictates of the national government.
81. Ibid., 176.
82. Brosnan, *History of the State of Idaho*, 129.
83. Ibid., 129.
84. Ibid., 129.
85. Meany, *History of the State of Washington*, 177.
86. Meany consistently reiterated these themes at crucial points in his narrative of the history of the State of Washington. Most of these cues came at the beginning of chapters. For example, Meany offered a thorough interpretation of the treaties and their effects at the beginning of chapter nineteen, dealing with the initial conflict on the Plateau after the 1855 treaty council. The inevitable progression of history was reinforced for the reader through a restatement of the basic frontier thesis. Savagery and civilization could not coexist for Meany and his contemporaries and conflict became inevitable in this situation.

87. Brosnan, *History of the State of Idaho*, 130. Any measure was justified if it was linked to the defeat of "generic" Indians.
88. Ibid., 131.
89. Meany, *History of the State of Washington*, 220. Wright, Steptoe, volunteers and regular army units fought for numerous reasons, but Meany sought to place their activities in the grand narrative of acquiring clear title to the land and encouraging the settlement of the Pacific Northwest.
90. Ibid., 221.
91. Ibid., 223.

NOTES TO CHAPTER FIVE

1. Phinney, *Nez Perce Texts*, 27.
2. Lucullus Virgil McWhorter, *Yellow Wolf: His Own Story* (Caldwell, Idaho: The Caxton Printers, 1940), 291. Yellow Wolf articulated the propensity of Anglo Americans to control the creation of history and he was fully aware of the power that this control over historical knowledge gave Anglo Americans.
3. Phinney, *Nez Perce Texts*, 27. While the Walla Walla Council and the ensuing treaty of 1855 guaranteed the Nez Perce most of their ancestral homeland, "Monster" would eventually return and consume Nez Perce land in one great inhalation. The United States government, through its ratification of the 1863 Thief Treaty, believed that the Nez Perce ceded close to seven million acres and reduced the size of the 1855 reservation to 1/10 of its original size. See Clifford Trafzer, *The Nez Perce*, 63 for more details on the 1863 treaty. For a full transcript of the 1863 Treaty see Slickpoo and Walker, *Noon Nee-Me-Poo*, 293-300.
4. Josephy, *The Nez Perce Indians*, 381. In no way does this imply that the Nez Perce and Palouse who lived within the confines of the 1855 treaty reservation had no contact with whites. On the contrary, cultural contact between the two groups continued, mainly at Walla Walla where Nez Perce, Palouse, Umatillas, Walla Wallas and other Indians peoples met and interacted with Anglo Americans.
5. Only a year before, the United States government failed to live up to treaty obligations with the Lakota and allowed miners to infiltrate into the Black Hills, a sacred place for the Lakota. Just as in the Northwest, the United States also attempted to renegotiate the treaty with the Lakota and, when that failed, turned to military force to protect white miners and adventurers.
6. Trafzer and Scheuerman, *Renegade Tribe*, 103 and Josephy, *The Nez Perce Indians*, 382-383. It should also be noted that Yakama Indians killed miners trespassing on Yakama land and the presence of miners was one of the reasons that led to the conflict called the Yakama War from 1856-1858. Greed and desire for material gain motivated many Anglo Americans to risk death if they were caught trespassing on Indian land supposedly guaranteed by treaty with the United States government.
7. Josephy, *The Nez Perce Indians*, 377-378. The Nez Perce people, both Christian and traditional groups, believed that the agreement reached in

1855 would protect their traditional homeland. The incursions of miners in the early 1860s upset many Nez Perce communities and eventually led to the Thief Treaty of 1863. After the treaty negotiations, the Nez Perce were principally divided into two groups, the Treaty Nez Perce and the Non-Treaty Nez Perce. Generally, the Treaty Nez Perce followed Lawyer as Chief, resided within the boundaries of the new reservation and accepted Christianity. The Non-treaty communities had many different leaders, like Eagle From the Light, Old Joseph, White Bird and others, and refused to sign the 1863 treaty. See Clifford M. Drury, *Chief Lawyer of the Nez Perce Indians, 1796-1876* (Glendale, California: Arthur H. Clark Company, 1979) for a detailed biography of Lawyer, leader of the Christian treaty faction on the Nez Perce Reservation.

8. See Josephy, *The Nez Perce Indians*, 384-385 and Trafzer and Scheuerman, *Renegade Tribe*, 103, for a more detailed discussion of the problems surrounding the discovery of gold on the Nez Perce Reservation created by the 1855 treaty.

9. According to Alvin Josephy, the name "Upper" Nez Perces referred to the titles given to the Nez Perce by Captain Benjamin Bonneville during his expedition in the Pacific Northwest in 1833-34. Originally the designation "Upper" Nez Perces referred merely to those groups that lived on the Idaho side of the Snake River while the "Lower" Nez Perces lived west of the Snake River. These designations took on different meanings as people in the "Upper" Nez Perce area responded to Christian missionaries and accepted Christianity and "Upper" Nez Perce began to be used to designate the Christian Nez Perce that lived principally along the Clearwater River and on the Idaho side of the Snake River. See Josephy, *The Nez Perces*, 103-104 and Slickpoo and Walker, *Noon Nee-Me-Poo*, 147 for in-depth discussions of the difference between "Upper" and "Lower" Nez Perces.

10. Slickpoo and Walker, *Noon Nee Me Poo*, 147 and 151. Allen Slickpoo, Sr. contended that the whole series of events leading up to the "Thief" Treaty of 1863 demonstrated the underlying desire of whites to obtain Nez Perce land by whatever means necessary.

11. Most Native Americans in the Western United States experienced an initial negotiation of a treaty and then renegotiation when white pressure for land became acute in a given region. For example, numerous Indian communities on the northern and southern Great Plains negotiated treaties in the late 1860s and early 1870s only to have the United States government fail to live up to treaty provisions. The government also lacked the will to protect Indian communities from white incursions on their lands and attempted to renegotiate treaties in order to supposedly protect Indians from whites. In reality, land was the real objective and renegotiation was the means to achieve the acquisition of Indian land.

12. Josephy, *The Nez Perce Indians*, 399. Alvin Josephy noted in his work on the Nez Perce that the United States government, as well as state and local government, saw only one way out of the growing crisis in Nez Perce Territory. He maintained "the military could not interpose itself between Indians and miners, white men would not withdraw from the mines, and

historic precedent said that in such cases the Indians must get out." The dishonesty of this stance must have confused and angered the Nez Perce. Not only had the government failed to live up to its side of the bargain, now the Nez Perce would have to pay the price for the government's unwillingness to oust miners and protect Indian land from incursions.
13. Trafzer and Scheuerman, *Renegade Tribe*, 104.
14. This paradox was present in many of the dealings of the United States with various Native American communities. The unwillingness of the government and army to live up to the terms of treaties allowed settlers, miners and other Anglo Americans to create situations that placed the government in an awkward situation as it tried to keep Native Americans happy or quiet and also placate Anglo Americans in their desire to exploit resources and gain ownership of land. Government officials and leaders often solved the problem by renegotiating treaties and threatening the use of military force if native peoples failed to cooperate. Talking out of both sides of their mouths, government representatives told Indians that they had to give up their land in order for the government to fulfill its original promises. Allen Slickpoo, Sr., mentioned the frustration and anger that these shifts elicited among Nez Perce people. This anger still exists.
15. See Slickpoo and Walker, *Noon Nee-Me-Poo*, 77-78 and Josephy, *The Nez Perces*, 406-407 for discussions pertaining to interpreters and translation. Interpreters and language have been root issues for Native Americans. The problem was that most treaties were written in English and interpreters did not generally read the treaties out loud but instead "explained" the treaty provisions to those present. At the Walla Walla Council in 1855 translation issues were exacerbated by the use of Chinook Jargon, a trade language that failed to express the subtleties of Nez Perce language. Every council and treaty negotiation caused great concern for Indians since they believed, often rightly so, that the government used the language barrier as a tool to trick and cheat them in the negotiations.
16. It must be reiterated that Old Joseph played important roles in the Walla Walla Council and led his people in the Wallowa area until his death in 1871. After Joseph's death, his son, Joseph, assumed his position and continued to voice Old Joseph's opposition to relinquishing any land to the United States government or to white settlers. Both men belonged to the Washani religion and were designated as "troublemakers" and "discontents" by white settlers, military officers like General Howard and others, and officials of the Bureau of Indian Affairs. Anglo Americans often grouped Old and Young Joseph in with other "Dreamers" like White Bird, Eagle from the Light, Toohoolhoolzote, Husis Husis Kute, and Young Chief. All of these men vehemently opposed giving up their land and voiced strong opposition to the government's positions in any councils called by military or civilian officials.
17. Trafzer and Scheuerman, *Renegade Tribe*, 104.
18. The confusion of the United States government representatives with the initial Nez Perce proposal demonstrated that the government was not dealing with the Nez Perce for only the land illegally occupied by miners, but used

the miners as an excuse to shrink the reservation and open the land to white settlement and use. Allen Slickpoo Sr., asserted that there was no proof to support Hale's assertion that all factions agreed to the treaty. In reality, there was a large body of evidence that non-treaty communities like those led by Old Joseph, Looking Glass, White Bird and others never agreed to the provisions of the treaty and absolutely refused to sign any agreement to give up or shrink their land base. Even United States government representatives, like General Oliver Otis Howard later observed that non-treaty groups had never agreed to or signed an agreement to give up their land. See Slickpoo and Walker, *Noon Nee-Me-Poo*, 147 and Josephy, *The Nez Perces*, 464.

19. Josephy, *The Nez Perce Indians*, 419.
20. Josephy, *The Nez Perce Indians*, 418-419. Allen Slickpoo, Sr. also noted that only the "Upper" Nez Perces signed the treaty. This group, according to Slickpoo, was called the "progressive," "Christian," or treaty group. Lawyer was generally recognized as their leader and they mainly resided in the Lapwai area. Slickpoo also maintained that the signing of the Treaty of 1863 by the Upper Nez Perces caused a split in the tribe. See Slickpoo and Walker, *Noon Nee-Me-Poo*, 147. Yellow Wolf used the term "Thief Treaty" when he referred to the 1863 Treaty. See McWhorter, *Yellow Wolf: His Own Story*, 35.
21. Robert H. Ruby and John A. Brown, *Indians of the Pacific Northwest*, The Civilization of American Indian Series (Norman: University of Oklahoma Press, 1981), 229.
22. L.V. McWhorter, *Yellow Wolf: His Own Story*, 35.
23. Trafzer and Scheuerman, *Renegade Tribe*, 105.
24. See Click Relander, *Drummers and Dreamers: The Story of Smowhala the Prophet and His Nephew Puck Hyah Toot, the Last Prophet of the Nearly Extinct River People, the Last Wanapums* (Seattle: Northwest Interpretive Association, 1986), for a thorough discussion of Smohalla and the Washani religion. Smohalla and other prophets, like the Nez Perce Toohoolhoolzote and the Palouse Husis Husis Kute, used the power of religious belief as the root for resistance. While each community, Wanapum, Nez Perce and Palouse, had its own religious traditions, they all shared a deep spiritual devotion to the land. General Howard's hostility toward Toohoolhoolzote and Husis Husis Kute at the 1877 Lapwai Council went back to their devotion to the Washani religion and the centrality of the land in their religious tradition. Howard's arrogance and disregard for Washani belief and practice led him to imprison Toohoolhoolzote and to insult many of the leaders present. Yellow Wolf noted that the War of 1877 resulted from the arrest of Toohoolhoolzote and Howard's "showing the rifle." It is important to note that Washani religion was not a "new" religion, but Smohalla and other prophets were calling Plateau peoples to return to older beliefs, give up Christianity and the contamination of white culture and beliefs.
25. Josephy, *The Nez Perces*, 448. While the goal of the United States government was to extinguish Indian title, the short-term requirements of this process generated a policy of restricting settlement in the Wallowa area and

removing settlers encroaching on Nez Perce lands. These short-term policies were highly unpopular among white settlers in northeast Oregon. According to Clifford Trafzer, white fears and animosity heightened as a result of the Modoc Rebellion in southwest Oregon. This conflict persuaded many Anglo Americans in Oregon that all Indians must be placed on a reservation in order to control their activities. The tensions and conflict in the Wallowa region confirmed this belief for local Anglo-American inhabitants and biased government officials against the non-treaty communities in the region. See also Clifford Trafzer, *The Nez Perce*, Indians of North America Series (New York: Chelsea House Publishers, 1992), 65-66.
26. Josephy, *The Nez Perces*, 449-450.
27. Josephy, *The Nez Perces*, 454.
28. Josephy, *The Nez Perces*, 456-457. The debates held among the leaders of the non-treaty Nez Perce highlighted the difficulty of finding a way to deal with white encroachment on Nez Perce land. The experience of these leaders failed to heighten their trust of the United States government or its representatives. As Allen Slickpoo, Sr. asserted, deception and dishonesty seemed to be common practice for Anglo Americans and the non-treaty leaders intimately knew the capacity of government officials to promise one thing to Indians while also promising something different to white settlers, miners, adventurers and businessmen. In the end, the inability of the United States government to deal with the Nez Perce and other Plateau peoples in an equitable and honest manner created great tension and difficulties for Joseph, Ollokot, White Bird and other non-treaty leaders who knew that their people were outnumbered and facing ever greater pressure to give up their land.
29. White Bird was an important chief, medicine man and warrior of the non-treaty faction. At the time of the Lapwai Council, White Bird was in his seventies and was, according to L.V. McWhorter, the oldest of the non-treaty chiefs. He held a place of honor during all councils and his experience and leadership skills increased his influence in non-treaty circles. Toohoolhoolzote was also an important chief and *tooat*. His people lived close to Joseph's people and supported the non-treaty faction. Toohoolhoolzote was one of the foremost religious leaders of the Nez Perce during the period before and after the Lapwai Council. Eagle From the Light led another non-treaty band and frequently traveled east over the Bitterroot Mountains with Looking Glass and his people to hunt buffalo. Eagle from the Light was present at the Walla Walla Council of 1855 and supported the non-treaty faction during the Lapwai Council. See Lucullus Virgil McWhorter, *Hear Me, My Chiefs!* (Caldwell, Idaho: The Caxton Printers, 1952),181-184 and Josephy, *The Nez Perce Indians*, 445.
30. Josephy, *The Nez Perces*, 464 and Trafzer, *The Nez Perce*, 67-70. General Howard was a hero of the Civil War, served as head of the Freedman's Bureau after the war, and commanded the expeditions against Cochise and the Apaches in the Southwest. Howard was a devout evangelical Christian, deeply infused with a sense of the superiority of Christianity *vis-a-vis* native religions. As Howard gained experience with Plateau peoples, his anger and frustration fell on the religious leaders of the non-treaty groups and he came

to regard them as both dangerous and misguided individuals who stood in the way of the Nez Perce and other Plateau communities' conversion to Christianity and immersion in American civilization. The twin themes of conversion and civilization were important components of Anglo-American ideology of the period, informing the doctrine of Manifest Destiny and the superiority of Anglo-American civilization. Historians like Edmond Meany and C.J. Brosnan would echo Howard's commitment to these themes in the early twentieth century. See Josephy, *The Patriot Chiefs*, 323.

31. Meany, *History of the State of Washington*, 220-221. Meany realized that the process of treaty making was necessary for Anglo-American possession of Indian land, but he also recognized that these treaties often contributed to the eruption of hostilities between the United States Government and Native Americans. According to Meany, Native American populations were small compared to the size of the land available and he stated that as whites came with their institutions, the clash between "civilization" and "savagery" was inevitable. The outcome of these clashes was also self-evident to Meany and most Anglo Americans in the early twentieth century. Meany believed that the government's policy of making treaties and attempting to assimilate Indians was the only course possible to prepare Native Americans for the "overwhelming changes fast approaching." See also Meany, *History of the State of Washington*, 176.

32. See Ruby and Brown, *Indians of the Pacific Northwest*, 229-230 for a discussion of the two 1866 Supreme Court decisions pertaining to United States Indian policy and President Grant's Peace Policy.

33. John B. Monteith took over the position of Indian Agent at Lapwai, Idaho in February 1871. The son of a Presbyterian minister, Monteith worked hard to demolish the last vestiges of Nez Perce culture and life. In particular, Monteith detested the *tooats* and their followers, seeing them as impediments to Nez Perce acculturation. See Josephy, *The Nez Perce Indians*, 431-432 for a more thorough discussion of Agent Monteith. The murder of Eagle Robe and one other Nez Perce person increased fears, particularly among government officials, that hostilities were imminent in the Wallowa region. For a discussion of the impact of Eagle Robes murder see Josephy, *The Nez Perce Indians*, 499.

34. *Tooats* is one of the Nez Perce words for spiritual leader. Leaders like Toohoolhoolzote and Husis Husis Kute played significant roles in the spiritual lives of the communities and often provided the most profound and sacred arguments against moving onto the Nez Perce Reservation. Civil and war leaders like Chief Joseph, Ollokot, White Bird, and Looking Glass often relied on tooats' guidance and rhetoric when confronting the United States government. Government officials like General Howard and Agent Monteith often used the derogatory term of "dreamer" to refer to the tooats and to those who followed their teachings.

35. Ruby and Brown, *Indians of the Pacific Northwest*, 242.
36. Trafzer and Scheuerman, *Renegade Tribe*, 106-107.
37. Ibid., 107.

38. For example, Toohoolhoolzote asserted "he had heard of a bargain, a trade between some of these Indians and the white men concerning their land; but I belong to the land out of which I came." Another example of Toohoolhoolzote's rhetoric regarding the land clearly illustrated the deep and abiding connection between the land and the Nez Perce people. He said, "The earth is part of my body, and I never gave up the earth." For Toohoolhoolzote, Husis Husis Kute, Smohalla and many other prophets, the land was much more than a place to gather food and live. The land was a part of them and giving up land meant breaking "the law of the earth" and breaking trust with the "chieftainship of the earth." See Trafzer and Scheuerman, *Renegade Tribe*, 107-108 for more references to Toohoolholzote's language.
39. "Showing the rifle" was an act of hostility, an act of war. General Howard's behavior at the Lapwai Council was not the behavior of a friend. Only enemies and those desiring conflict acted the way Howard had and those actions could only be interpreted as hostile. McWhorter, *Yellow Wolf: His Own Story*, 40-42.
40. Yellow Wolf was not the only Nez Perce person to note Howard's inappropriate behavior at the Lapwai Council. L.V. McWhorter interviewed Wo-to-len (Many Wounds) in July 1926. In the *Lament of Wotolen*, Wo-to-len noted, "This was bad. This was the same as declaring war." This was in reference to Howard's behavior and the ultimatum to move onto the reservation in 30 days. The Lapwai Council was not a negotiation, but instead Howard ordered the Nez Perce to comply with the government's dictates and refused to listen to the Nez Perce position. This was most clearly demonstrated by the arrest of Toohoolhoolzote. Lucullus Virgil McWhorter Collection, "The Lament of Wotolen," Washington State University Special Collections, Cage 55, Box 9, Folder 53.
41. Ruby and Brown, *Indians of the Pacific Northwest*, 243.
42. McWhorter, *Yellow Wolf: His Own Story*, 41.
43. Trafzer and Scheuerman, *Renegade Tribe*, 108. Yellow Wolf also asserted that none of the chiefs wanted to fight or go to war. He was so adamant about this that in the space of one page Yellow Wolf repeated four times that most Nez Perce did not want or expect to go to war with the United States Government. See McWhorter, *Yellow Wolf: His Own Story*, 41-42.
44. Ruby and Brown, *Indians of the Pacific Northwest*, 243.
45. McWhorter, *Yellow Wolf: His Own Story*, 41.
46. The Camas Prairie is located in the southeastern corner of the Columbia Plateau in present-day northern Idaho. The Prairie is separated from the Palouse Hills by the Clearwater Canyon to the north and by the Snake River to the west. The Camas Prairie has an undulating surface and is known for its deep soil and the rich beds of camas plants used by the Nez Perce and other Plateau communities as food. Tolo Lake was named *Eewahtam* (small body of water) by the Nez Perce, and the name Tolo Lake was given to the small lake after the Nez Perce War. Tolo was the name of a Nez Perce woman who warned miners in the Slate Creek area of the outbreak of hostilities. This was an act of commemoration by Anglo Americans of

Indians who helped whites at the beginning of the war. See Meinig, *The Great Columbia Plain*, 11, Josephy, *The Nez Perce Indians*, 504, and McWhorter, *Hear Me, My Chiefs!*, 176.

47. The author recognizes that the brief narrative of the Nez Perce War is only meant to give a cursory overview of the events that occurred in 1877. Three sources provide detailed and comprehensive narratives of the War. See Alvin M. Josephy, *The Nez Perce Indians and the Opening of the Northwest* (Lincoln: University of Nebraska Press, 1965) for the most comprehensive narrative of the War. The best Nez Perce sources concerning the war are L.V. McWhorter, *Yellow Wolf: His Own Story*, (Caldwell, Idaho: The Caxton Printers, Ltd., 1940) and Allen Slickpoo, Sr., and Deward Walker, Jr., *Noon Nee-Me-Poo: Culture and History of the Nez Perces, Volume One*, (Lapwai, Idaho: Nez Perce Tribe of Idaho, 1973). For a discussion of Palouse Indian involvement in the Nez Perce War see Clifford Trafzer and Richard Scheuerman, *Renegade Tribe: The Palouse Indians and the Invasion of the Inland Pacific Northwest*, (Pullman: Washington State University Press, 1986).
48. Trafzer and Scheuerman, *Renegade Tribe*, 109-110.
49. On the initial raid, Wahlitits was accompanied by his nephew Wetyetmas Wyakaikt and Sarpsis Ilppilp. For more thorough discussions of the raiding party see Trafzer and Scheuerman, *Renegade Tribe*, 110, Josephy, *The Nez Perces*, 499-501 and McWhorter, *Yellow Wolf: His Own Story*, 44-51.
50. Ruby and Brown, *Indians of the Pacific Northwest*, 243.
51. Trafzer, *The Nez Perce*, 79.
52. Yellow Wolf claimed that only 120 men of fighting age were in the camp at Camas Prairie, and of those only fifty fought in the war. L.V. McWhorter, in a footnote, noted that six to seven hundred people were at Camas Prairie, but most of this number were women and children. Also included in the footnote were references by General Howard and the War Department of three to four hundred Nez Perce warriors. See McWhorter, *Yellow Wolf: His Own Story*, 43.
53. Inflating the number of Nez Perce warriors played into myths about the Nez Perce War generated by Anglo Americans. There would be very little glory or heroism involved if the number of Nez Perce warriors were small. General Howard also contended that the Nez Perce managed to elicit help and manpower from other tribes in the region, but Yellow Wolf again denied these assertions and mentioned that only two men were not Nez Perce or Palouse. See McWhorter, *Hear Me, My Chiefs!*, 185-187.
54. Trafzer and Scheuerman, *Renegade Tribe*, 110-112.
55. Josephy, *The Nez Perce Indians*, 523-524. Peo Peo Thalekt was there and acted as a mediator. He was of Joseph's band and perhaps had accompanied Looking Glass and his people on their buffalo hunting expedition east of the Bitterroot Mountains. L.V. McWhorter also conducted an interview with Peo Peo Thalekt. The account given by Peo Peo Thalekt differed greatly from the formal written report filed by General Howard in 1877. See McWhorter, *Hear Me, My Chiefs!*, 262-272.

56. A number of engagements occurred before the Nez Perce arrived on Weippe Prairie. Some of these include the annihilation of Second Lieutenant Sevier M. Rain's scouting party, an engagement with a volunteer force under the command of Captain D.B. Randall, and a significant battle at the Clearwater River on July 11, 1877. See Josephy, *The Nez Perce Indians*, 516-548 for detailed descriptions of these and other battles before the retreat to Weippe Prairie.
57. Trafzer, *The Nez Perce*, 80.
58. Trafzer and Scheuerman, *Renegade Tribe*, 116.
59. Hahtalekin was a Palouse chief, who lived near the confluence of Snake and Palouse Rivers. According to L.V. McWhorter, Hahtalekin was a member of the buffalo hunter class and was esteemed for his bravery as a warrior. As with many non-treaty chiefs like Joseph, White Bird, and Eagle from the Light, Hahtalekin opposed the idea of war. See McWhorter, *Hear Me, My Chiefs!*, 172-173.
60. Trafzer, *The Nez Perce*, 83-84.
61. Wounded Head (Husis Owyeen) recounted the terrible devastation of the Big Hole Battle in an interview with L.V. McWhorter. He noted the death of Nez Perce warriors and a number of women and children, among them his own child. Gibbons, while initially winning the camp, eventually limped off the battlefield and could not pursue the Nez Perce after the Big Hole Battle. See McWhorter, *Hear Me, My Chiefs!*, 374.
62. Trafzer, *The Nez Perce*, 84.
63. Trafzer, *The Nez Perce*, 85 and Ruby and Brown, *Indians of the Pacific Northwest*, 246.
64. Ruby and Brown, *Indians of the Pacific Northwest*, 246.
65. McWhorter, *Yellow Wolf: His Own Story*, 215. Also see Trafzer, *The Nez Perce*, 86, Ruby and Brown, *Indians of the Pacific Northwest*, 246, and Josephy, *The Nez Perce Indians*, 595-508 for discussions of the Battle and Surrender at Bearpaw Mountain.
66. General Howard raised a company of treaty Christian Nez Perce as scouts during the Nez Perce War. In 1900, an investigation by the Indian Agent C.T. Stranahan found that fifty-seven treaty Nez Perce took part in the Nez Perce War and forty-one were given back wages for their participation. Among these scouts was James Reuben who would later go to the Indian Territory to help the exiles. Reuben was wounded in the arm in one of the engagements. See McWhorter, *Hear Me, My Chiefs!*, 621-626.
67. Trafzer and Scheuerman, *Renegade Tribe*, 118.
68. McWhorter, *Yellow Wolf: His Own Story*, 225.
69. See Ruby and Brown, *Indians of the Pacific Northwest*, 246 for descriptions of the death of Looking Glass and the flight of White Bird to Sitting Bull's camp in Canada.
70. Trafzer and Scheuerman, *Renegade Tribe*, 118-119.
71. Phinney, *Nez Perce Texts*, 28.
72. General Oliver O. Howard talked about these men and their roles in his articles for *St. Nicholas*. *The Famous Indian Chiefs I Have Known* series illustrates how other Native American groups suffered from the same si-

lencing and relegation of their stories to the narrative of one important leader. See Oliver O. Howard, *Famous Indian Chiefs I Have Known*, originally published in *St. Nicholas* magazine, November 1907 through October 1908, (Reprinted by Lincoln: University of Nebraska Press, 1989).
73. Slickpoo and Walker, *Noon Nee-Me-Poo*, 183.
74. For discussions of Indian policy in nineteenth century United States see, Robert A. Trennert, Jr., *Alternative to Extinction: Federal Indian Policy and the Reservation System, 1846-1851* (Philadelphia: Temple University Press, 1975), Francis P. Prucha, *American Indian Policy in the Formative Years: The Indian Trade and Intercourse Acts, 1790-1834* (Lincoln: University of Nebraska Press, 1962), Brian W. Dippie, *The Vanishing American: White Attitudes and U.S. Indian Policy* (Middletown, Connecticut: Wesleyan University Press, 1982), and Frederick E. Hoxie, *A Final Promise: The Campaign to Assimilate the Indians, 1880-1920* (Lincoln: University of Nebraska Press, 1984).
75. The following sources will be used to illustrate how Anglo Americans created their narrative about the non-treaty Nez Perce and the events leading up to the Nez Perce War of 1877: *Frank Leslie's Illustrated Newspaper*, Volume 64, June 16-November 10, 1877, *Letter from Nelson A. Miles, Brigadier General to the Assistant Adjutant General, Division of the Pacific, Presidio, San Francisco, California, May 6, 1885*, National Archives and Records Administration, Record Group 75, , Western Historical Publishing Company, *An Illustrated History of North Idaho Embracing Nez Perces, Idaho, Latah, Kootenai and Shoshone Counties, State of Idaho*, (Western Historical Publishing Company, 1903), Oliver O. Howard, *Famous Indian Chiefs I Have Known*, Originally Published in St. Nicholas Magazine, November 1907 through October 1908, (Reprinted by Lincoln: University of Nebraska Press, 1989), Kate C. McBeth, *The Nez Perces Since Lewis and Clark*, (New York: Fleming H. Revell Company, 1908), C.J. Brosnan, *History of the State of Idaho* (New York: Charles Scribner's Sons, 1926) and R. Ross Arnold, *Indian Wars of Idaho* (Caldwell, Idaho: The Caxton Printers, Ltd., 1932). There are other sources that discuss conditions before the war, events leading up to the war and the war itself, but these give a representative sample from the end of the war up to the 1930s.
76. Frank Leslie was born Henry Carver in Ipswich, Suffolk, England in 1821. He immigrated to the United States in 1848 and brought with him experience in illustrated newspapers and a new light-on-shade engraving technique. In 1855 he founded Frank Leslie's Illustrated Newspaper, the first paper in the United States to use the new method to illustrate the newspaper. The Lincoln Home website, created by the National Park Service, noted that Leslie pioneered the use of sensationalism to sell newspapers. The unofficial motto of the newspaper was "Never shoot over the heads of the people." Frank Leslie's primary competitor was Harpers Weekly, also an illustrated newspaper. The last issue of Frank Leslie's Illustrated Newspaper appeared in 1902 and Harpers Weekly ended publication in 1916. See John Popolis, http://www.nps.gov/liho/leslie.htm. "The New Indian War: Scenes of the

Recent Outbreak in Idaho. Types of Character and Views of the Country," *Frank Leslie's Illustrated Newspaper*, July 28, 1877, 353-354.
77. "The Cause of Trouble in Idaho," *Frank Leslie's Illustrated Newspaper*, September 1, 1877, 431.
78. "The Cause of Trouble in Idaho," *Frank Leslie's Illustrated Newspaper*, New York, September 1, 1877, 431.
79. "The Last Indian War: Home Life of the Defeated Nez Perces," *Frank Leslie's Illustrated Newspaper*, New York, October 27, 1877, Volume 65, 118-119.
80. "The Last Indian War: Home Life of the Defeated Nez Perces," *Frank Leslie's Illustrated Newspaper*, New York, October 27, 1877, Volume 65, 118-119.
81. Oliver Otis Howard, *Famous Indian Chiefs I Have Known* (Lincoln: University of Nebraska Press, 1989), 186. Howard's articles on these Indian leaders appeared originally in *St. Nicholas* magazine from November 1907 to October 1908.
82. Howard hated Toohoolhoolzote and other non-treaty *tooats* like Husis Husis Kute. For example, Howard noted that Toohoolhoolzote "hated white men." Toohoolhoolzote represented the intractable "long hair Dreamer," the Indian who resisted to the bitter end. Not only was Howard angry because of Toohoolhoolzote's religious influence but also because he stubbornly refused, in Howard's eyes, to see the futility of his situation. See Howard, *Famous Indian Chiefs I Have Known*, 191.
83. Ibid., 193 and xviii.
84. *An Illustrated History of North Idaho*, 44.
85. Narratives like the one in *An Illustrated History of North Idaho* also existed on a national level. The national narratives tended to lump all native peoples together and use Indian leaders, like Oliver O. Howard, as icons to understand the complex relations of the Anglo Americans with the United States. National and local narratives informed one another and their authors in disparate regions unconsciously worked together to reinforce the myth of Anglo-American cultural superiority.
86. *An Illustrated History of North Idaho*, 45.
87. Ibid., 45.
88. McBeth, *The Nez Perces Since Lewis and Clark*, 94.
89. Brosnan, *History of the State of Idaho*.
90. R. Ross Arnold, *Indian Wars of Idaho* (Caldwell, Idaho: The Caxton Printers, Ltd., 1932), 106-165.
91. See An *Illustrated History of North Idaho* and the other sources used in this section for examples of this tendency toward using Anglo-American sources exclusively. These sources drew from white settler testimony, government officials and army reports for information about the events leading up to the war and the events of the war.
92. Not once, in any of the above-mentioned narratives, does one hear a Nez Perce voice except for Joseph at the Bear Paw surrender. This silencing of Nez Perce voices would not end until the publication of L.V. McWhorter's *Yellow Wolf: His Own Story*.
93. *An Illustrated History of North Idaho*, 58.
94. Brosnan, *History of the State of Idaho*, 136.

95. Arnold, *Indian Wars of Idaho*, 115. It is important to note that despite the assertions in *An Illustrated History of North Idaho* and Arnold's *Indian Wars of Idaho*, L.V. McWhorter maintained, as well as Alvin M. Josephy, Jr., that massacres of civilians and settlers did not occur during the Nez Perce War and settler deaths were largely limited to the first few days of hostilities. See McWhorter, *Hear Me, My Chiefs!*, 226-230 and Josephy, *The Nez Perce Indians*, 500-508.
96. For an excellent discussion of the discrepancy of warriors attributed to the non-treaty Nez Perce see McWhorter, *Hear Me, My Chiefs!*, 184-187. McWhorter argued that every surviving Nez Perce warrior he was able to interview disputed General Howard's estimate of as many as 500 warriors. Howard's claims of 500 Nez Perce warriors and unsubstantiated claims of other tribes joining the Nez Perce led McWhorter to note, "All of this was a chimera of the General's imagination."
97. See Brosnan, *History of the State of Idaho*, 137-142. Brosnan's chapter on the Indian Wars of Idaho condensed the conflict between Native Americans and Anglo Americans into sixteen pages. The chapter is divided into various sub-headings and most of the divisions connected to the Nez Perce War contained Joseph's name in some form.
98. Western Historical Publishing Company, *An Illustrated History of North Idaho*, 44-71. Before the war, Joseph was mentioned numerous times in connection with negotiations and peace attempts. As soon as hostilities started, Joseph and all non-treaty people became "wily savages." The term wily savage allowed Anglo Americans in this narrative to recognize the intelligence and resourcefulness of their foes, while at the same time relegating them to the inferior status of savages. McBeth, *The Nez Perces Since Lewis and Clark*, 95-101. Howard, *Famous Indian Chiefs I Have Known*, 198.
99. See Figure 22 for the lithograph. "Montana – The Nez Perce War – Incidents in the Defeat and Capture of Chief Joseph by General Nelson A. Miles From Sketches by G.M. Holland," *Frank Leslie's Illustrated Newspaper*, November 3, 1877, 141.
100. Trafzer and Scheuerman, *Renegade Tribe*, 118. A letter from the wife of C.E.S. Wood, a young Lieutenant present at the surrender, is the only documentary evidence supporting the surrender speech. Mrs. Wood noted, "It was not General Miles who was responsible for the declaration of Joseph "From where the sun now stands" etc. It was none other than my husband! It was the young Lieutenant C.E.S. Wood who as aide de camp and adjutant in the field took down with a led pencil on a scrap of paper that famous surrender speech as the Interpreter (Arthur Chapman) pronounced it after Joseph. That scrap of paper formed the only record of that speech. At a later period my husband went to the War Department and asked to see that famous and precious piece of paper but it could not be found." "Letter From Mrs. C.E.S. Wood to Lucullus Virgil McWhorter, July 2, 1935," Lucullus Virgil McWhorter Collection, Cage 55, Box 15, Folder 92. By the time C.J. Brosnan wrote his *History of the State of Idaho*, the speech was well-entrenched in the narrative of the Nez Perce War. It was so important

that Brosnan included the full-text of the speech as remembered by Anglo Americans present at the surrender. See also Mark H. Brown, "The Chief Joseph Myth," *Montana* 22 (1972): 2-17.

101. Stories need to have markers to make them understandable to readers. These markers emerge as the result of the many different writers working independently, but all interconnected by shared cultural assumptions and beliefs. Anglo Americans needed these things to make sense of the story. Otherwise, the narrative would not have been accessible or intelligible to them. This is the last step in Trouillot's production of history, signifying or giving meaning to facts, archives and narratives. See Trouillot, *Silencing the Past: The Power and Production of History*, 26.

102. Both Meany's and Brosnan's narratives fit into the type of regional history encouraged by Frederick Jackson Turner during the late nineteenth and early twentieth centuries. The regional nature of these works determined the scope of action of their Indian characters and also marked out their final exit from the narrative.

103. See Trouillot, *Silencing the Past: Power and the Production of History*, 26-30 for a detailed description of the mechanisms involved in the production of history. Silence and silencing are integral parts of the narrative creation process. It is impossible to create a narrative without silencing some part of the story. Historical narratives can never achieve a total or complete description of the past and historians pick and chose the voices included in their narratives. During the late nineteenth and early twentieth centuries, Anglo Americans chose to only include Anglo-American voices in their stories and silence Nez Perce parts of the story.

104. Yellow Wolf recognized the power that Anglo Americans possessed in the creation of narratives about the Nez Perce War. Oliver W. Frank, the great nephew of Chief Joseph, also noted the importance that the Nez Perce played in Anglo-American historical imagination and narratives. During a speech given at the Stevens Treaty Centennial Ceremony on June 10, 1955, Oliver Frank noted, "Our tribe's folklore and history has helped to color the story of the building of the great Northwest." See Oliver W. Frank, "1955 Stevens Treaty Centennial Ceremony Address," *Indians Illustrated*, September 1967, 9-10.

NOTES TO CHAPTER SIX

1. Phinney, *Nez Perce Texts*, 28.
2. Trafzer and Scheuerman, *Renegade Tribe*, 119 and J. Stanley Clark, "The Nez Perces in Exile," *The Pacific Northwest Quarterly*, July 1945, Volume 36, Number 3, 213-216. Observers of the imprisonment of the Nez Perce noted that many of the people died from a combination of homesickness and disease. The effects of depression on the immune system have been well-documented and, combined with influenza, malaria, viral infections and other pathogens, depression helped to weaken immune systems and make death more likely. For a thorough discussion of these effects see Trafzer, *Death Stalks the Yakama*, 72-77. Allen Slickpoo, Sr., also asserted that the

government physician assigned to the exiled Nez Perce believed that "more Indians were sick in soul than in body. Death came from broken hearts as often as from malaria." Slickpoo and Walker, *Noon Nee-Me-Poo*, 106.

Kul-Kul Si-Yakth (Raven Spy) voiced the great despair and disappointment of the exiles in an interview with L.V. McWhorter in November 1925. Raven Spy referred to his time in the Indian Territory as a time of bondage and slavery. The pain and depth of his memories of Eekish Pah are evident in the concluding remarks of the interview: "I always think of our slavery in Indian Territory. I cannot forget it! Held in bondage till half of our band died in that hot, flat country, breeding place of malaria. I can never put its memory from my mind. The broken promise of General Miles that we return to our old home if only we lay down the gun. It is the same to this day, my mind, as when I was held a slave by this Government for so many years." See "The Narrative of Kul-Kul Si-Yakth (Raven Spy)" interview conducted by L.V. McWhorter, November 1925, Sam Lott Interpreter, Lucullus Virgil McWhorter Collection, Washington State University Special Collections, Cage 55, Box 7, Folder 38.

3. See Clark, "The Nez Perces in Exile," 218, Trafzer and Scheuerman, *Renegade Tribe*, and Josephy, *The Nez Perces*, 620-622 for brief descriptions of the trips to Washington D.C. by Joseph and Yellow Bull. Josephy's account also included the purported *North American Review* interview with Chief Joseph. L.V. McWhorter noted that the interview was highly edited and failed to communicate Joseph's intentions and desires. See McWhorter, *Hear Me My Chiefs: Nez Perce Legend and History*, Caldwell, Idaho: The Caxton Printers, Ltd., (1952), 502-503.
4. Slickpoo and Walker, *Noon Nee-Me-Poo*, 196. See Clark, "The Nez Perce in Exile," 216 and 222.
5. Agitation and efforts to return the exiled Nez Perce to the Pacific Northwest came from a number of different sources. For example, the national organization of the Presbyterian Church supported the return of the exiles. Petitions from around the country were sent to Congress, some of them with numerous signatures. J. Stanley Clark noted that during the spring 1884 Congressional session, almost every day some member would present a memorial or speech outlining the treatment of the Nez Perces and urging their return to the Pacific Northwest. July 4, 1884 Senator Henry L. Dawes sponsored the passage of an act to allow the Secretary of Interior to determine the disposition of the Nez Perce Indians in the Indian Territory. See Clark, "The Nez Perces in Exile," 228-229 and Clifford E. Trafzer, ed. *The Northwestern Tribes in Exile* (Sacramento: Sierra Oaks Publishing Company 1987), 49-51 and 62.
6. Trafzer, ed., *The Northwestern Tribes in Exile*, 50 and 61.
7. Trafzer, *The Northwestern Tribes in Exile*, 62-66. M. Gidley, *Kopet: A Documentary Narrative of Chief Joseph's Last Years*, (Seattle: University of Washington Press, 1981), 13-15. Salish-speakers like the San Poils vehemently opposed the settlement of the Nez Perce on the Colville Reservation. Skolaskin, the messianic leader of the San Poils, led this opposition and organized a large protest regarding Nez Perce settlement and the Indian

Agent, Major Rickard K. Gwydir called in a detachment of troops to restore calm and protect the Nez Perce from violence.
8. Slickpoo and Walker, *Noon Nee-Me-Poo*, 201.
9. Clark, "The Nez Perce in Exile," 222. M. Gidley, *Kopet*, 53.
10. M. Gidley, *Kopet*, 18.
11. Ibid., 43-44 and 54-61.
12. Ibid., 64 and 70.
13. Ibid., 72. Meany's inscription read as follows: (In raised letters on the base) Chief Joseph, (On one side of the shaft) Hin-mah-too-yah-lat-kekt, Thunder Rolling in the mountains, (On another side of the shaft) He led his people in the Nez Perce war of 1877. Died, 21 September 1904. Age, about 60 years, (On the back of the shaft) Erected 20 June 1905, by the Washington University State Historical Society.
14. Ibid., 78-82.
15. McBeth, *The Nez Perces Since Lewis and Clark*, 98. See Western Historical Publishing Company, *An Illustrated History of North Idaho*, 44-70 for the portrayal of Joseph as both hero and villain. The authors of that work managed to both admire his military skills and describe the lurid details of Joseph's supposed participation in the murder of a young girl and her mother.
16. J.W. Redington, "Protest From an Old Scout: Monument to Chief Joseph Declared Mockery to History," *The Oregonian*, undated editorial, possible date 1928. Found in Lucullus Virgil McWhorter Collection, Cage 55, Box 41, Folder 394.
17. Lucullus Virgil McWhorter, "Western Historian Insists Chief Joseph Is Maligned," *The Idaho Statesman*, Morning Edition, December 22, (1929): 2. Found in Lucullus Virgil McWhorter Collection, Cage 55, Box 15, Folder 89.
18. "Honor to Chief Joseph," *Yakima Republic*, Editorial, June 11, 1930. Lucullus Virgil McWhorter Collection, Cage 55, Box 15, Folder 89.
19. Undated newspaper clipping, "Five Great Idahoans Are Named: Four White Men and One Indian Listed," Lucullus Virgil McWhorter Collection, Cage 55, Box 15, Folder 89.
20. See Western Historical Publishing Company, *An Illustrated History of North Idaho*, 71, Brosnan, *History of the State of Idaho*, frontispiece and Arnold, *Indian Wars of Idaho*, frontispiece, for photographs of Chief Joseph.
21. Trafzer and Scheuerman, *Renegade Tribe*, 104.
22. "Report of Inspection of the Fort Lapwai School, Sanatorium, and Agency, Idaho, by Otis B. Goodall, Supervisor," Fort Lapwai, Idaho, October 1 to 13th, 1916. National Archives and Records Administration, Washington, D.C., Record Group 75, Bureau of Indian Affairs, CCF 1907-1939, Fort Lapwai, Box No. 27599-10-820 to 77493-18-930.

"Annual Report 1919." National Archives and Records Administration – Pacific Northwest Region, Seattle, Washington, Record Group 75 Bureau of Indian Affairs, Northern Idaho Agency, Superintendent Subject Files, 1907-46, Annual Reports, 1911-34, Merriam Reports, 1928, Box Number 0035; Folder: Annual Reports (FLA) 1919.

"Annual Report 1924." National Archives and Records Administration – Pacific Northwest Region, Seattle, Washington, Record Group 75 Bureau of Indian Affairs, Northern Idaho Agency, Superintendent Subject Files, 1907-46, Annual Reports, 1911-34, Merriam Reports, 1928, Box Number 0035; Folder: Superintendent Correspondence, ca. 1916-26.
23. "Report addressed to George Vaux, Jr., Chairman, Board of Indian Commissioners from Hugh L. Scott, member, Board of Indian Commissioners," Fort Lapwai, Idaho, September 5, 1922. National Archives and Records Administration, Washington, D.C., Record Group 75, Bureau of Indian Affairs, CCF 1907-1939, Fort Lapwai, Box No. 9893-15-150 to 60246-15-151.
24. Walker, *Conflict and Schism in Nez Perce Acculturation*, 53.
25. Slickpoo and Walker, *Noon Nee-Me-Poo*, 202.
26. Walker, *Conflict and Schism in Nez Perce Acculturation*, 66.
27. Ibid., 58.
28. "Letter from T.J. Morgan, Indian Commissioner, to Warren D. Robbins, Esq., U.S. Indian Agent, Nez Perces Agency, Idaho," June 25, 1891. National Archives and Records Administration – Pacific Northwest Region, Seattle, Washington, Record Group 75 Bureau of Indian Affairs, Northern Idaho Agency, Official Letters Received by Superintendent of Fort Lapwai Indian School from Office of Indian Affairs, 1889-1902, Box Number 7, Folder: Untitled – second in row.
29. "Letter from T.J. Morgan, Indian Commissioner, to Warren D. Robbins, Esq., U.S. Indian Agent," June 25, 1891.
30. "Letter from A.C. Tonner, Acting Indian Commissioner, to C.T. Stranahan, Superintendent, Fort Lapwai Indian School, Spalding, Idaho," April 19, 1902. National Archives and Records Administration – Pacific Northwest Region, Seattle, Washington, Record Group 75 Bureau of Indian Affairs, Northern Idaho Agency, Official Letters Received by Superintendent of Fort Lapwai Indian School from Office of Indian Affairs, 1889-1902, Box Number 6, Folder: Untitled – first in row.
31. Annual Report, Fort Lapwai Agency 1924, National Archives and Records Administration – Pacific Northwest Region, Seattle, Washington, Record Group 75 Bureau of Indian Affairs, Northern Idaho Agency, Superintendent Subject Files, 1907-1946, Annual Reports, 1911-34, Merriam Report, 1926, Box Number 35, Folder: Superintendent Correspondence, ca. 1916-26.
32. McBeth, *The Nez Perces Since Lewis and Clark*, 184.
33. Judith Ann Jones, "Women Never Used to Dance: Gender and Music in Nez Perce Culture Change," Dissertation, Washington State University, May 1995, 138-139.
34. Slickpoo, and Walker, *Noon Nee-Me-Poo*, 219.
35. Ibid., 202, 220.
36. Ibid., 202, 251.
37. Ibid., 223.
38. Walker, *Conflict and Schism in Nez Perce Acculturation*, 88.
39. "Synopsis of Report of Inspector Junkin on the Nez Perce Reservation dated January 4, 1893." National Archives and Records Administration, Wash-

ington, D.C., Record Group 75, Bureau of Indian Affairs, Letters Received 1877-1895.
40. "Synopsis of Report of Inspector Junkin on the Nez Perce Reservation dated January 4, 1893." National Archives and Records Administration, Washington, D.C., Record Group 75, Bureau of Indian Affairs, Letters Received 1877-1895.
41. "Employment Situation Among Nez Perce Men Between Ages of 18 and 65 years," December 1941, National Archives and Records Administration, Pacific Northwest Region, Seattle, Washington, Record Group 75, Bureau of Indian Affairs, Northern Idaho Agency, Box 209, Folder "Placement."
42. "Annual Report, Nez Perce Reservation," 1932, National Archives and Records Administration – Pacific Northwest Region, Seattle, Washington, Record Group 75 Bureau of Indian Affairs, Northern Idaho Agency, Decimal Files; 1911-51, Number 339.7, Monthly/Annual Forestry Reports, 1924-26; Number 350, Estates, 1926-29, Box Number 0023: Fort Lapwai.
43. "Inspection Report, Oscar H. Lipps, Supervisor, Fort Lapwai Training School, Idaho, December 20, 1910," National Archives and Records Administration, Washington, D.C., Record Group 75 Bureau of Indian Affairs, CCF 1907-1939, Fort Lapwai, Box Number 9898-15-150 to 60246-15-151.
44. Walker, *Conflict and Schism in Nez Perce Acculturation*, 83.
45. Ibid., 85-87.
46. Ibid., 78.
47. "Letter from Oscar H. Lipps, District Superintendent to the Commissioner of Indian Affairs," Fort Lapwai Indian Agency, Fort Lapwai, Idaho, December 24, 1926. National Archives and Records Administration, Washington, D.C., Record Group 75, Bureau of Indian Affairs, CCF 1907-1939, Fort Lapwai, Box No. 73458 07 225 to 13457-12-225, File No. 223.
48. McBeth, *The Nez Perces Since Lewis and Clark*, 88 and 102. Kate McBeth's book is still in print and available for purchase. At the Nez Perce Historical Park Visitors Center, McBeth's book was displayed prominently along with *Yellow Wolf: His Own Story* and other titles. The power of McBeth's narrative continued into the present as tourists purchased the book and read about the exploits of Christian missionaries and the Christian Nez Perce. The problem here is that McBeth's book is one of the few narratives that dealt with the reservation period.
49. McBeth, *The Nez Perces Since Lewis and Clark*, 163-183.
50. Ibid., 170-171.
51. Ibid., 183.
52. "Annual Report, Narrative Section, Section 1, Law and Order, 1919," National Archives and Records Administration – Pacific Northwest Region, Seattle, Washington, Record Group 75 Bureau of Indian Affairs, Northern Idaho Agency, Superintendent Subject Files, 1907-1946, Annual Reports, 1911-34, Merriam Report, 1928, Box Number 35; Folder – Annual Report, FLA., 1931, Narrative Section with photographs.
53. "Miscellaneous letters from Oscar H. Lipps, Superintendent, George Peo Peo Tha Likt, and the Nez Perce Talmaks Camp Meeting Association," 1924, National Archives and Records Administration, Washington, D.C.,

Record Group 75, Bureau of Indian Affairs, CCF 1907-1939, Fort Lapwai, Box Number 42566-12-056 to 1228-09-101.
54. "Letter from Geo. Peo Peo Tah Likt to E.B. Meritt, Commissioner of Indian Affairs," Spalding, Idaho, May 19, 1924, National Archives and Records Administration, Washington, D.C., Record Group 75, Bureau of Indian Affairs, CCF 1907-1939, Fort Lapwai, Box Number 42566-12-056 to 1228-09-101.
55. Letter from Oscar H. Lipps, Superintendent, to the Commissioner of Indian Affairs," June 18, 1924, National Archives and Records Administration, Washington, D.C., Record Group 75, Bureau of Indian Affairs, CCF 1907-1939, Fort Lapwai, Box Number 42566-12-056 to 1228-09-101.
56. "Letter from Willie W. Axtell, Secretary and James Hayes, President of the Nez Perce Talmaks Camp Meeting Association to O.H. Lipps, Lapwai, Idaho and Letter from OH Lipps to Commissioner of Indian Affairs," June 11, 1924, National Archives and Records Administration, Washington, D.C., Record Group 75, Bureau of Indian Affairs, CCF 1907-1939, Fort Lapwai, Box Number 42566-12-056 to 1228-09-101.
57. "Petition Addressed to Hon. Fred T. Dubois, U.S. Senate, Washington, D.C. From Allottees of the Nez Perce Tribe, Prepared by Starr Jacob Maxwell," undated, Latah County Historical Society, Orofino, Idaho, Starr Jacob Maxwell Collection.
58. "Petition Addressed to Hon. Fred T. Dubois, U.S. Senate, Washington, D.C. From Allottees of the Nez Perce Tribe, Prepared by Starr Jacob Maxwell," undated, Latah County Historical Society, Orofino, Idaho, Starr Jacob Maxwell Collection.
59. "Letter from Charles E. Monteith, U.S. Indian Agent, Nez Perce Agency, Idaho, to Hon. J.D.C. Atkins, Commissioner of Indian Affairs, Washington, D.C.," October 12, 1885, National Archives and Records Administration, Washington, D.C., Record Group 75, Bureau of Indian Affairs, Letters Received, 1882-1907.
60. "Letter from Oscar H. Lipps, Superintendent, to the Commissioner of Indian Affairs, Washington, D.C.," February 26, 1924, National Archives and Records Administration, Washington, D.C., Record Group 75, Bureau of Indian Affairs, CCF 1907-1939, Fort Lapwai, Box Number 9893-15-150 to 60246-15-151.
61. "Letter from Oscar H. Lipps, Superintendent, to the Commissioner of Indian Affairs, Washington, D.C.," February 26, 1924, National Archives and Records Administration, Washington, D.C., Record Group 75, Bureau of Indian Affairs, CCF 1907-1939, Fort Lapwai, Box Number 9893-15-150 to 60246-15-151.
62. "Letter from Oscar H. Lipps, Superintendent, to the Commissioner of Indian Affairs, Washington, D.C.," March 4, 1925, National Archives and Records Administration, Washington, D.C., Record Group 75, Bureau of Indian Affairs, CCF 1907-1939, Fort Lapwai, Box Number 9893-15-150 to 60246-15-151.
63. "Inspection Report of Fort Lapwai Indian Agency prepared by Hugh L. Scott, Member, Board of Indian Commissioners," September 5, 1922, Na-

tional Archives and Records Administration, Washington, D.C., Record Group 75, Bureau of Indian Affairs, CCF 1907-1939, Fort Lapwai, Box Number 9893-15-150 to 60246-15-151.
64. "Inspection Report of the Fort Lapwai Reservation prepared by Flora Warren Seymour, Member, Board of Indian Commissioners," September 20, 1926, National Archives and Records Administration, Washington, D.C., Record Group 75, Bureau of Indian Affairs, CCF 1907-1939, Fort Lapwai, Box Number 9893-15-150 to 60246-15-151.
65. "Inspection Report of the Fort Lapwai Reservation prepared by Flora Warren Seymour, Member, Board of Indian Commissioners," September 20, 1926, National Archives and Records Administration, Washington, D.C., Record Group 75, Bureau of Indian Affairs, CCF 1907-1939, Fort Lapwai, Box Number 9893-15-150 to 60246-15-151.
66. "Inspection Report of the Fort Lapwai Reservation prepared by Flora Warren Seymour, Member, Board of Indian Commissioners," September 20, 1926, National Archives and Records Administration, Washington, D.C., Record Group 75, Bureau of Indian Affairs, CCF 1907-1939, Fort Lapwai, Box Number 9893-15-150 to 60246-15-151.
67. "Inspection Report of the Fort Lapwai Reservation prepared by Flora Warren Seymour, Member, Board of Indian Commissioners," September 20, 1926, National Archives and Records Administration, Washington, D.C., Record Group 75, Bureau of Indian Affairs, CCF 1907-1939, Fort Lapwai, Box Number 9893-15-150 to 60246-15-151.

NOTES TO THE EPILOGUE

1. Phinney, *Nez Perce Texts*, 29.
2. Many Nez Perce people struggled to retell the narrative and recreate a place for themselves in the Pacific Northwest. Peo Peo Thalekt, Starr Jacob Maxwell, Archie Phinney, Yellow Bull and many others worked diligently to voice their perspectives and make their voices heard by the government and throughout American society. Unfortunately I cannot include their struggles and voices in this work. All of these lives and the lives of many other Nez Perce people deserve attention and research.
3. Steven R. Evans and Clifford E. Trafzer also noted that Yellow Wolf made money dancing at pow wows and making headdresses used by Hollywood actors. Undated private conversation between Steven Ross Evans and Clifford E. Trafzer.
4. See McWhorter, *Yellow Wolf: His Own Story* and Steven Ross Evans, *Voice of the Old Wolf: Lucullus Virgil McWhorter and the Nez Perce Indians*, (Pullman, Washington: Washington State University Press, 1996) for more thorough discussions of Yellow Wolf's life. These two works also relate a great deal about L.V. McWhorter, his life and his work among the native peoples of the Columbia Plateau.
5. McWhorter, *Yellow Wolf: His Own Story*, 18.
6. Horace P. Axtell and Margo Aragon, *A Little Bit of Wisdom: Conversations with a Nez Perce Elder*, Lewiston, Idaho: Confluence Press, 1997.

Bibliography

Arnold, R. Ross. *Indian Wars of Idaho, Illustrated*. Caldwell, Idaho: The Caxton Printers, Ltd., 1932.

Atwood, A. *The Conquerors: Historical Sketches of the American Settlement of the Oregon Country Embracing Facts in the Life and Work of Rev. Jason Lee*. Boston: Jennings and Graham, 1907.

Axtell, Horace P. and Margo Aragon. *A Little Bit of Wisdom: Conversations with a Nez Perce Elder*. Lewiston, Idaho: Confluence Press, 1997.

Bailey, Robert G. *Hell's Canyon: A Story of the Deepest Canyon on the North American Continent, Together with Historical Sketches of Idaho, Interesting Information of the State, Indian Wars and Mythology, Poetry and Stories*. Lewiston, ID: Lewiston Printing, 1984.

Bartlett, F.C. *Remembering: A Study in Experimental and Social Psychology*. Cambridge: Cambridge University Press, 1932.

Beal, Merrill D. *"I Will Fight No More Forever": Chief Joseph and the Nez Perce War*. Seattle: University of Washington Press, 1963.

Boyd, Robert, ed. *Indians, Fire and the Land in the Pacific Northwest*. Corvallis: Oregon State University Press, 1999.

———. *People of the Dalles: the Indians of Wascopam Mission: a Historical Ethnography Based on the Papers of the Methodist Missionaries*. Edited by Raymond J. and Douglas R. Parks DeMaillie. First ed., *Studies in the Anthropology of North American Indians*. Lincoln: University of Nebraska Press, 1996.

Brooks, Noah. *First across the Continent: The Story of the Exploring Expedition of Lewis and Clark in 1803-4-5*. New York: Charles Scribner's Sons, 1901.

Brosnan, Cornelius James. *History of the State of Idaho*. Revised ed. New York: Charles Scribner's Sons, 1926.

———. *Jason Lee: Prophet of the New Oregon*. New York: The Macmillan Company, 1932.

Brown, William Compton. *The Indian Side of the Story*. Spokane: C.W. Hill Printing Co., 1961.

Calvin, Martin. *The American Indian and the Problem of History*. New York: Oxford University Press, 1987.

Clark, J. Stanley. "The Nez Perces in Exile." *The Pacific Northwest Quarterly* 36, No. 3 (1945): 213-32.

Cole, Douglas. *Captured Heritage: The Scramble for Northwest Coast Artifacts.* Norman: University of Oklahoma Press, 1985.

———. *Franz Boas: The Early Years, 1858-1906.* Seattle: University of Washington Press, 1999.

Western Historical Publishing Company. *An Illustrated History of North Idaho Embracing Nez Perces, Idaho, Latah, Kootenai and Shoshone Counties, State of Idaho.* Boise: Western Historical Publishing Company, 1903.

Connerton, Paul. *How Societies Remember.* Cambridge: Cambridge University Press, 1989.

Coward, John M. *The Newspaper Indian: Native American Identity in the Press, 1820-90.* Edited by Robert W. and John C. Nerone McChesney, *The History of Communications.* Urbana: University of Illinois Press, 1999.

Davis, Russell and Brent Ashabranner. *Chief Joseph: War Chief of the Nez Perce.* New York: McGraw-Hill Book Company, Inc., 1962.

DeVoto, Bernard, ed. *The Journals of Lewis and Clark.* Boston: Houghton Mifflin, 1953.

Dippie, Brian W. *The Vanishing American: White Attitudes and U.S. Indian Policy.* Middletown, Connecticut: Wesleyan University Press, 1982.

Dowd, Gregory Evans. *A Spirited Resistance: The North American Indian Struggle for Unity, 1745-1815.* Vol. 4, *The John Hopkins University Studies in Historical and Political Science 109th Series (1991).* Baltimore: The John Hopkins University Press, 1992.

Evans, Steven Ross. *Voice of the Old Wolf: Lucullus Virgil McWhorter and the Nez Perce Indians.* Pullman: Washington State University Press, 1996.

Frykman, George A. *Seattle's Historian and Promoter: The Life of Edmond Stephen Meany.* Pullman: Washington State University Press, 1998.

Gidley, M. *Kopet: A Documentary Narrative of Chief Joseph's Last Years.* Seattle: University of Washington Press, 1981.

Goulder, W.A. *Reminiscences: Incidents in the Life of a Pioneer in Oregon and Idaho.* Boise: Timothy Regan, 1909.

Green, Keith and Jill LeBihan. *Critical Theory and Practice: A Coursebook.* London: Routledge, 1996.

Gulick, Bill. *Chief Joseph Country: Land of the Nez Perce.* Caldwell, Idaho: The Caxton Printers, Ltd., 1981.

Gunther, Erna. "The Westward Movement of Some Plains Traits." *American Anthropologist* 52, No. 2 (1950): 174-80.

Haines, Francis. *The Nez Perces: Tribesmen of the Columbia Plateau.* Norman: University of Oklahoma Press, 1955.

———. "The Northward Spread of Horses among the Plains Indians." *American Anthropologist* 40, No. 3 (1938): 429-37.

Halbwachs, Maurice. *On Collective Memory.* Edited by Lewis A. Coser, *The Heritage of Sociology Series.* Chicago: University of Chicago Press, 1992.

Hilden, Patricia Penn. *When Nickels Were Indians: An Urban, Mixed-Blood Story.* Edited by Arnold and Brian Swann Krupat, *Smithsonian Series of Studies in Native American Literature.* Washington D.C.: Smithsonian Institution Press, 1995.

Horsman, Reginald. *Race and Manifest Destiny: The Origins of American Racial Anglo-Saxonism*. Cambridge: Harvard University Press, 1981.
Howard, Oliver Otis. *Famous Indian Chiefs I Have Known*. Lincoln: University of Nebraska Press, 1989.
Hoxie, Frederick E. *A Final Promise: The Campaign to Assimilate the Indians, 1880-1920*. Lincoln: University of Nebraska Press, 1984.
Hoxie, Frederick E. and Joan T. Mark, ed. *With the Nez Perces: Alice Fletcher in the Field, 1889-92 by E. Jane Gay*. Lincoln: University of Nebraska Press, 1981.
Jennings, Francis. *The Invasion of America: Indians, Colonialism, and the Cant of Conquest*. New York: W.W. Norton & Company, 1975.
Josephy, Alvin M., Jr. *The Nez Perce Indians and the Opening of the Northwest*. Abridged ed. Lincoln: University of Nebraska Press, 1965.
— — —. *The Patriot Chiefs: A Chronicle of American Indian Resistance*. Revised ed. New York: Penguin Books, 1993.
Kapoun, Robert W. and Charles J. Lohrmann. *Language of the Robe: American Indian Trade Blankets*. Salt Lake City: Gibbs-Smith Publisher, 1997.
Katakis, Michael, ed. *Excavating Voices: Listening to Photographs of Native Americans*. Philadelphia: University of Pennsylvania Museum of Archaeology and Anthropology, 1998.
Kingston, Ceylon S. and J. Orin Oliphant. *An Outline of the History of the Pacific Northwest with Special Reference to Washington*. Cheney, Washington: State Normal School, 1926.
Kip, Lawrence. *Indian War in the Pacific Northwest: The Journal of Lieutenant Lawrence Kip*. Lincoln: University of Nebraska Press, 1999.
Klein, Kerwin Lee. *Frontiers of Historical Imagination: Narrating the European Conquest of Native America, 1890-1990*. Berkeley: University of California Press, 1997.
Lears, T.J. Jackson. *No Place of Grace: Antimodernism and the Transformation of American Culture, 1880-1920*. Chicago: The University of Chicago Press, 1981.
Martin, Calvin, ed. *The American Indian and the Problem of History*. New York: Oxford University Press, 1987.
Martin, Douglas Dale. "Indian-White Relations of the Pacific Slope, 1850-1890." Dissertation, University of Washington, 1969.
McBeth, Kate C. *The Nez Perces since Lewis and Clark*. New York: Fleming H. Revell Company, 1908.
McWhorter, Lucullus Virgil. *Hear Me, My Chiefs*! Caldwell, Idaho: Caxton Press, 1986.
— — —. *Yellow Wolf: His Own Story*. Caldwell, Idaho: The Caxton Printers, Ltd., 1940. Reprint, 6th Printing, Revised and Enlarged.
Meany, Edmond S. *A Block-Print History of the Northwest*. Seattle: University of Washington Book Store, 1928.
— — —. *History of the State of Washington*. New York: The Macmillan Company, 1910.

Meinig, Donald William. *The Great Columbia Plain: A Historical Geography, 1805-1910, The Emil and Kathleen Sick Lecture-Book Series in Western History and Biography.* Seattle: University of Washington Press, 1968.

Miller, Christopher L. *Prophetic Worlds: Indians and Whites on the Columbia Plateau.* New Brunswick, New Jersey: Rutgers University Press, 1985.

Nashone. *Grandmother Stories of the Northwest.* Newcastle, California: Sierra Oaks Publishing Company, 1987.

Nixon, Oliver Woodson. *How Marcus Whitman Saved Oregon: A True Romance of Patriotic Heroism, Christian Devotion and Final Martyrdom... With Sketchers of Life on the Plains and Mountains in Pioneer Days.* Chicago: Star Publishing Company, 1895.

———. *Whitman's Ride through Savage Lands with Sketches of Indian Life*: The Winona Publishing Company, 1905.

Novick, Peter. *That Noble Dream: The "Objectivity Question" and the American Historical Profession.* Edited by J.B. Schneewind Richard Rorty, Quentin Skinner, and Wolf Lepenies, *Ideas in Context*. Cambridge: Cambridge University Press, 1988.

Owens, Louis. *Other Destinies: Understanding the American Indian Novel.* Edited by Gerald Vizenor. Vol. 3, *American Indian Literature and Critical Studies Series.* Norman: University of Oklahoma Press, 1992.

Phinney, Archie. *Nez Perce Texts.* Translated by Archie Phinney. First ed., Vol. XXV, *Columbia University Contributions to Anthropology.* New York: AMS Press, 1969. Reprint, 1969 AMS Press, Inc.

Portelli, Alessandro. *The Battle of Valle Giulia.* Madison: University of Wisconsin Press, 1997.

———. *The Death of Luigi Trastulli and Other Stories: Form and Meaning in Oral History.* Albany: State University of New York Press, 1991.

Prucha, Francis P. *American Indian Policy in the Formative Years: The Indian Trade and Intercourse Acts, 1790-1834.* Lincoln: University of Nebraska Press, 1962.

Ray, Verne E. *Cultural Relations in the Plateau of Northwestern America.* Los Angeles: Southwest Museum, 1939.

———. "Native Villages and Groupings of the Columbia Basin." *The Pacific Northwest Quarterly* 27, No. 2 (1936): 99-152.

Relander, Click. *Drummers and Dreamers: The Story of Smowhala the Prophet and His Nephew Puck Hyah Toot, the Last Prophet of the Nearly Extinct River People, the Wanapums.* Seattle: Northwest Interpretive Association, 1986.

Rhonda, James P. *Lewis and Clark among the Indians.* Lincoln: University of Nebraska Press, 1984.

Robbins, William G. *Colony and Empire: The Capitalist Transformation of the American West.* Lawrence: University of Kansas Press, 1994.

———. "In Pursuit of Historical Explanation: Capitalism as a Conceptual Tool for Knowing the American West." *Western Historical Quarterly* 30, Autumn 1999 (1999): 282.

Ruby, Robert H. and John A. Brown. *Indians of the Pacific Northwest: A History, The Civilization of the American Indian Series.* Norman: University of Oklahoma Press, 1981.

Rupp, Virgil. *Let'er Buck!* Pendleton, Oregon: Pendleton Round-up Association, 1985.
Said, Edward. *Culture and Imperialism.* New York: Random House, Inc., 1993.
Schwantes, Carlos A. *The Pacific Northwest: An Interpretive History.* Lincoln: University of Nebraska Press, 1989.
Slickpoo, Allen P., Sr. *Noon Nee-Me-Poo (We, the Nez Perces): Culture and History of the Nez Perces, Volume One.* Lapwai, Idaho: The Nez Perce Tribe of Idaho, 1973.
Soule, S.H. *The Rand-McNally Guide to the Great Northwest, Containing Information Regarding the States of Montana, Idaho, Washington, Oregon, Minnesota, North Dakota, Alaska, Also Western Canada and British Columbia, with a Description of the Route along the Chicago and North-Western, Union Pacific, Oregon Short Line, and Oregon River and Navigation Co. Railways. Gives the Early History, Topography, Climate, Resourcs, and Valuable Statistics on the States Comprising the Great Northwest.* Chicago: Rand, McNally & Company, 1903.
Spinden, Herbert Joseph. "The Nez Perce Indians." *American Anthropological Association Memoirs* 2, No. 3 (1908): 168-274.
Taylor, Marian W. *Chief Joseph, Nez Perce Leader.* Edited by W. David Baird. First ed, *North American Indians of Achievement.* New York: Chelsea House Publishers, 1993.
Trafzer, Clifford E. *Death Stalks the Yakama: Epidemiological Transitions and Mortality on the Yakama Indian Reservation, 1888-1964.* East Lansing: Michigan State Universtiy Press, 1997.
— — —, ed. *Grandmother, Grandfather, and Old Wolf: Tamanwit Ku Sukat and Tradtional Native American Narratives from the Columbia Plateau.* East Lansing: Michigan State University Press, 1998.
— — —. *The Nez Perce.* Edited by Frank W. Porter, III, *Indians of North America.* New York: Chelsea House Publishers, 1992.
— — —, ed. *Northwestern Tribes in Exile: Modoc, Nez Perce, and Palouse Removal to the Indian Territory.* Sacramento: Sierra Oaks Publishing Company, 1987.
Trafzer, Clifford E. and Richard D. Scheuerman. *Renegade Tribe: The Palouse Indians and the Invasion of the Inland Pacific Northwest.* Pullman: Washington State University Press, 1986.
Trennert, Robert A., Jr. *Alternative to Extinction: Federal Indian Policy and the Reservation System, 1846-1851.* Philadelphia: Temple University Press, 1975.
Trouillot, Michel-Rolph. *Silencing the Past: Power and the Production of History.* Boston: Beacon Press, 1995.
Turner, Frederick Jackson. *The Frontier in American History.* Tucson: The University of Arizona Press, 1986.
U.S. National Park Service. *Nez Perce Country: A Handbook for Nez Perce National Historical Park, Idaho.* Handbook 121. Washington: Government Printing Office, 1983.
Walker, Deward E., Jr. *Conflict and Schism in Nez Perce Acculturation: A Study of Religion and Politics.* Moscow, Idaho: University of Idaho Press, 1985.

Williams, Raymond. *Keywords: A Vocabulary of Culture and Society.* Revised Edition New York: Oxford University Press, 1983.

Young, Robert. *White Mythologies: Writing History and the West.* London: Routledge, 1990.

Zucker, Jeff, Kay Hummel and Bob Hogfoss. *Oregon Indians: Culture, History and Current Affairs, an Atlas and Introduction.* Salem: Western Imprints, The Press of the Oregon Historical Society, 1983.

PRIMARY DOCUMENTS – REPOSITORIES

National Archives and Records Administration, Pacific Alaska Region, 6125 Sand Point Way N.E., Seattle Washington, 98115. Record Group 75 – Bureau of Indian Affairs, Fort Lapwai and Northern Idaho Agency.

National Archives and Records Administration, Washington, D.C. Record Group 75 – Bureau of Indian Affairs, Fort Lapwai and Northern Idaho Agency.

Washington State University, Holland Library, Manuscripts, Archives, and Special Collections, P.O. Box 645610, Pullman, Washington 99164-5610. Lucullus Virgil McWhorter Collection.

University of Washington, Manuscripts, Special Collections, University Archives Division, Allen Library, Box 352900, Seattle, Washington 98195-2900. Edmond Stephen Meany Collection and American Indians of the Pacific Northwest Collection (http://content.lib.washington.edu).

University of Idaho, Special Collections and Archives, University of Idaho Library, Moscow, Idaho 83844-2351. C.J. Brosnan Collection and Historical Photograph Collection.

Clearwater Historical Museum, 315 College Avenue, P.O. Box 1454, Orofino, Idaho 83544. Starr Jacob Maxwell Collection

Idaho Historical Society, Historical Library and Archives, 450 North Fourth Street, Boise Idaho 83702-6072. Lizzie Crawford Collection.

Index

A

Ahtanum Creek, 92
Aleiya, *see* Lawyer
   role as crier, 86
   agreement to terms of 1855 treaty, 88
allotment, 168-172, *see also* Dawes Act
American Board of Foreign Missions, 74
American Fur Company, 58
Anderson, Major Albert M., 152
Anglo-Saxon race, 135-136
annual reports of the Office of Indian
      Affairs, 163, 176, 167
Apostle Paul, 72
Arikara Indians, 55, *see also* Lewis and Clark
      Expedition
Arnold, R. Ross
   Indian Wars of Idaho, 130
   Nez Perce War, 137-139, 160
assimilation, 146, 173
Assiniboin Indians, 55, *see also* Lewis and
      Clark Expedition
Astor, John, 58
Atkins, J.D.C., 178
Atlantic Ocean, 133
Axtell, Horace
   spiritual power, 24
   autobiography, 189

B

Baker City, Oregon, 2
Bancroft, Hubert Howe, 60
bannock, 46
Battle of Clearwater, 140
Battle of Four Lakes, 93
Battle of Spokane Plains, 93
Battle of Whitebird Canyon, 118, 140
Bear Paw, 147
   battlefield, 162
   mountains, 124-125, 128, 140
Big Hole River, 120, 123
Bitterroot Mountains, 18, 20, 56, 102, 104,
      120
Bitterroot Valley, 47, 56, *see also* Lewis and
      Clark Expedition
Blackfeet, 20, 47
Black Hills, 104
Black mountain huckleberry, 35
Blanket Indians, 166
Blue Mountains, 18
Board of Missions, 166
Boas, Franz, 16
Bolon, Andrew Jackson, 91
Bonneville, Captain , 66, 68
Boone, Daniel, 79
Bourne, E.G., 80
Boyd, Robert, 47, 49, 51
Britain, 58
Brosnan, Cornelius J., 8, 60-61, 70, 77, 160
   background of, 80-81
   Nez Perce War, 128, 136, 142
   number of Nez Perce warriors, 139-140,
      160
   Treaty of 1855, 74
   Yakama War, 94-97, 100-101
Buchanan, James, 103
buffalo hunting, 35
buffalo robe, 158
Bumppo, Natty, 79
Bureau of Indian Affairs, 176
   Nez Perce exile, 127, 147
   Nez Perce Reservation, 165, 169
Burke Act, 169

239

C

Cain, A.J., 103-104
California, 102
Cameahwait, 55, *see also* Lewis and Clark Expedition
Camp Fortunate, 55
Canada, 123-125
    Grandmother Country, 123
    Yellow Wolf's escape to, 186
Canoe Indian, 64
Carlisle Indian School, 140
Carson, Kit, 79
Cascade Mountains, 18, 38
Catholic Missionaries, 71, 74
Cayuse, 3, 95, 102
    Columbia Plateau religion, 52
    Nez Perce War, 117
    relationship to the Whitman Mission, 75
    Sahaptin language, 36, 38
Celilo Falls, 20, 57
Charles Wilkes Expedition, 66
Cheyenne Indians, 123-125
Chief Albert, 145
Chief Joseph, 36, 120, 140, 177
    Big Hole and escape, 123-125
    conflict in Wallowa region, 107-109
    councils with government officials, 111-112
    death of, 153-154
    exile of, 146-147, 151
    interpretations of Joseph's role in Nez Perce War, 127-130, 132-134
    role in Nez Perce War, 117-118
Chief Yellow Bull, 147-149
Chinook jargon, 38, 85-86
Chinook salmon, 32, 34
Chinook wind, 19
Christian Advocate Journal and Zion's Herald, 72
Christian Nez Perce, 163-165, 172
    allotment, 168
    Fourth of July celebration, 174-175
    prohibiting immoral practices, 167
Civil War, 107
Clark, J. Stanley, 149
Clark, William, 56, *see also* Lewis and Clark Expedition
Clearwater River, 20, 56, 73, 103-104
Clearwater Valley, 26
Cochise, 128
Columbia Plateau, 5, 7-8, 97
    description of, 18-21
    Treaty of 1855, 94-95
Columbia River, 18, 20, 34, 54,
Colville Reservation, 150-154, 186
Colville, Washington, 150
Conner, Edward J., 167
Continental Divide, 48, 55, 56, *see also* Lewis and Clark Expedition
conversion of Treaty Nez Perce, 165-166
Cook, Captain James, 64
Coeur d'Alene, 36
Coyote, 20, 30, 109, 127
    importance to Nez Perce, 39-41
Coyote and Monster story, 68, 70, 98, 146, 163, 183
    Archie Phinney's version of, 13, 43, 69, 99, 145, 185
    religious importance of, 52-53
    swallowing of Coyote, 143-144
Craig, William, 76
Crazy Horse, 128, 160
Crockett, 79
Crow Indians, 120, 123
Curtis, Edward S., 154
Custer, George Armstrong, 104, 123

D

Dalles, the, 57, 91
dancing, 163
Dawes Act, 169, 171-172
De Smet, Father Pierre Jean, 74
Department of Interior, 150
Dinges, Bruce J., 135
disease, 30, 49
Disoway, G.P., 72
Dowd, Gregory, 23
Drake, Sir Francis, 64
Dubois, Fred T., 178

E

Eagle From the Light, 103, 105, 108, 109
Eagle Robe, 111, 117, *see also* Tipyahlanan Siskan
Eekish Pah, 13, 127
    exile of Nez Perce to, 146-149
Evans, Steven Ross, 189

Index

F

Faulkner, Dr. W.H., 150
firearms, 46
Five Crows, 88
Flatheads, 36, 71, 74
Fletcher, Alice C., 169-170
Fort Astoria, 58
Fort Clapsop, 57
Fort Colville, 91
Fort Fizzle, 120
Fort George, 58
Fort Keogh, 125
Fort Lapwai, 111, 114
Fort Laramie, Treaty of 1868, 104
Fort Leavenworth, 125, 127, 147
Fort Mandan, 55, *see also* Lewis and Clark Expedition
Fort Simcoe, 92
Fort Vancouver, 58, 84
Fort Walla Walla, 92-93
Foucault, Michel, 6
Frank Leslie's Illustrated Newspaper, 130
    reporting of Nez Perce War, 130-136, 138-139
fur trade, 57-59

G

gambling, 163
Gay, Jane, 169
Geary, Edward R., 104
Geronimo, 128, 160
Gibbon, Colonel John, 120, 123
Gidley, Mick, 152-153
Gilliam, Colonel Cornelius, 76, 83
Gold Rush, 1849, 102
Goodall, Otis B., 163
Goodwin, F.M., 183
Gospel of John, 1
Granger, Idaho, 23
Grant, Ulysses S., 108
Gray, Robert, 64
Great Basin, 38
Great Depression, 171
Great Falls of the Missouri River, 55, *see also* Lewis and Clark Expedition
Great Plains, 19
Green River, 72, 73
guardian spirit, 23, *see also wyakin*

H

Hahtalekin, 120, 123
Hale, Calvin, 105-107
Haller, Major Granville O., 91, 92
Harvard, 169
Hawkeye, 79
headman, 27
Hear Me My Chiefs!, 159
Heart of the Monster, 39
Heinmot Hihhih, or White Thunder 24
Hill, Tom, 124
horse(s), 20, 35, 38, 46
Horse Indians, 64
Howard, Oliver Otis, 8, 140, 147, 162
    confrontation with Toohoolhoolzote, 112-115
    Famous Indian Chiefs I Have Known, 133-135
    Nez Perce War, 117-125
    role in Pacific Northwest Indian policy, 109-112
Howe, Indian Agent 106
Hudson's Bay Company, 58-59, 73
Hunn, Eugene, 18
    change in Columbia Plateau culture, 45-46
    Columbia Plateau Native American religion, 21-25
    disease and epidemics, 49
    edible plants, 34
    gender roles, 29-31
    horse culture, 46-47
    impact of disease on religion, 50-52
    kinship and family relationships, 28
    seasonal round, 31-35
    women and salmon run, 34
Husishusis Kute, 107, 112, 127, 134, 147, 149, 150

I

Idaho, 101
    Camas Prairie, 115, 117, 118
    Frank Leslie's Illustrated Newspaper, 127-133
    Grangeville, 115
    Lapwai, 105, 111
    Lewiston, 102, 104, 106
    Salmon River, 117, 118, 120
    Tolo Lake, 115
Idaho Statesman, 159

Illustrated History of North Idaho, An, 70, 128
   Chief Joseph, 140-143
   "civilizing" aspect of missions, 73
   narrative of exploration and fur-trade, 65-66
   narrative of Nez Perce War, 135-136, 138
   Whitman myth, 77-78
Indian Claims Commission, 17
Indian Commissioner, Atkins, 150
Indian Department, 108, 109
Indian Rights Association, 149
Indian stick-game, 167
Indian Territory, 4, 114, 125, 162, 186
   Nez Perce exile to, 147-150
Iroquois, 71, 84

J

Jason, 106
Jefferson, Thomas, 54, *see also* Lewis and Clark Expedition
Jerome, Lieutenant Lowell H., 124
Jesus Christ, 165
John Day River, 57
Jokias, Captain John, 124, 162
Jones, Judith Ann, 168
Joseph's War, 99, 127, 128
Josephy, Alvin M. Jr., 91, 108, 189
   acquisition of horses by Plateau Indians, 46-47
   attack on Looking Glass village, 120
   discovery of gold, 102
   Treaty of 1863, 106
Junkin, William M., 170-171

K

Kamiah, Idaho, 34, 39, 154, 165, 166
Kamiakin, 97
   Walla Walla Council and Treaty, 84-86
   Yakama War, 90-92
Kansas, 125
keh-kheet, 34
khem-mes, 34, *see also* camas root
Kelley, Hall Jackson, 66
Kelly, Colonel Thomas, 92
khouse, 34
Klein, Kerwin, 14, 21, 64, 67, 68

L

Lakota Indians, 47, 104, 123
Lane, Joseph, 83
Lapwai, 13, 137, 152, 165
   Spalding Mission, 73, 79
Lapwai Council of 1863, 105-106
Lapwai Council of 1877, 112, 118, 134
Lapwai Reservation, 134
Latham, Edward H., 154
Lawyer, 95, 130, 132
   role in Treaty of 1863, 103-107
Lawyer, Archie, 148-149
Lean Elk, 123
Lears, T.J. Jackson
Lee, Jason, 72, 73, 79, 81
Lemhi Pass, 55, *see also* Lewis and Clark Expedition
Lewis and Clark Expedition, 43, 49-50, 59, 66, 68, 183
   Arikara Indians, 55
   Assiniboin Indians
   Bitterroot Mountains, 56
   Bitterroot Valley, 56
   camas root, 56
   Cameahwait, 55
   Camp Fortunate, 55
   Celilo Falls, 57
   Clearwater River, 56
   Continental Divide, 55, 56
   Corps of Discovery, 55, 56, 57
   the Dalles, 57
   Fort Clatsop, 57
   Fort Mandan, 55
   Great Falls of the Missouri River, 55
   John Day River, 57
   Lemhi Pass, 55
   Lolo Trail, 56
   Louisiana Purchase, 54
   Louisiana Territory, 54
   Mandan Indians, 55
   Meriwether Lewis, 55
   Missouri River, 55
   Napoleon, 54
   narrative of, 53-58
   Nez Perce Trail, 56
   Oregon Territory, 54
   salmon, 56
   Shoshoni Indians, 55, 56
   St. Louis, 57
   Tetoharsky, 56, 57
   Thomas Jefferson, 54

Index

Twisted Hair, 56, 57
Walla Walla Indians, 57
Wanapum Indians, 57
Watkuweis, 56
Weippe Prairie, 56
William Clark, 56
Wishram people, 57
Yakama Indians, 57
Yellowstone River, 57
Lewis, Meriwether, 55, *see also* Lewis and Clark Expedition
Lipps, Oscar H., 172-173, 176-177, 178
Little Ice Age, 45
Little Rocky Mountains, 124
Lolo Trail, 56, 120, *see also* Lewis and Clark Expedition
Looking Glass, 90, 114
    leadership during Nez Perce War, 118-125
Louisiana Purchase, 54, *see also* Lewis and Clark Expedition
Louisiana Territory, 54, *see also* Lewis and Clark Expedition
Lukens, Fred E., 159

M

MacArthur, A.T., 178
Mackenzie, Alexander, 48, 58, 59, 66, 68
Mandan Indians, 55, *see also* Lewis and Clark Expedition
Manifest Destiny, 4, 8, 46, 71
    Treaty of 1855, 101, 109, 110, 114
    Nez Perce War, 128, 137, 142
    exile of Nez Perce, 145-146
Marshall, W.I., 80
Martin, Calvin, 6
Maxwell, Starr Jacob, 178
McBeth, Kate, 8, 70, 128, 174-175
    allotment, 168
    arrival of missionaries in Pacific Northwest, 71-72
    arrival of Sue McBeth, 174-175
    images of Chief Joseph, 158, 160
    Nez Perce War, 136-136, 139-140
    Whitman Massacre, 77
McBeth, Sue, 13, 101, 165-166, 174
McClellan, Captain George B., 84
McLoughlin, John, 58
McWhorter, Lucullus Virgil, 158-159, 186-187

Meany, Edmond S., 8, 100, 101, 110, 133
    background and importance, 60-62
    death of Chief Joseph, 152-160
    narrative of discovery and exploration, 62-68
    Nez Perce War, 142
    Walla Walla Treaty of 1855, 94-95
    Whitman Myth, 70-71, 77-80
    Yakama War, 96-97
Medicine Dance, 24, *see also* Winter Dance
Meinig, Donald, 18-20
    climate and seasons, 18-19
    description of Columbia Plateau, 18-20
    human geography, 19
Meopkowit, 124, 162, *see also* Old George
Mexico, 46
Miles, Colonel Nelson A., 147, 159
    Battle of Bearpaw, 123-125
    end of Nez Perce War, 139-140
Miller, Christopher, 45-46
Missouri River, 55, *see also* Lewis and Clark Expedition
Monster, 99, 101, 109, 127, 129
Montana, 104
    Missoula, 120
    Fort Fizzle,
Camas Meadows, 123
    Milk River, 124
Monteith, Agent, 150
Monteith, Charles E., 178
Monteith, John B., 110-114
Morgan, T.J., 166
Murphy, Patty, 86

N

Napoleon, 54, *see also* Lewis and Clark Expedition
Napoleon of Indians, 159
Napoleon of the Northwest, 159
New England Granite and Marble Company, 154
New Mexico, 46
New York, 130, 133
Newell, Robert, 105
Nez Perce Camp Association, 176
Nez Perce delegation, 71, 72, 183
Nez Perce Indians
    gender roles, 29-30
    land and religion, 22
    marriage, 28-29
    religion, 21-26

religion, change in, 50-53
social and political life, 26-30
Nez Perce Reservation, 115, 125, 130, 137, 149, 152
   allotment, 168-169
   description of, 163-165
   dissolution of, 177
   inspection of, 170-172
   population of, 172
Nez Perce Trail, 56, see also Lewis and Clark Expedition
Nez Perce War of 1877, 8, 95, 183, 186
   councils leading up to, 100-112
   narrative of, 117-144
      Chief Joseph myth, 151
   Nez Perce scouts and, 162
noble savage, 78
North American Review, 148
Northern Idaho Agency, 171
Northwest Company, 48, 58-59
Numipu, 146, 185

O

Office of Indian Affairs, 147, 162, 178
   exile of Nez Perce, 147, 150
      Colville Reservation and Chief Joseph, 153
      relationship to Christian Nez Perce, 166-167
Ogden, Peter Skeen, 83
Oklahoma, 125, 146
Old Chief Joseph, 88, 130
   Treaty of 1863, 103-107
Oliver, Frank, 143
Ollokot, 108, 112
   meetings with General Howard, 117-118
   role in Nez Perce War, 123-124
Omaha Indians, 169
Oregon, 107
   Congressional delegation, 108
   Northeast, 107, 108, 127
   Pendleton, 112
Oregon Country, 58, 79, 82
Oregon Territory, 54, 79
Ott, Larry, 111, 117, 138
Owhi, 88, 93, 97

P

Pacific coast, 46
Pacific Northwest, 107, 110, 127, 129
Pacific Ocean, 133
Pacific Railroad survey, 84
Pahka Pahtahank, 123
Palmer, Joel, 87, 90, 98, 110
Palouse Indians, 36, 38, 82, 83, 97
   killing of Palouse horses, 93
   Nez Perce War, 107, 115, 117-118, 125, 127
Parker, Samuel, 73
Paul, Jesse, 182
Peo Peo Mox Mox, 88, 92, 97
Peo Peo Thalekt, 120, 177
Perry, Captain David, 118
Phinney, Archie, 39, 189
Pierce, Ellias D., 102, 103
Pilgrim Fathers, 97
Pilot Knob Peak, 23, see also *Tuhm-yo-leets-yeets-mekhs*
Place of the Butterfly, 73, 74, 75, 76, 82, see also Waiilatpu
Plains culture, 47
Ponca Agency, 127, 147-148
Pontiac, 128
Portland Oregonian, 150
Presbyterian Church, 166, 168
prophecy, 51-53
Puget Sound, 85-86

Q

Qualchin, 91, 93
Quapaw Agency, 125, 127, 147

R

Rainbow, 123
Rains, Major Gabriel, 92
Ray, Verne, 32, 36
   Native American oral history sources, 15
   Nez Perce villages, 26-27
   work for Indian Claims Commission, 17
Red Napoleon, 127, 139
Red Thunder, 153
Redington, Colonel J.W., 158-159
Reuben, James, 148-149, 162
Rhonda, James, 55, 56
Robbins, Warren D., 166
Robbins, William, 5
Rocky Mountains, 47
Ruby, Robert and John Brown, 115, 117, 120, 123

S

Sahaptin language, 28, 36, 38
Said, Edward, 6
Salish, 36, 38
salmon, 19, 20, 33, 35, 56
Salmon River, 138, 139
Schwantes, Carlos, 57, 59
Scott, Hugh L., 163-164, 182-183
seasonal round, 26, 27, 30-35
    women and, 31-32
    buffalo hunting, 35
Secretary of the Interior, 108, 149-150, 169
Selam, James, 29, 46
Seymour, Flora Warren, 183
shaman, 24-25
shamanism, 22
Sherman, General William T., 125
Shoshonean culture, 20, 47
Shoshoni Indians, 47, 48
Sitting Bull, 123, 124, 125, 127, 160, 186
Slacum, William, 66
Slickpoo, Allen, Sr., 129, 143, 189
    Alice Fletcher, 170
    allotment, 168-169
    arrival of missionaries, 73
    death rituals, 29
    duties of headman, 27
    gold rush on Nez Perce Reservation, 104
    Nez Perce exile, 148-149
    Nez Perce marriage, 28
    opposition to Walla Walla Treaty, 90
    plant harvesting, 34
    power of spiritual beings, 23
    return of exiles to Lapwai, 150
    Sue McBeth, 166
    Walla Walla Council, 86
    Watkuweis and Lewis and Clark, 56
    wyakin, 23-24
smallpox, 49, 51
Smith, Jedediah, 67-68
Smohalla, 76, 85, 107, 117
Snake River, 19, 115, 124
Social Darwinism, 78
Sioux Indians, 123, 124
Spalding, Eliza, 78
Spalding, Henry Harmon, 72, 105, 183
    Whitman myth, 77-79
special power song, 23
Spinden, Herbert, 16, 25, 26, 30, 32
Spirit Sickness, 25
Spokane, 97
Spokane Plains, 93, *see also* Battle of Spokane Plain
Spokan Indians, 36
Spotted Eagle, 105
Steele, Henry, 145
Steptoe, Colonel Edward, 92-93, 97
Stevens, Isaac I., 110
    biographical information, 84
    Brosnan's interpretation of, 95-97
    Meany's interpretation of, 94-94
    Walla Walla Council and Treaty, 85-90
St. Louis, Missouri, 3, 57
St. Paul, Minnesota, 84
Stranahan, C.T., 167
sweat bath, 23

T

Tecumseh, 128
Territory of Oregon, 83
Tetoharsky, 56, 57
"Thief" Treaty of 1863, 129, 130, 134, 163
    Wallowa region and, 107, 110-112
Treaty of 1863, 100, 128, 130, 132
    Wallowa region and, 107, 109
thlee-than, 34
Thomash, 117
Thompson, David, 59
tiewets, 24
Timothy, 106, 107
Tipyahlanan Siskan, 111, 117, *see also* Eagle Robe
Tongue River Cantonment, 123
tooats, 24, 111, 112, 114, 124, 166, *see also tiewets*
Tonner, A.C., 167
Toohoolhoolzote, 85, 109, 134
    involvement with councils, 111-115
    Nez Perce War, 118, 124
    Treaty of 1863, 106-107
Trafzer, Clifford, 51
    gold rush on Nez Perce Reservation, 102
    Nez Perce War, 120, 123-125
Trafzer, Clifford and Richard Scheuerman, 125, 189
    Agent Bolon's murder, 91
    Chief Joseph's surrender speech, 142
    Isaac I. Stevens, 84
    Kamaikin, 86-87
    Nez Perce delegation, 72
    Wallowa and Councils, 111, 115, 117
    Treaty of 1863, 105-107

Whitman and measles, 75
Yakama War, 91-93
Treaty Nez Perce, 162
Trouillot, Michel-Rolph, 7, 8, 83, 143
tsa-weetkh, 34, *see also* wild carrot
Tuhm-lo-yeets-mekhs, 23, *see also* Pilot Knob Peak
Turner, Frederick Jackson, 95, 153
  Edmond Meany, 60, 62, 67, 77, 78
Twisted Hair, 56, 57, *see also* Lewis and Clark Expeditioin

U

Umatilla Indians, 3, 36, 38, 102
Umatilla Reservation, 112
Uncle Sam, 133
United States
  Army, 109, 111, 139, 146, 147
    enforcement of Walla Walla Treaty, 100-102
    Nez Perce War, 117-118, 120, 123-125, 127-128
  Congress, 83, 149, 169, 183
    Treaty of 1863, 105, 107
  Constitution, 110
  Court of Claims, 183
  Government, 117, 123,129, 130, 133, 171
    consequences of Walla Walla Treaty, 102-110
    Second Lapwai Council, 112, 114
  Indian policy, 104, 107, 130, 132
  Senate, 103
University of California, Berkeley, 81
University of Idaho, 136
University of Washington, 61, 153
University of Wisconsin, 153

V

Vancouver, Washington, 58

W

Wah Tee Tash, 20
Wahlitits, 117, 123
Waiilatpu, 3, 82, *see also* Place of the Butterfly
  Whitman Mission, 73-76
Walker, Deward, 189
  Christianity and Nez Perce, 165-172

wyakin, 23-25
Walker, William, 72
Walla Walla, 74, 82, 102, 112
Walla Walla Council of 1855, 85-87, 101, 105
  interpretations of, 94-95
  revisions of 109-112
Walla Walla Indians, 57, 102, 117
Walla Walla River, 73
Walla Walla Treaty of 1855, 90, 99, 111
  interpretations of, 94-98
  Nez Perce War, 130-136
  provisions of, 90
  violations of, 102-106
Walla Walla, Washington, 2, 3
Wallowa, 132, 173, 186
  Chief Joseph's return to, 153-154
  conflict over, 107-111
Wallowa region, 147
Wallowa Valley, 26, 183
Wallula, Washington, 150
Wanapum Indians, 57, 117
War of 1812, 58
Washani religion, 26
  Nez Perce exile, 149, 152
  Nez Perce War and, 107
  Toohoolhoolzote, 111, 112
Washington, D.C., 79, 147-148, 174
Washington State, 61, 101
Washington State Historical Society, 154
Washington Territory, 84, 85
Water, Charlie, 170-171
Watkuweis, 56
Weippe Prairie, 34, 56, 120, *see also* Lewis and Clark Expedition
Whipper, 28
Whipple, Captain Stephen, 118, 120
White Bird, 111, 114, 125
  Treaty of 1863, 105, 106, 108
White Bird Canyon, 118, *see also* Battle of White Bird Canyon
White, Dr. Elijah, 73
White Thunder, 24
Whitman, Dr. Marcus, 72-80
Whitman Massacre, 2-3, 43, 49, 76, 183
Whitman Mission, 2,3
Whitman, Narcissa, 76, 78
Whitman, Perrin, 105, 106, 112
Whitman-Saved-Oregon-Myth, 80
wild carrot, 34, *see also tsa-weetkh*
Willamette Valley, 72
Williams, Mark, 148

Winter Dance, 32, 36, *see also* Guardian Spirit Dance
Wishram people, 57
witches, 3
Wootolen, 120, 143
Wright, Colonel George, 92, 97, 125
wyakin, 23-25, 28
Wyeth, Nathaniel, 66, 68
Wyoming, 104, 120, 123, 125

Y

Yakama Indians, 57, 102
Yakama War, 94-97, 101-103
Yakima country, 20
Yakima Republic, 159
Yakima Valley, Washington, 187
Yellow Wolf, 1, 8, 14, 143, 159
   acquiring his power, 24
   Chief Joseph's surrender, 124-125
   dilemma of Nez Perce history, 100
   events leading to Nez Perce War, 114-118
   McWhorter and, 184-187
   number of Nez Perce warriors, 139
   showing the rifle, 134
Yellowstone River, 57
Young Chief, 88, 117
Young, Robert, 6, 7

Printed in the USA/Agawam, MA
October 25, 2012